The Guide to the Vineyards of Britain

The Guide to the Vineyards of Britain

THE GUIDE TO THE VINEYARDS OF BRITAIN

DON PHILPOTT

MPC

Published by:
Moorland Publishing Co Ltd,
Moor Farm Road, Airfield Estate,
Ashbourne, Derbyshire
DE61HD, England

British Library Cataloguing in Publication Data
Philpott, Don
The guide to the vineyards of Britain.
1. Great Britain. Vineyards
I. Title
941.085'8

ISBN 0 86190 322 6

Cover photograph:
Lamberhurst Priory Vineyard (Patrick Eagar Photography)

Illustrations have been supplied as follows: M. Caldwell p126 (top); J. Holmes p71; MPC Picture Collection pp47, 51 (both), 67 (both), 110, 112, 117, 119, 127 (bottom), 134, 135, 138 (bottom), 154 (bottom).
All other illustrations have been supplied by the vineyards.

Colour and black and white origination by:
Scantrans, Singapore

Printed in the UK by:
Butler & Tanner Ltd, Frome, Somerset

— Contents —

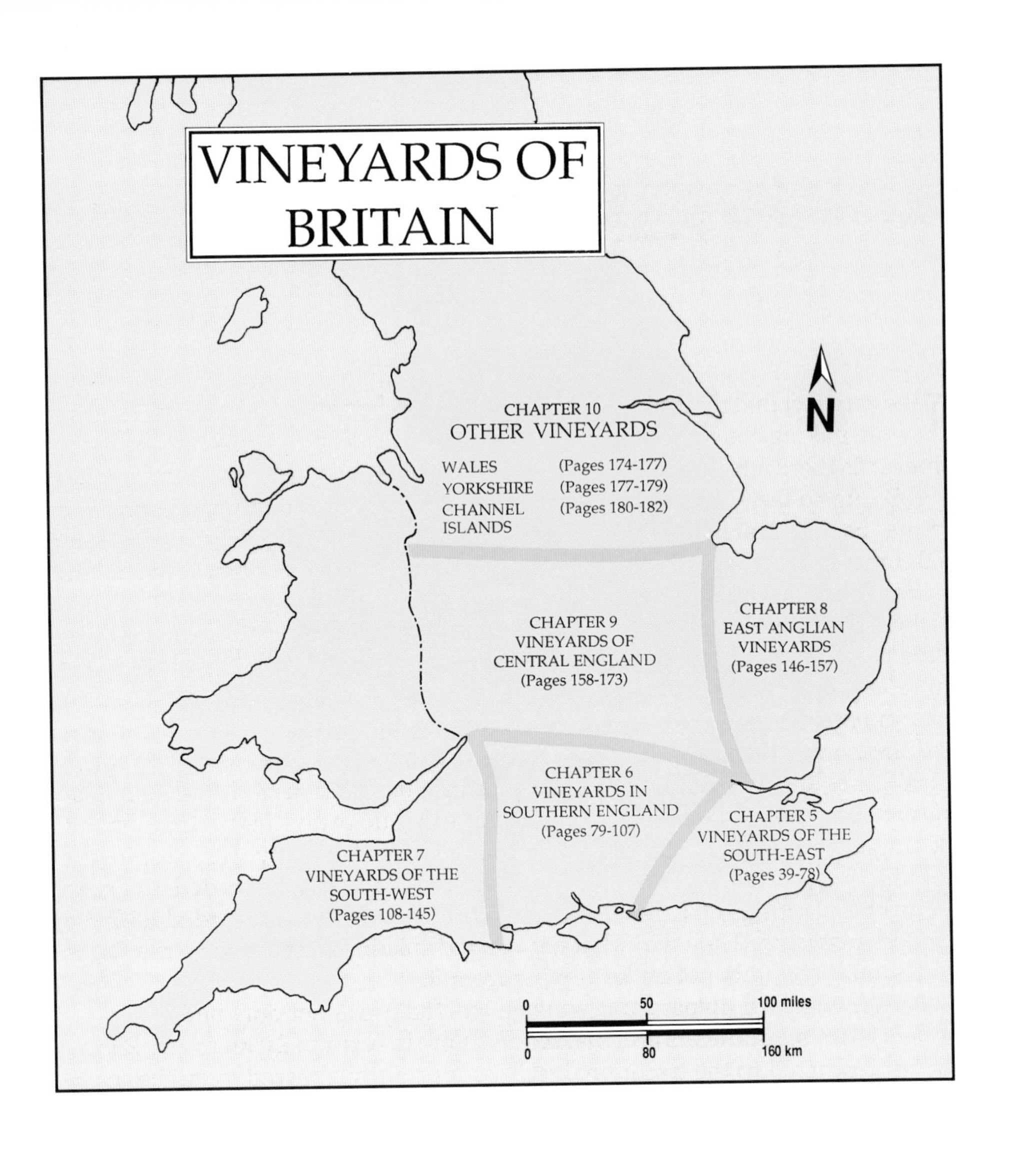
VINEYARDS OF BRITAIN
CHAPTER 10
OTHER VINEYARDS
WALES (Pages 174-177)
YORKSHIRE (Pages 177-179)
CHANNEL ISLANDS (Pages 180-182)
N
CHAPTER 8
EAST ANGLIAN VINEYARDS
(Pages 146-157)
CHAPTER 9
VINEYARDS OF CENTRAL ENGLAND
(Pages 158-173)
CHAPTER 6
VINEYARDS IN SOUTHERN ENGLAND
(Pages 79-107)
CHAPTER 5
VINEYARDS OF THE SOUTH-EAST
(Pages 39-78)
CHAPTER 7
VINEYARDS OF THE SOUTH-WEST
(Pages 108-145)
0 50 100 miles
0 80 160 km

— *Foreword* —

The very fact that this book is considered necessary shows just how far English winemaking has come in the last few years. No one knows for sure how many vineyards there now are in Britain because the number and acreage under vines is growing so fast. It is certainly well over 1,000 however, and expanding at a greater pace than at any time since the post-war revival began. There are at least 300 commercial vineyards and of these, more than a third are open to the public.

English wine must never be confused with British wine. English wine is exclusively produced from grapes grown in this country, while British wine is often made from a hotchpotch of imported grape concentrate and is not in the same league at all. English wines, however, are not the sole preserve of the English, and there are now vineyards producing English wine to be found in Wales and the Channel Islands. Vineyards are also to be found in the Irish Republic.

Winemaking in Britain is not the eccentric occupation of a few cranks or simply something to do for those wishing to while away their retirement, or looking for a hobby. For most people though, it never really was, despite the popular image of a few years ago. The dedicated pioneers who started this latest revival by planting the first vines after World War II, were regarded with the deepest suspicion. They would never make drinkable wines, and so the critics said, would certainly not make a living from it.

British vineyard owners and winemakers today are not only highly professional growers, producers and marketeers, but also extremely innovative. They are not restricted to the traditional techniques rigidly adhered to on the continent, and can and do experiment to bring an added character to English wines.

Marvellous *Méthode Champenoise* wines produced in Sussex have won the plaudits of French winemakers, while German producers have praised the fresh, fruity style that typifies so many of the English wines.

At long last English winemaking is being taken seriously by other producing countries, and while England will never rival the huge volumes of most of its competitors, it can match quality time and time again. Today, the best English wines can compete on equal terms with the finest foreign wines. English wines are to be found in the finest restaurants in London, Paris and New York. They are served during banquets at 10 Downing Street and at British embassies around the world, and are being exported to every continent.

This guide has been written to encourage more people to visit British vineyards and see just how good the wine has become. Many of the vineyards can be visited by following the well signposted wine routes that have been established in several parts of the country. This guide tells you how to find these and the many other vineyards which are open to the public but not so well publicised.

Often the vineyards are in the heart of beautiful countryside, and a visit can be part of a day's outing taking in other places of interest as well. The guide also gives advice on recommended places to eat and stay if you wish to extend your visit. English wine has come of age and I hope this guide will lead you on an unforgettable journey of discovery.

Montagu of Beaulieu
(President of the English Vineyards Association)

— Preface —

A couple of years ago I was rooting about in the cupboard under the stairs when I came across a bottle of 1975 Lamberhurst Müller-Thurgau. The wine had been bought shortly after bottling and had lain forgotten and undisturbed for all that time. Obviously we opened it although we expected it to have gone off long before. Not a bit, the wine was wonderful. It was no longer fresh but it was still fruity and had acquired a lovely bouquet and soft bottle age. It brought home in the nicest possible way, just how far English winemaking has come in the last couple of decades or so.

Alas, far to much English wine was sold quickly because, with such small production, the growers and winemakers had to get their money back as soon as possible to finance the next year's vintage. A great deal of wine that was made had excellent ageing potential, and few people really had the chance of experiencing this.

Today the wine industry in Britain can really be said to have come of age. The wines have scored many notable successes against big-name foreign rivals in blind tastings in this country and abroad. Winemakers now have the confidence to lay their wines down, some are ageing in wood, and almost all are experimenting and innovating with new techniques in the vineyard and winery.

The winemaking scene in Britain is now more exciting than at any time in the last 2,000 years and the next few years promise to be more exciting still. New varieties are being tried, winemaking methods are being refined even more, and the vineyard frontiers are constantly being pushed further north.

In the last 40 years winemaking in Britain has been transformed from a tiny industry to one that has attracted international interest. Since the last war a handful of people have played a crucial role in the great English wine revival—people like Edward Hyams, Ray Barrington Brock, George Ordish, the Gore-Brownes and Jack Ward.

Today, we are producing fine sparkling wines. English red wines, once considered a joke, are now being taken seriously, and new cold climate grape varieties hold out the chance of even greater advances. White wines to suit all tastes are being produced and every year, despite the vagaries of the weather, standards continue to improve.

English winemaking has developed both in size and quality, so much in the last few years that it is no longer dismissed as an offshore cottage industry by the Common Market officials in Brussels. A list of all British vineyards is being drawn up and English wine will soon be subject to all the controls our European competitors face. This may be bad news for English winemakers because of all the extra red tape, but it does mean that English wine has at last come of age, and is now ranked alongside French, German, Italian and Spanish wine as a force to be reckoned with.

The future lies in the hands of many more people than those who planted the first vines three and four decades ago, but the new army are just as dedicated and devoted to producing the best English wine they can.

This guide has been a delight to write and would not have been possible without the help of the growing army of British winemakers, most of whom gave up precious time to answer my almost endless list of questions. To all of them my grateful thanks. My thanks, too, for the wine they make and long may they do so.

I hope this guide encourages more people to learn about the vineyards of Britain and to discover for themselves just how good many of our English wines are.

Don Philpott

Chapter 1
The History of English Wines

The history of winemaking in Britain has been remarkably well documented over the centuries but there is still doubt about how the first vines were introduced to English shores. It is generally thought, however, that it was the Romans who imported them to Britain together with the art of winemaking almost 2,000 years ago.

The grape producing vine *Vitis vinifera*, is not a native of Britain and the first stocks may well have been planted illegally in England by corrupt Roman officials. It is known that Emperor Domitian, who reigned from AD81-96, issued a decree banning the planting of vineyards outside Italy. He also ordered that all existing vineyards outside Italy be halved in size. There were a number of reasons for this policy which continued for almost 200 years after the emperor's death. Firstly, the armies of the Empire were becoming increasingly stretched and the availability of imported wine, especially in northern Europe and Britain, encouraged the local population to rebellious behaviour. There was also considerable concern in Rome that wine production had become so lucrative throughout the Empire that farmers were planting vineyards rather than cultivate cereals, and food shortages and empty stomachs were a sure recipe for insurrection. Finally, wine was taxed by price in Rome, and by creating a virtual monopoly throughout the Empire, the cost shot up as did the income flowing into treasury coffers.

Although there are a number of historical works about life in Roman Britain under Julius Caesar, whose armies overran *Gaul* and then subdued Britain in 54BC, there is no mention of vineyards in England or of vines being grown during his time. So it is probable that the first vines planted in Britain were imported by Roman officials towards the end of the first century AD in defiance of the imperial decree. The vines, probably from Italy, would have been totally unsuitable for the British climate, even in the south of the country, which may explain why the acreage did not grow very large.

Some historians have suggested that the climate was so inhospitable for the production of wine, that the grapes may have been eaten as fruit, either fresh or dried. As the climate has not changed that dramatically over the last 2,000 years, and now some excellent wines are produced, this argument does not seem valid.

Wine, however, would certainly have been imported even before the Roman invasion. Large storage jars found in the tombs of tribal chiefs almost certainly held wine. The chieftains were famed for their lavish hospitality and at feasts the strong wine would have been drunk neat. It was the Romans who introduced them to the idea of diluting it by adding water.

The irony of the Domitian decree was that the Britons, who had long enjoyed their tipple, had a wide choice of other alcoholic drinks available. Beer, mead and liqueurs were all produced, often at much higher alcoholic strengths, but there is no evidence that the imperial ruling did anything to stem the flow of imported wine. It was a further irony that the decree, originally designed to push up prices, had to be repealed by the Emperor Probus in AD276 because wine cost so much, causing considerable unrest.

There were other reasons of course, for its repeal. The decree could not be enforced. The wine lobby was a very powerful and influential one, and there were sound economic and political reasons as well. The influence of the Roman Empire was already on the wane and there was no longer a need for such large invasion armies so unemployment became a problem as soldiers were demobilised. Repeal of the decree meant a massive expansion of the vineyards which created jobs and as the Romans also had a virtual monopoly on the latest winemaking techniques there was money to be made by hiring out experts to provinces and neighbouring states. It also meant the emperor could have his own 'spies' in the enemy camp.

Probus unknowingly signed his own death warrant by repealing the Domitian decree. In AD282 he was killed when Roman soldiers mutinied after being ordered to help plant the new vineyards. Although the extent of vineyard plantings in Roman Britain is unknown, there was certainly no shortage of wine. All Romans enjoyed their wine. It was drunk by the rich and powerful, as well as by the ordinary soldiers who were each allowed a daily ration, or *posca*, similar to the traditional daily tot of rum for sailors in force until a few years ago.

In the first days of the Roman occupation of Britain, wine would have been brought in using massive amphorae. These have been found in almost every villa excavated, and examples can be seen in virtually every museum serving an area which has a Roman past. There are also records of vine stocks being discovered during excavations. One such find was made at a villa at Boxmoor in Hertfordshire. No evidence has yet been found, however, of winemaking equipment such as presses or vats.

A lot of wine would have been exported to Britain aboard ships from the Roman province of *Aquitania* (modern-day Bordeaux) or Germany, where it would have been transported on river barges and then across the Channel.

Shipment of wine in these vessels would have been a risky business. After a long journey the wine could easily have gone off, and this had two effects on the trade. It encouraged producers and shippers to look for more suitable containers, and concentrated the minds of consumers on ways of getting a better product. The shippers came up with the idea of wooden casks, and the consumers decided to cut out the middle men and produce their own wine.

There were plentiful supplies of Moselle wine in the second and third centuries AD and some of it was shipped in barrels. Traces of barrels made from Pyrenees fir found in Silchester and London, most probably contained wine from Gascony. The Romans did not rate these wines very highly so exported them from their French colonies anywhere rather than Italy.

Aurelius Lunaris, a rich merchant who traded in Lincoln and York, erected an altar in Bordeaux in AD237 to celebrate his safe arrival by boat from York. He traded in wine and sold it to both the civilian and military populations. Although there were vineyards in Britain during the reign of Domitian, the boom really occurred after AD276 with the repeal of his decree. It specifically mentioned

Britain as one of the provinces from which the vine growing restrictions were lifted.

Vineyards appeared across southern England, often planted next to the villas of the local Roman governors. It is most likely that the rootstock for these new vineyards came from Italy and did not prosper. Therefore, this first surge of English winemaking was relatively short lived, lasting for only about 150 years.

When the Romans started to pull out of Britain, at the beginning of the fifth century, the vineyards went into decline and many disappeared altogether. However the winemaking tradition did not die out. Some vineyards survived and gradually wine became popular again so that by the time of the Norman Conquest it was being produced in most of the southern counties of the country.

The Venerable Bede in his *Ecclesiastical History of the English Nation* mentions vines growing in various parts of England and Ireland, and the Saxons even called October the Wyn Moneth — the month of the wine harvest. The Saxon King Alfred (849-900) passed a law which ruled that 'anyone damaging another's field or vineyard must pay compensation to the owner at an exact valuation', and in 955 King Edwy made a gift of a vineyard to the monks of Glastonbury Abbey.

The Vikings also loved wine, with many references to it in the old Norse *Sagas* and imported it to Britain from the Rhine vineyards. A great deal about the role of wine in society can also be gleaned by the many references to it in English literature, including Chaucer's *Canterbury Tales* and Shakespeare's *The Tempest* which refers to the Goblet system of pruning and training.

There were so many vineyards around Ely at the time of the conquest — the French named the area 'L'Isle des Vignes' — and the *Domesday Book* (published in 1086), recorded forty-five English vineyards in fourteen counties. Some of the vineyards were on fertile ground just outside the city of London. Those listed include Hatton Garden and Holborn, in the palace garden of the Bishop of Ely, in an area just to the north of Holborn Circus. The vineyards were on a gentle south sloping hill which ran down to the Fleet river. During the reign of Elizabeth I, the monarch transferred the land to the ownership of Sir Christopher Hatton. The area still bears his name and is one of the world's leading diamond centres.

Some indication of the fertility of these vineyards comes from the records of Raleigh, an Essex vineyard mentioned in the *Domesday Book*, which produced 540l of wine an acre.

This revival started around the beginning of the ninth century, and William of Malmesbury, the twelfth-century historian who chronicled life in Anglo-Saxon England, wrote: 'no county had so many or so good vineyards as Gloucestershire either for fertility or for sweetness of grape.' The wine he said had 'no unpleasant tartness or eagerness, and is little inferior to the French in its sweetness.'

There were a number of vineyards around Winchester and early historians argued that this was how the city came to be named. It was called *Vintonia* by the Romans, subsequently *Wintonia*, and then re-named by the Saxons as Winchester.

The second boom period for English wine followed the Norman Conquest. The Norman aristocracy planted their own vineyards, and installed Benedictine monks in monasteries throughout the land. The Benedictines had a long pedigree of winemaking, not only for devotional use, but as a source of revenue for their order.

Huge volumes of wines were needed to help celebrate the mass. From the ninth to the thirteenth centuries all the congregation took wine at communion, but this was outlawed in 1281 by the Synod of Lambeth which decreed that only the celibrant should take wine. After Henry VIII's break with Rome, he ruled that all the congregation should once again take wine to celebrate communion.

Both the nobles and the church established vineyards, even though large quantities of wine were still being imported from France. Bordeaux passed to the English crown in 1152 when Henry II married Eleanor of Aquitaine, the divorced Queen of France. It was part of her dowry and provided Henry II with huge quantities of claret. He was still a great supporter of English wine, and even had his own vineyards on the Royal estate around Windsor Castle. Bordeaux remained under the English crown until 1453.

In 1291 Martin of Ray, a local mason, was paid £66 13s 4d to build a 74ft long wine cellar at the royal palace at King's Langley, Herts, the home of Queen Eleanor of Castile, wife of Edward I. The records show that local coopers were employed to build barrels to store the wine produced from grapes grown in the palace vineyards. For centuries, the archbishops of Canterbury maintained a number of palaces, each with their own vineyard, so that wine would be available when they were travelling the country. In Kent, for instance, the archbishops had palaces and vineyards at Sevenoaks, Otford, Faversham and Teynham.

At the end of the thirteenth century, English white wine was sold for considerably less than imported wine and was nowhere near as plentiful. According to the historian Pegge, in 1420 red wine from Vasconia sold for 8 *denarii* while English wine fetched 6 *denarii*.

For almost 500 years English winemaking was to flourish as the monasteries extended both their influence and their landholdings. Because the monasteries were meticulous with their records, a great deal is known about the production and movement of wine during this period. It is known that the vineyards grew mostly white wine varieties, but as red wine was essential to celebrate the mass, elderberries were added to get the right colour. Important strides were also made in storage techniques although few monks had any real knowledge about the chemistry of wine and why it turned to vinegar.

Smaller barrels were introduced to try to keep the wine in better condition because the monks realised that once the bung was loosened and the tap opened the wine started to deteriorate. For centuries, new wine commanded higher prices than the old, simply because there was no satisfactory way of ageing wine without it being contaminated, oxidised or acidified. Bishop Haman, who owned a vineyard at Halling in North Kent, sent a gift of his own wine to the 19-year-old Prince of Wales — later to become Edward II — in 1303 when he was staying at Bockingfold.

Although most of the monastic orders were broken up on the orders of Henry VIII at the time of the Dissolution, a number of the vineyards survived. The monastery lands, including their vineyards and wineries, were simply transferred to the ownership of favoured lords and nobles. The extent of the vineyards can be traced in some degree by the number of places still called 'The Vine'. The name can be found over and over again in counties throughout the south of England.

For the next 400 years English winemaking did continue with some notable innovations. Winemakers from different areas of Europe were invited by the British nobility to run their estates, new vine stocks were introduced and new, lighter styles of wines developed. Attempts were also made to establish vineyards further north.

Pegge quotes references to vineyards at Over-Arley, Staffordshire, where wine was made 'altogether undistinguishable from the very best French wines by the most judicious palates,' and at Darley Abbey in Derbyshire.

In 1610 Robert Cecil, the first Earl of Salisbury, started a vineyard at Hatfield on the banks of the river Broadwater. The eminent botanist John Tradescant was sent to Flanders by Cecil to find suitable vines and the following year the French ambassador in London arranged for 30,000 vines to be shipped to Hatfield, which was later visited by Samuel Pepys and recorded in his diaries.

The diarist Thomas Philpott wrote in 1659 that Captain Nicholas Toke had a vineyard at Godington, Great Chart, in Kent, where he 'hath so industriously and elegantly improved our English wines, that the wine pressed and extracted out of their grapes seems not only parallel, but almost to out-rival that of France.'

There were two major developments in the seventeenth century that boosted English winemaking. While vineyard techniques had been steadily improving, not too much progress had been made in the winery itself. The two developments were chaptalisation, the addition of sugar to improve the balance of the wine, made possible by imports of relatively cheap cane sugar from the plantations in the West Indies, and the first 'hydrometer' which gave some indication of the strength of the must. The hydrometer was a fresh egg and Sir Kenelm Digby wrote in 1669 that honey should be added to the must 'until a fresh egg floats to the depth of twopence'. The more sugar that was added, the higher the egg would float. The other great innovation at the end of the eighteenth century was the widespread introduction of the cork which prevented the deterioration of wine once it had been bottled, and allowed stocks to be kept to mature.

Glasshouses had also become very fashionable on many of the large estates and it is likely that more attention was paid to growing vines indoors during this period rather than on the outdoor varieties in the vineyard. There is also evidence that many vineyards were still being planted with unsuitable varieties which discouraged many growers. Some are thought to have planted dessert varieties even though they wanted the grapes for winemaking.

The noted French winemaker David Geneste was persuaded to leave his estate at Guienne in 1739 to oversee the Honourable Charles Hamilton's vineyard at Painshill, Cobham. The 35,000 vines yielded both red and white wines, and hundreds of hogsheads were produced over the next 30 years.

General James Oglethorpe, who founded Georgia in North America for imprisoned English debtors, built a walled vineyard at his home at Westbrook Place, Godalming, and produced a 'wine like Rhenish'. A similar style wine was made there for 100 years from 1720, although the general died in 1784 at the ripe old age of 89.

Contemporary accounts record that in the 1760s, the Duke of Norfolk produced 28,350l (sixty-three pipes) of red wine from his vineyards at Arundel Castle in Sussex. Production continued until the 1820s, and the vineyards were replanted in 1970 after a rest of 150 years.

According to the records, Arundel wine was said to be similar to those from Burgundy while the white wine produced by the Marquis of Bute at Cardiff Castle in Glamorgan between 1873 and 1913, from his vineyards at nearby Castle Coch, were said to resemble 'still champagne'. In 1887 he made 3,600 bottles, and production had risen to 12,000 bottles by 1893. He also made red wines and appointed leading London wine merchant Hatch Mansfield to sell it.

There were many books published on English vineyards during the eighteenth century by such authorities as Sir Edward Barry, William Speechley and Philip Miller.

In the seventeenth century alone almost a score of books were written on English wine, including one by John Rose, King Charles II's head gardener at St James's. He mentions six vine varieties, a new white grape (presumably a seedling developed for the English conditions), White Muscadine, the Parsley grape, the Muscadelle and red and white Frontiniaq. His ideal conditions for vines were for a light sandy soil about 2ft deep with a stony surface, and a bottom of chalk or gravel free from springs. The vines should be planted on a south or south-west facing slope and be protected from the north by hills or trees. Brambles were always a good indication that the soil was suitable for vines. He pointed out that vines could be planted in loamy soil but warned that the growth would be too vigorous which would reduce yields.

The vines were planted during the winter at 2ft intervals in rows 3ft apart and running from east to west, giving a density of 7,260 vines an acre. Pruning took place in January and a sort of early Guyot system of training was adopted. In the summer shoots were snapped off and leaves removed to aid ripening of the grapes, the bunches of which were limited by trimming.

Phillip Miller was the gardener to the Apothecaries, the garden of which can still be visited alongside the Chelsea Embankment in London. He lived from 1691-1771 and his most famous work was *The Gardeners' Dictionary*, which contained a 65,000 word section on vines with many columns devoted to English vineyards. Miller promoted a less intensive system of viniculture with the vines planted at intervals of 6ft, in rows 10ft apart giving a density of 726 vines to the acre. The large spaces between the vines helped the air to circulate thus reducing the risk of disease, he argued. Although American mildew did not reach Britain until the nineteenth century, there might already have been problems with botrytis (mould).

He did a great deal of work on improving winemaking techniques, and experimented with sulphur fumes as a disinfectant, and other additives to control the wine. He used egg white, milk, ashes and even flour as fining agents, powdered alabaster, marble and chalk to clarify it and reduce acidity, and sulphuric acid to increase acidity levels. Miller was not averse to the addition of boiled beetroot or elderberry juice to improve the colour of red wines, and flavours were enhanced by adding beech bark, cloves, cinnamon, nutmeg, ginger, saltpetre and many other substances. But he did stress that a lot of these additives were unnecessary if care was taken in making the wine by keeping equipment clean and sterilising with sulphur fumes. His book also contains two prints depicting giant wine presses. Based on the traditional cider press, the grapes were wrapped in cloth then laid on the floor of the press and each layer of grapes was separated by a layer of wooden battens.

One of the most famous vineyards of the day was that owned by the Honourable Charles Hamilton at Pain's Hill, Cobham in Surrey. The workings of the vineyard were vividly recorded by Sir Edward Barry in his *Observations, Historical, Critical on the wines of the Ancients and the Analogy between Them and Modern Wines*, published in 1755.

It is known that initially red wine grapes were grown, the Black Cluster, or Pinot Noir, which was introduced from Champagne, and the Auvernat, probably from Auvergne, although exactly what it was is not clear.

The wines were 'very harsh and austere' and not really fit to drink, but there was the suggestion of a flavour similar to that found in some French white wines.

He uprooted the vineyards, planted white wine varieties and in his first year of production proclaimed, 'it nearly resembled the flavour of Champagne'. After a further 2 or 3 years as the vines developed, he said of his white wine, 'it has a finer flavour than the best Champagne I ever tasted'.

Most of the people who tried the wine agreed with him, including his French aristocratic guests, but he remarked, 'such is the prejudice of most people against anything of English growth, I generally found it most prudent not to declare where it grew, till after they had passed their verdict upon it.' The wine was so popular that he was able to sell it to wine merchants for fifty guineas a hogshead (207l or about 480 bottles), and they sold it on for up to 10s 6d a bottle.

Grapes were picked at the last possible minute and transported to the winery in small quantities. All rotten grapes were thrown out and the remainder put into the press. The free run was kept separate and the must placed in tightly sealed reinforced hogsheads where fermentation started within a few hours. The hogsheads were overwintered in a barn, and the wine racked into clean barrels only on cold days. Isinglass was used for fining if needed, and the wine was bottled at the end of March.

Storing the wine in the cold barns did help retain some of the gas from the first fermentation, and this reacted with the residual sugar as the weather got warmer to set off secondary fermentation in the bottle. This produced a lively, fresh wine usually drunk within 6 weeks of bottling, although the experts believed it reached its peak after about a year. After 2 years in the bottle it started to decline, losing its flavour and sweetness, but Barry reports that he kept some for 16 years and said it could easily have been mistaken for old Hock.

A great opportunity to boost the popularity of English wines was lost at the beginning of the nineteenth century during the Napoleonic Wars. Throughout this period there was a prohibition of trade with France, but smuggling was rife and wine continued to flow into the country, especially from the merchants in Bordeaux. Rather than develop English wines, there was a great vogue in the country to copy continental styles. Books were published with instructions on how to make a gooseberry wine, said to be similar to Champagne but in reality could not have been more different, although there is today a winery producing a very good sparkling gooseberry wine. The winemakers rightly feel no need to compare it with anything else.

The technique for producing the nineteenth-century gooseberry wine however, left a lot to be desired. About 3lb of sugar was added for every gallon of must, and after fermentation 2.25l of brandy was added for every 22.5l of wine. The finished product would have been a sweet, clinging liqueur with an alcoholic strength of 22° or more.

There was a gradual decline in the popularity of vineyards towards the end of the nineteenth century, partly because of the introduction of diseases, such as American mildew, both powdery and downy, and phylloxera which was already devastating the vineyards on the continent. Powdery mildew was first discovered in a Margate glasshouse in 1845 and quickly spread round the country. Commercial vineyards could control it by applying sulphur dust but the disease killed off thousands of domestic vines. Downy mildew made a first brief appearance in England in 1894 and did not reappear for another 32 years. It is controlled by spraying with Bordeaux mixture, a blend of copper sulphate and lime. Phylloxera was found first in Europe in Hammersmith in 1863 and did not cause significant damage to English vines at the time but it has appeared again and is posing a threat in the 1980s after being discovered in a number of vineyards. Fortunately the spread of phylloxera can now be controlled. Insects and bugs can be protected by insecticides, unwanted weeds and other growth controlled by herbicides or ploughing in, but there is a growing interest in organic wines which has been fuelled by the recent concern about food safety. An increasing number of producers are now offering organic wines. Another reason for the decline of the vineyards was the liberalisation of taxes on imported wine in 1860 when the duty on French wine was slashed from 1s a bottle to 2d, making it very much cheaper.

At the turn of the century, most of the attention was being devoted to producing dessert grapes. In the Channel Islands the table grapes were grown under glass and the houses were known as vineries. It was only when cheaper imported grapes became available that these greenhouses were switched to producing tomatoes. Most of the large houses and estates had their own heated vineries, coal for heating was plentiful and like the labour was cheap. The Marquis of Bute's Castle Coch Vineyard survived until World War I. The onset of war meant all the land was needed to grow crops and most of the remaining vineyards were grubbed out. There was a shortage of sugar anyway, and not enough labour to man the vineyards had they survived.

So by the beginning of the 1900s many of the commercial vineyards producing wine had already gone out of business, although a few staggered on. One of the many casualties of World War I was the vineyard industry in Britain, and it was to be almost 30 years before it was to embark on its current and greatest revival.

Chapter 2
The Great Revival

Records do not show exactly when the last bottle of English wine was made during World War I but the last commercial vineyard certainly closed down before 1918 with no record of any production over the next 30 years. In fact, during those three decades English wine became something of a joke. Few people could remember the fine English wine they had drunk before the war, any bottles laid down were drunk, and by the start of the World War II, English wine had totally lost its identity and was considered by many to be in the same league as home made fruit wines.

Strangely it was World War II which really encouraged the revival in English winemaking. It gave many soldiers stationed overseas a taste for wine, and some of these experimented with small private vineyards when they returned home. It was Ray Barrington Brock who during 1946, set in motion the steps needed to restore English viticulture to its former glory. From his home in Oxted, and at his own expense, he started to examine scientifically the 2,000 or so varieties of wine producing vines to see which were suitable for the British climate. Using his training gained while working as a research chemist with the photographic firm Ilford he set about isolating the most suitable vines and his findings, together with the publication in 1949 of *The Grape Vine in England,* by Edward Hyams (another revivalist vineyard owner), proved the stimulus that was needed.

Major General Sir Guy Salisbury-Jones was encouraged to plant a 3-acre vineyard at Hambledon in Hampshire in 1952. With the help of winemaker Anton Massel, he produced the first commercial English wine for more than 30 years. The great English wine revival had started and is continuing to go from strength to strength.

Although Hambledon was the first commercial vineyard in production, many other people had started to plant vines and experiment with winemaking techniques. However it is useful to go back a few years, and see how the revival came about.

George Ordish, author of *Vineyards in England and Wales,* which is still regarded as a text book on British viticulture, planted his first vines in 1936. He took cuttings from vines growing locally and augmented these by buying stock from a local nurseryman who recommended Black Hamburg which he was to discover were useless for outdoor purposes. He had been interested in winemaking for many years producing fruit and flower wines, but it was a spell in Champagne working on pest control experiments in the vineyards that fired his imagination. He noticed that the climate in Champagne was very similar to that of southern England although winters were much milder this side of the Channel.

Throughout the south of England there were still traces of old vines mostly growing on old houses. The vines were being killed by powdery mildew, but had obviously flourished at one time so the climate and soil must have been suitable. Ordish set about planting his vines and cuttings on the sunny walls of the house but also used a 'High Culture' system with wires running across the garden. Mildew was controlled by dusting with sulphur and the first vintage was gathered in 1940 — enough to produce 270l for home drinking. He quickly realised that he could make better white wine than red, although in three exceptional years — 1945, 1947 and 1949 — he produced 'some good red'. His main variety was Brant, which had a slight labrusca flavour, and was late ripening.

Edward Hyams had already planted small vineyards near Canterbury, Kent, and at Ashburton in Devon, before writing his book. He had also discovered that a vine growing up the wall of a cottage beside the main road in Wrotham, Kent, was a strain of Pinot Noir, a variety he considered very suitable for England.The discovery led to a lot of media coverage with numerous articles and broadcasts about the possibilities for English wine. The nurserymen were quick to note the growing public interest and set about providing vines suitable for planting out of doors.

It is clear from Ordish's account, however, that little testing was done to see how suitable the vine varieties were for the climate, and in the early days it is likely that many of the vines were not even correctly labelled.

It was around this time (1946) that Ray Barrington Brock started his scientific studies of the different vine varietes. He set up the Viticultural Research Station at Oxted in Surrey, and funded all the work himself. He catalogued the various vines, published his findings and held open days to encourage growers. He answered more than 2,000 postal enquiries a year and sold vines which showed promise.

Brock discovered enormous confusion about the vines available because same varieties were often sold under a large number of different names. He also became the first person in Britain to be granted a licence to produce brandy. He had found a number of varieties of grape which he thought would make wine suitable for distillation, but it took almost a year of constant battling with customs before they would agree to give him a licence. Even then, they imposed the ludicrous restriction that none of the brandy produced was to be drunk but immediately destroyed. The revenue men did relent a little, however, and allowed small quantities to be tasted 'for experimental purposes', and by all accounts some very good brandy was produced.

The authorities did not take his work seriously and refused all applications for grants, so he continued to fund the operation himself until 1970. By this time he had completed most of the research he had wanted to do and closed the station. As so often happens, it was about then that the authorities realised the importance of his work and its enormous potential. Staff at the Ministry of Agriculture's research station at Long Ashton in Somerset, and researchers at Wye Agricultural College in Kent, continued his work. Although the station closed down he continued to grow his approved varieties, and the revival of English winemaking since the last war owes an enormous debt to his dedication and foresight.

Another of the early pioneers was Jack Ward who founded Merrydown at Heathfield, just on the Sussex side of the border with Kent, in 1946. The company

Cutting ripe grapes from the vine at Loddiswell Vineyard, Devon

made cider and fruit wines and in the early 1950s marketed a cider with about 12 per cent alcohol. It was in effect an apple wine, but as cider did not attract any duty at this time, neither did the apple wine. It became hugely popular and the government introduced speedy legislation in 1956 to apply excise duty to cider over 8.55 per cent alcohol.

The company went ahead and planted its own vineyard and started to produce wine from its own grapes, offering winemaking facilities to other nearby vineyard owners. The number of British vineyards grew, not just through the south of England but northwards and into Wales. English wine began to be recognised again in its own right and was no longer considered a curiosity. Sir Guy Salisbury-Jones, who was marshal of the Diplomatic Corps in London, did an enormous amount to establish the credentials of English wine. In 1967 the English Vineyards Association (EVA) was founded with Sir Guy Salisbury-Jones as its first president, and Jack Ward as chairman, a position he held for 14 years. In all that time he missed only one meeting, and that was when he went to Buckingham Palace in 1978 to receive his OBE for services to English viticulture. There were fifteen founder members who between them had 10 acres of vineyards, although membership had risen to twenty by the end of the first year.

Jack Ward said, 'I do not think we shall ever produce a Château Latour, but we can produce a good wine. Our climate, awful though it is, is no problem. We can overcome the bird problem, which is bad in England. We can just about absorb the heavy duty imposed by the government. But it is the acceptance by the public and by the trade that is the really dodgy issue. There are two main requirements for growing wine in Britain: good drainage and protection from the wind. A vine needs only 150 days of about 50°F (10°C) during its growing season. It can grow on almost any type of soil, including chalk, as indeed all Champagne vines are'. Another of the great pioneers of the revival were the Gore-Browne's who helped found the EVA and whose trophy is the most prestigious award.

In 1968 Jack Edgerley planted the first vineyard in Suffolk at Kelsale. A retired barrister, he planted the vineyard as an experiment, but it was one that paid off because in 1974 he won the gold medal for English wine in the International Wine and Spirit Competition. The wine was marketed by Adnams of Southwold, who had no difficulty selling the 2,500 bottles produced each year.

A near neighbour was soon to be Kevin Fitzgerald, a director of Suffolk vineyards which had about 20 acres under wine, and managed 50 acres more for other growers. The company opened its winery in the autumn of 1975 at Bruisyard, with storage facilities for up to 200,000 bottles.

Also in 1968 Ken Barlow planted his 8-acre vineyard at Adgestone on the Isle of Wight. His first commercial harvest was in 1970 when he produced 6,000 bottles and the following year 24,000. The winemakers looked for a yield of at least 2 tons of grapes an acre in an average year, and expected to produce 1,000 bottles of wine from each ton of grapes gathered. In 1969 Prince Charles was presented with a bottle of Welsh wine thought to be the first produced in the principality for more than half a century. It came from a small hillside vinery at Pembrey, Carmarthenshire, and was laid down in the wine cellar at Buckingham Palace. The prince was recommended to drink it in 1971.

Pembrey '67 was surprisingly a light red wine and Master of Wine Michael Broadbent who tasted a bottle at the time, said it was 'a light, pleasant drink, slightly sweet, nice acidity, well made but not a classic dinner wine. A wine to be drunk by itself rather than with a meal. Like a Loire red in character, reminding one perhaps of a Bourgeuil'. He thought a reasonable price for the wine would be 16s a bottle (80p), which included 5s (25p) duty. The 5s duty was a particular stumbling block for the early producers. Once a vineyard owner had registered his property by paying a 5 guinea fee, he had to pay the 5s duty on every bottle of wine sold.

Pembrey Vineyard, formed in 1969, was the oldest of twenty-six, most of them small, that had been planted in Wales by enthusiasts after experts had pronounced the terrain and climate suitable for viticulture. It was planted by Mr George Jones, known locally as Jones the Grape, and the father of Welsh viticulture.

Most of the Welsh vineyards were too small to produce wines commercially. The largest was owned by Wing Commander Lewis Mathias, who farmed near Pembroke. His 2.5 acres produced 90l, about 120 bottles, in 1969.

By 1971 English winemakers were being taken seriously on the continent as well. Peter Noble, chairman of the Wine and Spirit Association, told a five nation conference in Copenhagen that there were at least 200 acres of commercial vineyards in the UK, and that the acreage was increasing rapidly. Merrydown, he said, produced one of the best '*château* bottled English wines' from its Sussex vineyards, a white wine called Anderida. 'That more land is not under vines in the UK is because it is usually more profitable to grow something else, than because the soil or the climate is unsuitable. It is difficult to grow a red wine here, but the same could be said for West Germany,' he told the conference.

Also in 1971 Britain was negotiating to join the Common Market and the

English Vineyards Association applied for a government approved Certification Trade Mark for English wine. The standards of quality laid down were harder to obtain than the German *Qualitätswein*, or the French QPSR, as it was then. Although the English were striving to produce quality wines, they still had to include the words 'table wine' on their labels. The EVA Certification Trade Mark, now known as the Seal of Quality, has been in force since 1979 and sets the target to which all English winemakers aspire.

In 1973 Sir Guy Salisbury-Jones notched up another milestone in the English revival by deciding to export the wine from his 4-acre Hambledon vineyard to France and Germany. At the same time, he threw HM customs and excise into turmoil. Customs had piles of forms for wine being imported into Britain, but they had never had to deal with wine going the other way, not for several hundred years at least. Sir Guy, who was still president of the EVA, claimed to be the first Englishman 'brave enough to tackle the French and Germans at their own game for 300 years'. The wine was simply labelled 'Hambledon Wine', and despite such modest packaging, he succeeded in winning orders from wine merchants in Paris and Hamburg. 'The customs chaps here seemed to be confused by the fact that I actually wanted to export wine. They didn't seem to know which forms to send me,' said Sir Guy. He dispatched five cases of wine to a merchant in Paris but because of the customs confusion, they took more than 5 weeks to arrive. The export was a success however, and within months, the vineyard was sending small consignments as far afield as Japan and the USA. Sir Guy also attempted to break down prejudices by inviting parties of French and German schoolchildren to visit his vineyards. 'It is ironic that after 20 years of viticulture I find continental wine growers are more likely to take English wine seriously than the wine drinkers on my own doorstep,' he said. Despite this, most of his wine was bought on the English market and 1973 was the first year he had to introduce rationing, partly because of a small crop the previous year (the weather was always the major problem, and bad weather wrecked the vintages between 1972 and 1974), but mainly because of the wine's popularity. His aim throughout was to produce quality wines which is why in 1974 when he came to replace some of his vines, he substituted his hybrid Seyve Villard with a bigger proportion of the 'nobler' Chardonnay and Pinot Noir vines.

He was selling his wines for about £1.50 a bottle and prices were helped by the government's recognition early in 1973 that there was a difference between genuine English wines and British wines made from imported concentrate, reducing the excise by half. It was something for which Sir Guy and the other vineyard owners had been campaigning for years.

By 1973 there were 300 members of the EVA, almost all of them non-commercial. The following year there were forty commercial viticulturalists registered, tending 385 acres of vines from Lincolnshire in the north to the Isle of Wight, and from Cornwall in the west to Suffolk in the east.

In 1964 total production of English wine was estimated to be 1,500 bottles but by 1971 had increased to 30,000, had doubled to 60,000 in 1975 and reached 200,000 in 1976. Total English wine production in 1978 topped 500,000 bottles a year, certainly higher than the levels reached at the industry's previous zenith during the Middle Ages.

A blind tasting by experts concluded at Christie's in London contained six English wines and six each from Germany and France. All were unlabelled and cost between £1.50 and £2 a bottle. Most of the experts were unable to distinguish between the English and continental wines, and many placed the English wines at the top of their preference lists.

By the summer of 1975 there were 516 acres of English vineyards, mostly in the south-east and eastern parts of the country, and almost all devoted exclusively to the production of white wine.

In 1977 membership of the EVA had grown to 385 and there were more than 600 acres of commercial vineyard between Sheffield and Southampton and the vintage that year yielded 400,000 bottles.

Although English wines were contributing £1 million a year to the Treasury, a delegation of winemakers travelled to London in July of that year to protest to the government that they were not being taken seriously. 'English wine is by far the most profitable side of British agriculture as far as the Chancellor of the Exchequer is concerned, but the industry suffered all the disadvantages of the Common Market's agricultural policy, while the government denied it any of the advantages. Wine was cheap on the continent, but heavily taxed in Britain. Growers had to work on overdrafts to pay the tax too' said Sir Guy Salisbury-Jones, who led the delegation as president of the EVA. The press were invited to a splendid meal which consisted of: Elham Park from Norfolk and Hambledon '75 as apéritifs; an experimental Hambledon '76 with the avocado mousse; Adgestone with the sole Veronique; New Hall from Essex and Lamberhurst Priory from Kent with the cold meats, Wootton from Somerset, and Magdalen from the Isle of Wight with the English cheeses.

In 1978 the government got into the English wine business but only as an experiment to find out whether the revival of commercial grape growing was economically viable. An acre of young vines planted at the ministry's Efford Experimental Station, near Lymington in Hampshire, bore their first fruit, and the grapes were taken to the Long Ashton research station in Bristol, which had its own winery. The quality and palatability were both assessed as high.

The number of commercial vineyards of more than an acre topped 115, and the total acreage of vineyards was expanding so fast that the EVA, which now had 525 members, admitted it was unable to keep track. The acreage with new plantings covered about 750 acres.

At an important wine tasting held on the Moselle in August 1979, high quality vintages from seven countries including France and Italy were assessed by a panel of international wine judges. The one that stood out head and shoulders above all the others was a white wine from Shepton Mallet in Somerset. The EVA membership was over 700 and English wine was being exported throughout the continent.

In 1978 Pilton Manor Vineyard at Shepton Mallet, Somerset started exporting wine to Italy. The first order was for 200 cases of Riesling Sylvaner which was sold in northern Italian towns. 1979 was another landmark because it was the year that the EVA's Seal of Quality, England's own Appellation Contrôlée, was officially recognised after years of fighting with government departments. Although the EVA applied for the seal in 1971 it took 8 years before it got official blessing, and in September 1979 eight English wines were awarded certificates for excellence.

The wines underwent eight different laboratory tests before being judged by a panel of experts for colour, clarity, bouquet and above all, taste. The vineyards to receive an award were: Adgestone, Isle of Wight, Cavendish Manor and

Glyndwr Vineyard, Cowbridge, South Glamorgan

Highwaymans (both in Suffolk), Horam in Sussex, Lamberhurst and Penhurst (both in Kent), New Hall in Essex and St Ethelreda in Cambridgeshire.

Winner Kenneth McAlpine, owner of Lamberhurst Priory, which with 33 acres was the country's largest vineyard, said 'I'm delighted because it is very important that the British public has some way of telling the better and sometimes very poor English wines apart. Otherwise they may taste a poor one and assume all taste the same.'

Although the quality scheme was officially recognised in Britain, it still did not have the blessing of the Common Market. Under EC Appellation Contrôlée regulations, a vineyard must have been in production for a minimum of 10 years, and must have a reputation for quality going back at least 10 years.

As far as Brussels was concerned, English vineyards were still in the experimental stage. The English vineyards had to conform with most EC viticulture and winemaking regulations from 1978 when Britain became a full member of the community after the 5-year transition period, although there were a number of important exemptions. The UK became part of the community's wine growing area Zone A, which also included West Germany, Luxembourg, Holland and Germany.

By 1979 there were 220 registered vineyards of half an acre or more and it was the year that a tiny English vineyard trounced the most illustrious French and German *châteaux* to win the accolade of producing one of the world's finest wines.

The Wootton '78 from North Wootton, near Wells, Somerset, came first in the Traminer section of the Wine Olympiad, organised by the French gourmet magazine *Gault-Millau*. To dent Gallic pride even further, Wootton Vineyard, owned by retired army major Colin Gillespie, and his wife Susan, consisted of only 6 acres of grubbed-up orchard of which only 3 acres were in production. The vineyard only made 9,500 bottles in 1978. Their wine 'crisp and flowery' sold at the door for £3.15 a bottle, and Major Gillespie said he had no idea how the wine came to be entered in the Olympiad. The blind tasting by 62 wine experts involved 330 wines in 22 categories from 34 countries. France took top honours in ten categories, mostly for red wines. Also in 1979 Pieroth, Germany's biggest wine company, acquired a 28-acre vineyard in Sussex, near Uckfield. They planned to increase production from 70,000 to 250,000 bottles a year and make it 'an international showplace for English wine'.

English wine production in 1980 slumped because of the poor summer and many producers made a loss with average yields down to about a quarter of those from an average year. The industry had not enjoyed a really good vintage since 1976 and put 1980 down with 1978 and 1972 as the worst in its short history. Only about eighty of the 230 English vineyards were commercially viable, but even the succession of poor harvests did not discourage new entrants, or increased plantings. Bill Carcary, the manager at Hambledon, said the economic cost of wine produced at his vineyard would be £75 a bottle, but it was clearly impossible to charge customers that sort of price. Most English wines retailed at between £2.40 and £4.

English ingenuity at winemaking showed no bounds. In October 1980, the grapes from a vine brought to England from Malta by Royal Engineers on their way home from the Crimean War in 1856, were put on show in Farnborough. The vine had flourished for more than a century in the greenhouse of the government-owned Vine House, in Farnborough Road, Aldershot. Queen Victoria used to eat the grapes and fed them to her royal guests. Members of the Farnborough Wine Circle heard about the vine and persuaded the authorities to let them take over responsibility for it. The grapes were displayed at their annual harvest dance, and then rushed off to produce a gallon of red wine. History does not record what the wine tasted like.

The wet summer of 1980 washed out the Welsh wine harvest. Doctor Idris Thomas, owner of Wales's biggest vineyard with 1,500 vines at Llanarth, near Cardigan, produced fewer than eighty bottles, having lost 80 per cent of his crop. His wine was usually exported to the USA where it was quickly bought up by expatriate Welshmen. 'I expect the 1980 vintage will cost substantially more than a bottle of champagne,' he said.

Total production in 1981 was about 250,000 bottles but the following year the 1,000 plus vineyards, of which 220 were producing wines commercially, were gearing up for a record harvest — the first to top a million bottles. In 1976 record yields of 10 tons of grapes an acre were achieved, but 1983 was hailed as the vintage of the century. About 3 million bottles were produced and Sussex winemaker David Carr Taylor, vice-chairman of the 550-strong EVA actually reduced the price of his wines. He cut the prices of wine from his 21-acre vineyard at Westfield, near Hastings, by 50p a bottle because of the bumper harvest. The price of a varietal wine went down to £3.30, and a blended wine, produced from up to five or six varieties, down to £2.40. Exceptionally favourable conditions had given English growers a fantastic crop, he said. Parts of his own vineyard had yielded up to 15 tons of grapes an acre, nearly four times the normal average. Trellises were breaking under the strain. In 1982 he produced 56,000 bottles and quadrupled this in 1983.

There were still complaints from the wine growers about the unfair treatment they considered they were getting from Brussels and the lack of support from Westminster. English wine was still dearer than it need be because each bottle carried up to £1.40 in tax charges or interest costs. The government did not recognise the English wine industry as an agricultural concern, although it was treated as such throughout Europe giving continental producers considerable competitive advantages. On his own vineyard in 1983 David Carr Taylor had to pay £250,000 in excise duty, and the interest charge alone on this amounted to a further 7p to 10p a bottle. Excise duty was 85p a bottle and VAT ranged from 35p to 45p a bottle.

The excise duty on British wine, however, was 50 per cent less and in addition the industrial producers received 16p a litre grant from the Common Market for the privilege of using grape concentrates from EC countries.

Earlier in 1983 David Carr Taylor took the bull by the horns taking 300 cases of wine to exhibit at Sial in Paris, France's top agricultural show, to show the French just how good English wine had become. 'Good English wine is unique. It has the locked in flavour of summer days, crisp mornings and long cool evenings,' he said.

By 1984 the vineyard acreage topped 1,000 acres, and many of the vines planted in the mid-1970s were reaching maturity and this was reflected in the quality of the wines produced. The wine was being drunk in the House of Commons and at top London hotels such as the Ritz and the Dorchester. It was stocked at Harrods and in the major supermarket chains. The wine was increasingly exported to all parts of the world, and its reputation was growing fast.

There was concern, however, that the industry, with one record vintage under its belt, was fast approaching the production ceiling which would mean it losing the exemptions negotiated in Brussels as a small producer. The UK had been able to gain a number of concessions from the Common Market so that it did not have to comply with a number of the EC wine regulations. These concessions excluded Britain from strict controls on the types of vine which could be grown in different areas. About twenty different vine varieties were being cultivated commercially at this time by English growers. According to the Ministry of Agriculture, the concessions applied only to countries producing less than 25,000 hectolitres, or about 3.5 million bottles of wine a year.

The great dilemma for many growers was which vines to plant. Most growers had started out planting Müller-Thurgau irrespective of soil and local climatic conditions, and there was now a great deal of experimental work going on trying out new clones and different varieties, and the industry was very concerned not to lose its experimental status.

The EVA estimated there were just over 200 commercial vineyards of more than half an acre in England and Wales, with the main concentration in Kent, Sussex, Hampshire, Somerset, Wiltshire, Essex, Suffolk and Norfolk. The association also said vineyards needed to be at least 5 to 7 acres to provide a living, while some growers said at least 10 to 15 acres are required to make the initial capital investment worthwhile.

Kenneth McAlpine of Lamberhurst Priory, was the country's largest winemaker, producing about 750,000 bottles a year. He said it takes at least 6 years to get into profit after planting, and the vines take about 10 years to reach maturity.

The costs of planting alone, exclusive of land costs, work out at about £3,500 an acre in 1984. The greatest constraint on producers said the very most English vineyards could yield was about 10 million bottles a year.

In the last 5 years, the industry has gone from strength to strength, the acreage under vine has continued to expand, and the weather has continued to interfere with yields. An example of the interest in English wine came when Hambledon vineyard went on the market after the death of Sir Guy Salisbury-Jones. It was sold for well in excess of the £400,000 asking price. The vineyard at Windmill Down, Hambledon, had an annual production of between 15,000 and 20,000 bottles, and the selling agents reported intense competition for the vineyard from home and abroad.

Britain's first commercial sparkling wine to be made strictly by the *Méthode Champenoise* was launched, made from gooseberries. It was produced by Hugh Rock at his winery, Twyford, Berkshire, where 100 cases of wine were released. The first true sparkling wine made strictly by the Champagne method, using grapes, came from David Carr Taylor.

In 1985 the Ministry of Agriculture launched an investigation to discover whether phylloxera was spreading through Britain. The disease, which almost destroyed the wine industry in Europe at the end of the last century, was found in three Somerset vineyards. Investigations indicated that the disease had been imported into England on vines of the Madeleine Angevine variety, and these were the ones considered most at risk. Another vulnerable variety was the French-American hybrid Seyval Blanc.

By 1986 there were 1,220 acres of vineyards; 890 acres in production and the rest still to yield grapes. Production in 1985 fell to 870,000 bottles, less than half the total in 1984, because of the poor summer. It was an excellent vintage but a low crop. The 1986 harvest was about 1,250,000 bottles.

Gay Biddlecombe of St George's Vineyard at Heathfield in East Sussex, was one of the industry's most energetic and forceful promoters. Her wines were drunk in the House of Commons, sold in the Mitsukoshi stores in Japan, and served on flights by Continental Airways of the USA.

A growing number of tourists from the continent started to visit Britain just to see vineyards at work and taste the wine. Mrs Paula Abbs, of Syndale Valley Vineyard at Faversham said, 'we are finding German tourists flocking here. They are taking away hundreds of our £2.99 bottles which are worth something like £6 in their own country.' Although their production was only 15,000 bottles in 1986, Mrs Abbs said, 'we have been saying English wine is the best in the world for years. It seems everyone else is finally taking notice.'

In 1987 four of England's award winning vineyards joined forces to sell their wines to China where they are considered the ideal accompaniment to their finest dishes. The consortium, Wines UK, had already won export orders to Japan and Singapore. The four vineyards are Adgestone (on the Isle of Wight); Astley, (Stourport Hereford and Worcester); Wickenden (Taplow, Bucks) and Wootton (near Shepton Mallet, Somerset). 'There is an enormous potential for English wines in this part of the world and connoisseurs in the Far East have told us that our wines are the ideal accompaniment to the very best Chinese cuisine', said marketing director Mr Raymond Salisbury-Jones before leaving for Hong Kong for talks with Chinese buyers.

An English 'Beaujolais Nouveau' even appeared in November 1987, courtesy of Geoffrey Rose of Potters Bar, Hertfordshire, who produced the grapes from vines grown on his two nearby allotments. The British even reversed the traditional Beaujolais Nouveau race and offered prizes to see who could be the first to deliver the best of English wines to the heart of Paris.

The last three vintages have all been hit by miserable summers. Vineyards in the south-east were badly hit by the hurricane which swept up from the continent in October 1987 but even though many vines were destroyed, pickers were out at first light to salvage what grapes they could and some wine was made.

Today there are more than 650 members of the EVA, both commercial vineyard owners and associates who make wine for fun or have very close ties with the industry. The vineyard acreage is in excess of 1,500 acres and is still expanding fast, said chief executive Commander Geoffrey Bond.

One of the great problems today is knowing exactly how many vineyards there are in Britain. There are at least 1,000 vineyards because not all belong to the EVA, and about a third of these are producing wines commercially either in their own wineries, or by sending them to a neighbour who makes the wine under contract. The exact acreage is also unclear because new plantings are taking place at a rapid rate.

For many of the small vineyard owners, the making of wine is a relaxation, but a growing number rely on it for their living and this has led to a new breed of entrepreneur producers who are not only first class winemakers, but also professional marketeers.

Until even quite recently there were a number of reasons why the emerging British vineyard industry was treated quite casually by officialdom. Before Britain joined the Common Market, production of English wine was limited and posed a threat to no one, while nobody was too interested in it. As far as customs and excise was concerned, most vineyard owners were producing wine for their own consumption and that did not attract duty.

For a number of years after Britain joined the community, the number of English vineyards and their production was so small that again it posed no threat, but the Ministry of Agriculture deliberately underplayed the real situation so as not to attract the interest of the Brussels bureaucrats. The British government did not want to be saddled with even more EC regulations and controls, on top of the already complicated tangle of red tape surrounding all other agricultural sectors.

The extent of production is still not great when compared to other member states, but Brussels has been taking an increasing interest in the growth of British vineyards and it is only a matter of time before winemakers in Britain fall further under their bureaucratic control.

English wine can now be drunk on every continent, in many of the finest hotels and restaurants while the quality improves with each vintage. There is no doubt that English wine is now enjoying the greatest period in its long and fascinating history.

Chapter 3
Viticulture in Britain

The weather is the greatest problem facing viticulturists in Britain, but experience has shown that in good years, excellent wine can be made. Although the industry has now been flourishing for almost two decades, it is still in its infancy and there is a great deal yet to be learned, particularly about the varieties of vine planted. There is no doubt that many early varieties planted were not suitable for the UK, and a great deal of experimentation is still taking place.

Geography and climate are crucial and vineyards are ideally planted to catch maximum sunlight. They should be protected from frosts, especially spring frosts which if very severe can kill the vine. Hail and torrential summer rain can also seriously damage the crop and it is interesting to compare conditions with some of the vinegrowing areas across the Channel. Bordeaux, for instance, enjoys a temporate climate similar to that of the south of England although it enjoys warmer summers and milder winters. Over the last 30 years, the region has averaged 35in of rainfall a year, and 1,090 hours of sunshine, although there are of course enormous local variations. Burgundy can have very unpredictable weather with very hot summers and frequent bitter cold winters. It rains in Burgundy 155 days a year on average, there can be heavy falls through the summer, and June and October are the wettest months. Hail is also a problem. July is the hottest month with temperatures averaging between 70°F (21°C) and 75°F (24°C) and around Dijon there are an average 60 days of frost a year, usually between December and February. Rainfall averages 27in to 29in a year, and there are an average 2,000 hours of sunshine a year. Champagne is the most northern major vineyard region of France, and the average annual temperature is 50°F (10°C), about the lowest temperature at which vines can flourish, but the slight elevation of the vineyards on the gentle slopes protects them from all but the most severe spring frosts. It has an annual average rainfall of 26in over 176 days and 1,537 hours of sunshine.

England and Wales has an annual rainfall of 35in (average for the last 40 years), and Scotland 56in. Average daily temperature in England and Wales is 50°F (10°C) and in Scotland 48°F (9°C). England and Wales enjoys an average 1496.5 hours sunshine a year (4.1 hours a day), compared with 1,277.5 hours (3.5 hours a day) in Scotland.

A vine needs about 150 days of about 50°F (10°C) on average and about 19in of annual rainfall to flourish. It needs sunlight as well as heat but the warmth of the sun decreases the further north one travels, even though the hours of summer sunlight increase in some areas. Thus, vine growing becomes less suitable the further north one goes because there is not enough warmth to ripen the grapes. It is clear therefore that vines can be grown over most of the southern half of the

Collecting the grapes at Wickham Vineyard, Hampshire

country and well up into Central England, but it becomes questionable if it is viable beyond, unless there is a special microclimate.

After climate, siting, drainage and wind protection are the next important considerations. Although the sun is never directly overhead in Britain, a vineyard planted on a slope at the correct angle can get as much direct sunlight as if it were. So vineyards are ideally planted on south facing slopes so they literally point at the sun.

Although northern vineyards have longer days and therefore more sunshine than those further south, the strength of the sun is not that great so siting is critical to ensure maximum sunlight for photosynthesis and ripening. It is also important to prevent shading of some vines although this can also be prevented by reducing the density of planting or introducing a different system of training for the vines.

If it is not possible to plant on a south facing slope it is better to plant on flat ground. North facing slopes are clearly out, and both eastern and western slopes have serious disadvantages in that they get considerably less sunshine. West facing slopes are often exposed to damper conditions which could encourage disease, and eastern slopes often suffer from early morning mist which is a further block to sunlight. Rows planted north to south get maximum sunlight during the middle part of the day but first thing in the morning only the east facing vines get sun and these shade the rest, while the reverse is true in the afternoon as the sun starts to sink in the west. When the vines are planted east to west, most of the rows are shaded early in the day by their northern neighbour. This alignment, however, does encourage the grapes to form on the south side of the vines, and these are usually of higher quality than those growing on the north facing side of the vine. The east-west alignment also affords the vineyard protection against the prevailing south-westerly winds. Windbreaks can reduce damage to the vines, and most growers protect their vineyards by planting hedges or trees, or siting them so that they get natural protection from hills, woods and so on.

English wine growers tend to produce for quality and this influences the density of planting in the vineyard. In exceptional years 15 tons of grape to an acre have been gathered, but most growers look to yields of about 5 tons an acre from mature wines.

Mechanisation is another influence. Densely planted vineyards mean a great deal more work because there are more vines, it makes the use of mechanisation impossible and the task of gathering grapes very difficult even if hand picking.

The number of vines per acre varies according to the system of training used. The Geneva Double Curtain system involves a density of about 450 vines an acre, while the Lenz-Moser system needs between 750 and 1,050 and the Double Guyot method about 2,500. There are many other training systems including modified Lenz-Moser, Umbrella, modified Kniffen, and two tiered Single and Double Cordon. There is a great debate amongst growers as to which is the best system. Certainly the Geneva Double Curtain, favoured by many of the top growers, consistently brings in higher yields than the Guyot, which is still recommended by a number of authorities, including the Ministry of Agriculture. It may well be that training experiments being carried out in Australia and New Zealand could end all the argument by persuading growers to switch gradually to completely new systems. It is possible to operate a commercial vineyard with about 2 acres, but most growers today would say that at least 5 acres is preferable.

Yields vary enormously from almost nothing in atrocious years to that staggering 15 tons in record years. Average yields vary between 2 tons for most growers, to 8 tons, and this compares with Germany's average of 6 tons, and Luxembourg's 8 tons.

Having decided on site and tested soil suitability, drainage has to be installed before the vineyard can be planted with the selected varieties. Vines like quick draining land, which is why it is often necessary to install drainage. They do not like water logged soils because it restricts growth, and although they like rich soils this is not good for grape production because the growth is too vigorous, especially of leaves and shoots.

Stony soils have the advantage that the stones can trap the sun's warmth during the day and then slowly release it during the night encouraging further growth. Many of the world's greatest wines come from vineyards with very stony soils.

According to research by Dr Alex Muir, there are some remarkable similarities between the soils of some English vineyards and some of the great wine producing areas of France. The stony soil in the Graves area of Bordeaux is similar to Hampshire soils around Beaulieu Abbey, and Raleigh in Essex. The Thames Valley and Reading gravels are comparable to the brick-earth found in a number of Bordeaux vineyards, while the chalky downland soils of parts of Kent, Sussex, Dorset and Hampshire resemble those of Champagne. Chalky soils are good for producing light wines with good bouquet, and noble varieties do well in them, but hybrid or grafted wines usually require a chalk-tolerant root-

Vine Varieties

The most common grape varieties found in British vineyards are as follows:

White

Bacchus: a Riesling, Sylvaner and Müller-Thurgau cross, much better suited to the English climate. Produces a flowery, fragrant wine which can be quite sharp. Strong flavours of elderflower.

Ehrenfelser: a Riesling and Sylvaner cross developed at Geisenheim in 1929. Can be left on vines for late harvesting, but lacks acidity so not suitable for great ageing. It is very suitable for northern wine regions and is disease resistant.

Guttenborner: a Müller-Thurgau cross and Chasselas Napoléon cross. A neutral, bland grape, quite late budding and early ripening. Needs sheltered sites. High but very variable yields.

Gewürztraminer: trial plantings at Barton Manor on the Isle of Wight. Great potential but yields expected to be low.

Huxelrebe: growing in popularity. A cross between Gutedal and Courtillir Musqué. In good years can be honeyed with good acidity if late picked. It is often used for blending. Can have a grapefruity flavour.

Kerner: a Riesling and Trollinger cross and already very promising. Can produce style similar to a light Mosel.

Madeleine Angevine: grown as a dessert grape in many areas of the world but produces good green, acidic wines in England. Can have a pleasing elderflower nose, and if late picked, develops a more honeyed style.

Müller-Thurgau: the backbone of the English wine industry for years. A Riesling-Sylvaner cross. Can produce a very good dry varietal with good acidity which mellows and becomes honeyed with age. Often blended with a more aromatic variety.

Ortega: makes lovely, full perfumed wines, good for blending and better suited to England than the Mosel.

Reichensteiner: a multiple cross between Madeleine Angevine, Müller-Thurgau and Calabrese, now the second most planted vine in the UK. Can produce a good dry wine with elderflower fruit flavours, and makes pleasant slightly sweeter wines with hints of smokiness and honey. Good ageing potential.

Schönburger: a Pinot Noir, Chasselas Rosé and Hamburg Muscat cross which is doing very well in England. Makes a fat, fruity wine with hint of Gewürztraminer and good acidity. Difficult wine to make but tremendous when it comes off.

Seyval Blanc: a hybrid very well suited to the British climate because it is resistant to frost and is a late ripener. Can produce a dry wine with good acidity and a hint of Sauvignon, which becomes smooth and honeyed with age. Good for blending.

Siegerrebe: grown mainly for its strong aromatic properties which are used in blends.

Red and Rosé

Cabernet Sauvignon: the classic grape now being grown on Guernsey at the island's two vineyards. Potential unknown but worth following.

Pinot Noir: the great red grape of Burgundy. Has been planted by a number of vineyard owners but the red wines produced tend to be a bit thin. Much greater potential for producing rosé, and some decent pinks have been made after blending.

Seibel: a long wine from Provence where it is more generally planted, but produces a good rosé.

Triomphe D'Alsace: a hybrid which developed in Alsace. Good potential for rosé.

Wrotham Noir (or Wrotham Pinot): developed in England from Pinot Noir and Pinot Meunier. Has been used for red and rosé production.

stock. Originally varieties were planted on their own rootstock, but the emergence of phylloxera has led to vines being grafted on to resistant American rootstock.

There are a score of Common Market recommended and authorised varieties, both pure *Vitis vinifera cultivars* and hybrids, which are the result of crossing *vinifera* with many of phylloxera and others pest resistant American varieties.

The varieties recommended by the EC for use when the UK became a full member of the community were Auxerrois, Bacchus, Chardonnay, Ehrenfelser, Faber, Huxelrebe, Kanzler, Kerner, Madeleine Angevine, Madeleine Royal, Madeleine Sylvaner, Mariensteiner, Müller-Thurgau, Ortega, Perle, Pinot Noir, Ruländer (Pinot Gris), Seyval Blanc, Siegerrebe and Wrotham Noir.

Others grown or tested have included Gutedel, Guttenborner, Optima, Pinot Blanc, Reichensteiner, Riesling, Scheurebe, Schönburger, Seibil, Würzer and Zweigeltrebe.

Some time ago, the EVA also suggested the following varieties of white grapes: Précoce de Malingre and Perle de Czaba for early varieties, and Albalonga, Chasselas, Rabaner, Regner and Septimer for mid-season. Initially Müller-Thurgau, Reichensteiner and Seyval Blanc dominated the plantings and no one was really concerned with producing a red wine. In the last 15 years many of the other recommended varieties have been planted, especially Madeleine Angevine, Huxelrebe and Schönburger.

Many growers have increased their plantings of the noble varieties but the hybrids are still important because as most are late ripening varieties the grapes have more chance to develop during the fickle British summer and autumn.

Some red grape varieties are being grown, especially Pinot Noir and Wrotham Noir, and a few drinkable wines produced, although they do tend to be a little 'thin' after poor ripening years. There is also great excitement at the potential from some of the Russian varieties. Some of these cultivars from Georgia in particular, have been planted on an experimental basis for nearly 15 years by growers and research institutes. These include Gagarin Blue, Kuibishevsky and Tereshkova, all of which grow well around the Black Sea where there are bitterly cold winters and scorching hot summers. These varieties have been chosen not because the climate in Britain is similar to that in Georgia, but because the vines are so hardy to survive such extremes of temperature, that they should be able to cope with the British weather.

Chapter 4
The Winery

The Making of White Wine

A ton of grapes should produce about 675l or 960 bottles, so in a good year, when a grower with 5 acres is getting 5 tons to the acre, he or she can expect to make 27,000l of wine, enough for at least 38,000 bottles.

The basic technique for making white wine has changed little over the centuries but it has become much more sophisticated, special equipment has been produced to control the various stages of production and new materials have helped reduce the risk of contamination. It is all a far cry from some of the 'wineries' used by the pioneers of the English wine industry in the first two decades or more since the end of the last war. Many winemakers used dairy parlour equipment designed for milk collection and adapted it to their own specialist uses — and some still do.

As production increased, however, and more attention had to be paid to quality control, modern wineries were built. Because of the huge capital cost involved not all growers could afford their own wineries, so those who had, started to produce wines on a contract basis for those who had not. Still today, the majority of small vineyards do not have their own wineries and a growing number are prepared to let the experts with modern facilities produce their wines for them.

The vintage in the UK starts in October but exactly when depends on the weather. The grapes are normally picked in the first two weeks of the month, but if the weather is fine, the grower might risk delaying harvest because the longer the bunches are on the vine, the more sunshine they will receive and the more sugar will be produced. If the weather is wet or forecast to be, the grapes will be picked as soon as possible before rot can spread through the crop. It is a nail-biting time because heavy rains can dilute the sugar in the grapes and strong winds can break down the vines and damage the fruit.

The sugar content of the grape at the time of picking is the most critical factor in determining the initial alcohol content, and thus the quality of wine. The vine-yard owner, who is often the winemaker as well, will keep a very careful watch on the development of the grapes in the run up to the harvest. He or she will use a refractometer in the vineyard to test the sugar level in the grapes, and may also crush a few grapes to determine the specific gravity using a hydrometer.

The grapes are picked by hand usually when it is dry, and picking is limited each day to the quantity that can be handled by the winery. If there is a dew the pickers will wait until the moisture has left the surface of the grapes. It is important to pick the grapes carefully so that they are not damaged. Most grapes

The modern winery at Barkham Manor Vineyard, East Sussex

have only a short distance to travel to the winery for pressing.

Before pressing the winemaker must know both the sugar and acidity levels. As the grape ripens, the acidic juices are slowly converted to sugar but in the UK, as in Germany, the sun rarely shines long enough through the summer to ensure this happens. Because the grapes do not ripen fully, the natural sugar is low and the natural acidity level high—not the best ingredients for producing good wine. As a result wine growers here, as in many other countries, are allowed to enrich the must by adding sugar, and controlling the acidity by using calcium carbonate, or some other approved alkali. This has to be done before pressing or before fermentation takes place. Grapes for white wine are usually crushed and stalks pressed, but some producers de-stalk. All grape juice is white and the colour comes from keeping the juice in contact with the skins.

White wines do not normally spend much time in contact with the skins but can extract extra tannin from the stalks. Red wines spend much more time on the skins both to get colour and tannin, and are almost de-stalked first because they do not need extra tannin from them, and it can sometimes add some bitterness if not controlled very carefully.

After crushing to ensure maximum extraction of juice, the crushed grapes, or 'must' is passed to the press. Ideally, the must should be transported through tubes so that it is not exposed to the air which could cause oxidation problems.

Few wineries no longer rely on the old wooden screw presses that would have been used in the monasteries 500 years ago. Winemakers now know the importance of keeping their juice as protected as possible. Presses are enclosed and usually mechanically controlled to ensure the correct pressure is applied for optimum extraction.

The French Vaslin press is widely used throughout Europe and has found favour with a lot of UK winemakers. It is a horizontal stainless steel press which slowly rotates while the two end plates move towards each other. The juice is pressed out under pressure and then taken away by centrifugal force. After this first pressing the plates are returned to their original positions and the process repeated. The first pressing is generally considered to produce the wine, but most winemakers will use the juice from a second and third pressing.

Large wineries often use continuous presses which are ideal for coping with large quantities of grapes. An Archimedes screw delivers a steady stream of grapes into the press where the juice is extracted under pressure, runs off and collected.

There are other sorts of presses. Some consist of perforated steel tanks which contain a bladder. The grapes are placed in the press and then air is gradually pumped into the bladder so that it inflates. The grapes are pushed against the side of the tank and the juice pressed out.

The must is usually treated with sulphur as soon as it comes from the press to prevent oxidation, and to kill off any bacteria and wild yeasts. Sulphur dioxide is used and the Common Market regulations control maximum levels. Sulphuring has an important role to play but it has become a thorny question in recent years. Certainly the over-use of sulphur in cheap continental white wines has caused a problem. If used unwisely it can taint the wine and give you a nasty headache the day after. Good winemakers keep their use of sulphur dioxide to a minimum.

After sulphuring, the must is then usually passed through a centrifuge which gets rid of suspended matter in the juice, such as bits of skin, pips and so on. Fermentation then takes place mostly in large stainless steel tanks and a starter is normally used to get it going. This is usually a dose of actively fermenting yeast which acts as a catalyst and starts the chemical reaction whereby the sugar is converted to alcohol. Fermentation was once a very haphazard affair, but now it is strictly controlled by temperature. The cooler and longer the fermentation process, the greater is the intensity of flavours in the wine.

After fermentation, the wine is drawn off from the sediment which has settled at the bottom of the tank. This sediment is known as the 'lees' and winemakers have different theories as to how the long wine should be kept on them to extract flavour.

The drawing off or 'racking' usually takes place in December and a second racking may occur in February or March after a second settlement has taken place. This is normally all that is needed to produce a clear wine, but if it is still not clear, it can be fined. This process involves passing it through a filtration unit or centrifuge to get rid of the suspended solid particules which cause cloudiness. A number of fining agents are also allowed such as egg whites, gelatine and isinglass. These substances 'wrap' themselves round any unwanted solid particles and then sink to the bottom. After settling the clear wine can be racked off and the sediment disposed of.

The winery at the Chilford Hundred Vineyard, Cambridge

The racked wine is stored in sterilised barrels or tanks until ready for bottling. If a sweet or medium sweet wine is required, a little concentrated grape must is added at this stage. This addition or 'dosage' is allowed under EEC regulations.

Commercial wineries have automated bottling lines. The bottles are sterilised by boiling water or steam and the wine is pumped into the bottling hall in pipes so that there is no contact with the air. Corks, labels and capsules are all usually applied automatically in the larger wineries. A great deal of the commercial wine produced by British vineyards is still sold on their own premises. Most is sold young because the producer needs to get a quick return on his or her money. Luckily most English wine is made to be drunk young, but it can age remarkably well. As the industry develops and becomes more profitable, winemakers will be able to lay aside more of their stocks for ageing, and many of the wines will benefit as a result.

Chapter 5
Vineyards of the South-East

Kent

ASH COOMBE VINEYARD

Paul and Isabel Lucas
Coombe Lane, Ash
Canterbury CT3 2BS
☎ (0304) 813396

The vineyard is a member of the EVA and Canterbury Winegrowers and at present extends to 1.5 acres of Schönburger vines, now in their third year. A further 1.6 acres are being planted in 1989 and a further 4 acres will be added in about 2 years time. The new acreage this year consists of an acre of Seyval Blanc and a third of an acre each of Dornfelder and Kernling.

The vineyard is sited on a gentle south facing slope and gets cold winters and hot summers with relatively low rainfall. The soil is a sandy loam.

The vines are trained on the Double Guyot system and there is a programme of planned spraying at intervals during the growing season.

The vineyard is still waiting for its first harvest, but is already making plans to extend its acreage and provide facilities for visitors. The vineyard by 1991 should cover about 7 acres and there will be facilities for tasting as well as a vineyard shop.

Visiting times: visitors are welcome but because the vineyard is still in its infancy, people are asked to ring or write to make an appointment.

How to get there: take the A257 from Canterbury towards Sandwich. At Ash take the fork right signposted to Eastry. Just past the last houses, turn right into Coombe Lane which is narrow and continue until you see the vineyard.

BARDINGLEY VINEYARD

H.B. Smith and I. Winter
Bardingley Wines of Kent
Babylon Lane, Hawkenbury
Staplehurst TN12 0EG
☎ (0580) 892264

The vineyard (a member of the EVA and the Weald and Downland Vineyards Association) is run by the owners and Dr J. Gibson from Bearsted Vineyard who assists with the winemaking. The vineyard covers 2.5 acres. Main varieties are Huxelrebe, Reichensteiner, Seyval Blanc, Zweigeltrebe, Seibel 13053, Triomphe D'Alsace and Leon Millot, which each account for 15 per cent of production, and the remaining 5 per cent comes from Seibel 5455. In recent years some of the Huxelrebe has been replaced by Seyval and there is a further acre of new, but as yet unproductive, vines.

It was planted between 1979 and 1981, and all the vines are trained on the high Geneva Double Curtain system. The founder of the vineyard was determined to produce a good English red wine and many grape varieties have been experimented with. This pioneering work is being continued with encouraging results and the owners hope to plant a further 2.5 acres within the next few years. The vineyard also has a reputation for high quality blackberries and is situated 50ft above sea level on flat ground in the flood plain of the river

Beult. It is sheltered from severe winds on a sandy loam soil.
The vineyard year is as follows:
January-March: pruning according to the Geneva Double Curtain training system.
April-May: new vines are planted, the spray programme starts and continues at approximately 2 week intervals until just before harvest in October.
June-July: vines flower.
August: leaves are removed to expose the grapes to maximum sunlight.
October: harvesting takes place.

The harvest normally starts in the second week of October with Huxelrebe. About a week later the main pick of the season takes place with all the other white varieties being gathered except Seyval Blanc. The red varieties are then picked and finally Seyval. The main pick usually lasts about 2 weeks.

The grapes are crushed manually, destrigged and then tranferred to a 660lb Vaslin screw press. Fermentation takes place in stainless steel and glass fibre tanks.

The wines are checked for stability and after the initial racking and blending, fining is carried out if necessary. The wine is then filtered, tasted for sweetening and sterile filtered prior to bottling. The vineyard's aim is to achieve EVA Gold Seal standards for all its wines.

Production in 1987 was 2,330l of wines and quality was average. Production in 1988 was 3,000 litres and quality was good.

Wines produced currently are: Bardingley Blend-White, a medium dry wine, having good fruit character and dry finish; Huxelrebe, a dry, full, balanced white; Zweigeltrebe, a popular dry white with light blush colour; Estate Rosé, a dry rosé, very well balanced and Estate Red, an unusual light dry red, smooth and well balanced.

The wine is sold in local shops and off-licences, is exhibited and sold at wine shows, and county shows in the south-east, as well as direct sales, including exports if required.

There is a small winery in the grounds of Elizabethan Hall House and vineyards are listed in the area in the *Domesday Book.*

Visiting times: weekends and bank holidays only. Summer 10am-5pm, winter 11am-4pm. Wine tastings can be provided and there are ample grass areas for picnics and walks.

How to get there: take the A274 south out of Sutton Valence which lies to the south of Maidstone, but try to avoid the county town. Take the first turning on the right, and turn right again at the fork which leads to Babylon Lane and Bardingley which is about a third of a mile down a long lane.

Recommended pubs, restaurants and hotels in the area: Hare and Hounds (pub), Hawkenbury for bar snacks, and The Shant (restaurant, East Sutton), for hotel and bar meals.

BEARSTED VINEYARD

John and Elizabeth Gibson
24 Caring Lane, Bearsted
Maidstone ME14 4NJ
☎ (0622) 36974

The vineyard is a member of the EVA and the Weald and Downland Vineyards Association and covers 4 acres. It is fully planted but not all the vines are yet in production. The acreage is as follows: Bacchus 1.2 acres (29 per cent of total planting), Seyval 1.1 acres (26 per cent), Kerner 0.8 acres (19 per cent), Faber 0.7 acres (16.5 per cent), red varieties 0.3 acres (7 per cent) and experiment vines 0.1 acres accounting for 2.5 per cent of total planting.

The red varieties consist of Leon Millot and Triomphe D'Alsace, and a number of varieties are being tested on the experimental plot. The first vines were planted in 1986, and all but the Kerner are now productive.

The vineyard is 180ft above sea level on a south facing promontory in the valley of the river Len, which joins the river Medway at Maidstone. The soil is a fine sandy loam, varying in depth from 27in to 39in, over Kentish ragstone which is calcareous in nature and drains well without the need for assistance. The site is protected from the west by trees, from the south by Arnold Hill on the other side of the valley, and from the north by the North Downs.

The site is favoured by good air and water drainage and well protected from the prevailing winds. The vineyard was formerly an orchard, and lies within a mile of a Domesday vineyard.

Winters are cold enough to guarantee complete dormancy and can be severe enough to damage young vines. Spring frosts are a danger until late May. Summers are mild to warm with only moderate rainfall, and protracted autumns ripen the wood well and the grapes slowly, allowing the retention of full flavour and acidity.

The vines are trained high to a single wire and cordon-pruned so that the new shoots fall as a single curtain. This method is preferred to the more popular Geneva Double Curtain method because it provides good light intensity for the whole height of the vine on both sides, and congestion and shading between two curtains is avoided. It is more expensive however to establish with rows only 8ft apart and vines 6ft apart in the row.

Pruning is done in two stages to avoid too early a bud break, the first stage beginning in early January and the second being completed by the end of March. Regular spraying against fungal diseases takes place fortnightly throughout the growing season until a few weeks before harvest. The varieties were chosen because of their different ripening times in order to spread the harvest and the winemaking over several weeks from mid-October.

Picking normally takes place over four weekends starting with Bacchus, then Faber, Seyval and finally Kerner, but the exact dates depend on the levels of sugar and acid in the grapes, the amount of botrytis in the bunches, and the ravages of the birds. Nets are put over the crop in mid-September when the grapes begin to ripen but are never 100 per cent effective in keeping the birds away. Pickers work under the nets, picking into plastic buckets which are emptied into bins.

Grapes are transported in 55lb bins to the winery for crushing. After a brief maceration period in contact with pectin-releasing enzymes, the mash is pressed and the juice allowed to settle for 24 hours. Only the clear decantate after settling is fermented. The yeast is selected for a number of attributes such as slow, non-foaming, quick settling and minimal hydrogen sulphide producing. Fermentation usually takes 2 to 3 weeks to complete at about 59°F (15°C).

The wine is racked off its lees as soon as possible after fermentation has stopped, and left for 5 to 6 weeks to clear. Protein stability tests are carried out and fining with Kieselsol gelatine is undertaken if necessary, followed by a further racking and coarse filtering.

The wine is allowed to rest during the coldest part of winter for tartrates to deposit before final sterile pad-filtering and cold sterile bottling in March or April.

The vineyard has only had one vintage to date and the single wine produced is medium dry, fruity, with a pleasant bouquet, moderate body and fair finish. It has been awarded the EVA Seal of Quality.

The vintage was collected in one weekend because only half the vineyard was mature enough to produce fruit, and even that was controlled to produce a light crop. It is important at this stage in the vine's life that most of the energy goes into producing a strong, permanent framework capable of carrying heavier crops in future years. The grapes picked, however, were in excellent condition, and in spite of an indifferent summer, reached a respectable sweetness level of 65 Oechsle.

The vintage was vinified by the Gibsons at another vineyard. In the future they plan to create their own winery in a building

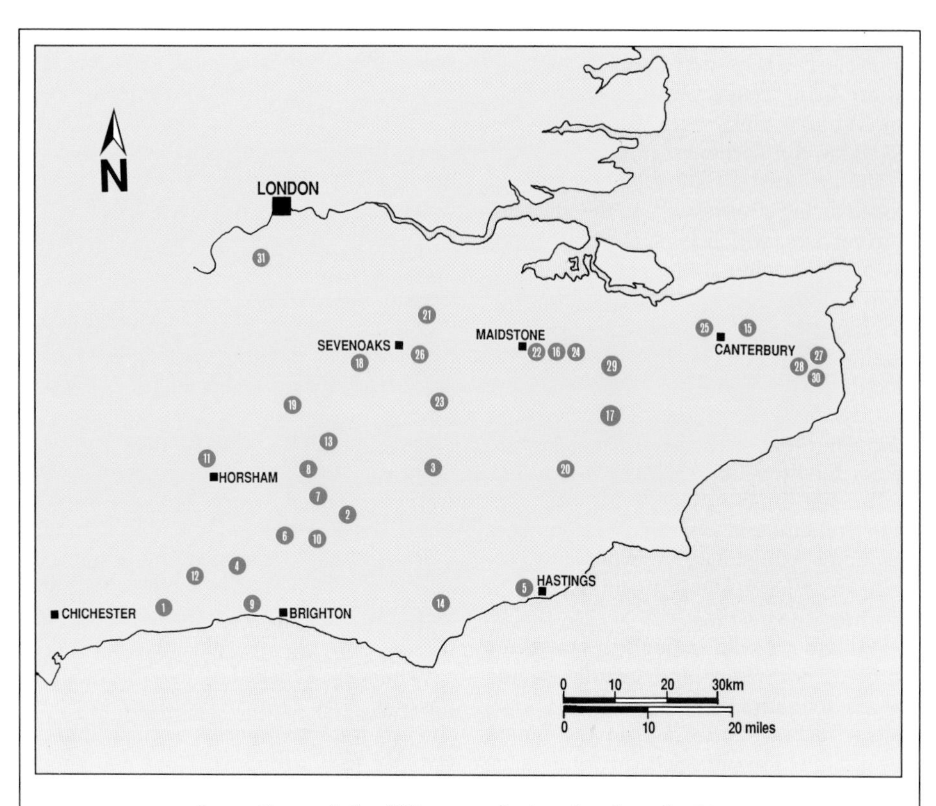

— Location of the Vineyards in the South-East —

Sussex
1 Arundel
2 Barkham Manor
3 Burwash Weald
4 Bylsborough
5 Carr Taylor
6 Downers
7 Flexerne
8 Hidden Spring
9 Nyetimber
10 Rock Lodge
11 Seymours
12 Steyning
13 St George's
14 Berwick Glebe

Kent
15 Ash Coombe
16 Bearsted
17 Biddenden
18 Chiddingstone
19 Bardingley
20 Harbourne
21 Ightham
22 Knowle Hill
23 Lamberhurst Priory
24 Leeds Castle
25 Mount Ephraim
26 Plaxtol
27 St Nicholas of Ash
28 Staple
29 Syndale Valley
30 Three Corners

Surrey
31 Thorncroft

originally constructed as a cold store for apples. It has excellent insulation.

The vineyard expects to sell almost all its production at the farmgate or at winefairs. The Single Wire trellis and Single Curtain training system is of interest to visitors, and the Gibsons believe it is potentially better than the very popular Geneva Double Curtain, especially as its full potential has not yet been realised.

Elizabeth Gibson is responsible for the growing with the help of some casual labour at busy times, while John, who is a chartered chemist, makes the wine. Several thousand vines have been planted in other English vineyards using the Bearsted Planter, a hand tool developed by the Gibsons and which they are now marketing to

The house at Bardingley Vineyard

other growers.

The vineyard also sells a few vines because they maintain their own surplus stock for replacement purposes.

Visiting times: by appointment only between 11am and 5.30pm Monday to Saturday, and 12noon to 5.30pm on Sundays. There are tasting facilities for customers and at present wine is only sold by the case. Visitors may wander around the vineyard on a self-guided tour with the help of a descriptive leaflet, free of charge. Escorted tours for groups of between five and twenty can be arranged for a small charge and are followed by a tasting. There is a grass area in front of the vineyard for picnicking.

How to get there: the vineyard is situated 3 miles east of Maidstone just off the A20 in Bearsted. If you are driving from Maidstone the turning into Caring Lane is on the right and the vineyard is about half a mile down the lane.

Nearby attractions: Leeds Castle and Stoneacre House (National Trust) are both within 2 miles.

Recommended restaurant and hotels in the area: The Great Danes Hotel, Tudor Park Hotel and Golf and Country Club are both within a mile of the vineyard.

BIDDENDEN VINEYARD
Richard A. Barnes
Little Whatmans, Biddenden

Ashford TN27 8DH
☎ (0580) 291726

The vineyard is a member of the EVA and the Weald and Downland Vineyards Association, was established by the Barnes family in 1969 when a half acre plot was planted, and is Kent's oldest commercial vineyard. It covers 22 acres and further expansion is possible. The varieties grown are Ortega 12 acres, Müller-Thurgau 3 acres, Reichensteiner 2 acres, Dornfelder an acre, Gamay an acre and Huxelrebe, half an acre, with the balance made up by other varieties, some of them experimental.

There have been no changes to the varieties in recent years but 5 acres of new vines have recently been planted but are not yet in production. This comprises 4 acres of Ortega and an acre of Schönburger.

The vineyard is at an altitude of 200ft, on sandy loam over clay. The slopes have either south-west, south or south-east aspects in a sheltered, shallow valley.

Both the Double Guyot and Geneva Double Curtain systems of training are used, and spraying takes place at 14-day intervals from the first green leaf stage.

The harvest normally starts on or about 10 October with Ortega, followed by Müller-Thurgau, Reichensteiner, Huxelrebe, Dornfelder and finishes with Scheurebe in the first week of November, allowing all the varieties to be picked at their optimum time. The grapes are picked by hand and taken to the winery by trailer. A Vaslin press is used and the must is passed through a centrifuge and fermented in glass fibre tanks. The wine is stabilised in early January and bottled in March or April.

Every vintage has produced good wine although there have been variations in style because of different weather conditions. An indication of the vulnerability to weather can be seen from the production figures for the last 5 years. Production was 85,000 bottles in 1983, 45,000 in 1984, 9,000 in 1985, 16,000 in 1986, 3,000 in 1987 and 14,000 in 1988.

Individual wines are made from each variety. Müller-Thurgau produces a crisp, fruity medium dry white wine and fragrant nose, and together with Ortega comprise the main production. The Biddenden Ortega 1986 received the Gore-Browne Trophy in 1987 as English Wine of the Year. Half the wine produced is sold at the vineyard gate and the remainder is sold through hotels, restaurants and wine merchants. The vineyard has a wine shop and a vineyard trail. Vines are on sale to visitors as is Biddenden Cider which is produced at the vineyard.

Visiting times: visitors are welcome to stroll around the vineyard at leisure and to call at the shop for a tasting of wine or cider. It is open daily for the sale of wines by the bottle or case, and also sells cheeses and gifts. The winery shop is open May to October, Monday to Friday 9am-5pm, Saturday 11am-5pm. Sunday 12noon-5pm, bank holidays 11am-5pm; November to April, Monday to Friday 9am-5pm, Saturday 11am-2pm, Sunday closed.

Arrangements for guided tours for parties between twenty-five and fifty should be booked in advance for any weekday during June, July and August. A small charge is made for a visit which includes a vineyard walk, winery talk and tasting of wine and cider. Tour times are between 10.30am and 4pm.

There are also Christmas tastings which include mulled wine and mince pies. The winery is open each Saturday in December from 10am-6pm.

How to get there: follow the A262 south out of Biddenden and follow the right hand lane signposted to Benenden, not the main road which swings east. Take the first turning on the left and the vineyard is signposted a little way down.

Nearby attractions: the Kent and East Sussex Railway, Biddenden village with half-timbered houses and thirteenth-century grey stone church. Many historic gardens and castles.

Recommended pubs and restaurants in the area: Ye Maydes (restaurant, Biddenden), Three Chimneys (pub, Biddenden), The Bell (pub, Smarden).

CHIDDINGSTONE VINEYARD

J.M. and D. Quirk

Vexour Farm, Chiddingstone Edenbridge TN8 7BB ☎ (0892) 870277

This vineyard is part of a 400-acre farm with cereals, sheep and white cattle and ownership of the land can be traced back to 1280. It is a member of the EVA and produces wines closer in style to the French than the German.

Wines produced are Pinot Noir pressed white and blended with a little Gutedal to produce a white Burgundy style; a Seyval Blanc blend with Kerner to produce a Sancerre style, and Pinot Noir fermented red as a rosé to produce a Provence rosé style with a *goût de terroir.*

The family-run vineyard covers 21 acres with 6 acres each of Seyval Blanc and Madeleine Angevine, 4.5 acres of Pinot Noir, 2 acres of Gutedal and 1.5 acres of Kerner.

The vineyard is planted on brickearth and alluvium over river gravels beside the river Eden, a tributary of the Medway. The rows run north to south, and the aspect of the slopes is often slightly north.

The vineyard is between 80ft and 150ft above sea level, and the south-west and south-east winds reduce the ambient air temperatures in the vineyard. Winter pruning starts every Boxing Day afternoon — snow or shine — and continues until the end of March.

First Double Guyot trainings have been converted to Geneva Double Curtain and all later plantings have followed this system. A few vines in rocky and hot situations remain Double Guyot.

Spraying takes place every 7 to 14 days during the growing season, about ten or twelve times in all. Starlings are a major pest in October and buzzbirds are used to drive them away, quite successfully.

Harvesting starts on the last Friday in October and continues until the first Saturday in November. It is a very late harvest for a frosty river valley but the most valued varieties are late ripening, and even if the sugar levels do not go on rising, the acid falls steadily. Gutedal hangs well on the vine, and together with the Kerner and the Pinot Noir is picked last. Seyval often has to be picked earlier than preferred because once botrytis is visible it spreads rapidly.

The grapes are picked into buckets, tipped into half-filled barrels and taken by trailer to the winery where they are augured from the reception bin into the 4-ton press. It is lightly pressed and pumped into settling tanks of 4,000l capacity for 24 hours. It is then transferred to 2,000l and 1,500l fermentation vessels and kept by water cooling at a constant 61°F (16°C). The fermentation in stainless steel or glass fibre takes between 2 and 3 weeks. Chaptalisation and the addition of acidex and bentonite takes place before fermentation. By letting the temperature rise to between 68°F (20°C) and 72°F (22°C), malolactic fermentation is then induced. Some red wine is fermented on the skins.

The wine is then racked and coarse filtered into holding tanks where it is kept for a year before bottling. The wines stay for 6 months in bottle, in the case of Seyval and 12 months for Pinot Noir before labelling, capsuling and boxing for sale. Wine is sold by the case only and mostly through recommendations and the annual production averages about 1,000 cases a year.

Visiting times: there are no listed visiting hours, but visits are welcomed from seriously interested amateurs of wine, even at short notice, although a telephone call first is appreciated. Tastings are available. The winery buildings are very attractive, and wine is sold from the winery door because there is no shop.

How to get there: once clear of Penshurst Place, take each left hand turn, except the station approaches. The route takes you on to the B2027 through Chiddingstone Causeway, and then left on to the road signposted Chiddingstone and Cowden. Take the left hand fork just past the iron gates by a humpback bridge over the river. From Leigh take the first turning on the left after Chiddingstone Causeway sports ground.

Nearby attractions: Hever Castle (3.5 miles), Penshurst Place (4 miles) and Chiddingstone a fourteenth-century NT village.

Recommended pubs and restaurants in the area: Little Brown Jug (restaurant, Penshurst Station), Thackerays House

A selection of wines produced by the Harbourne Vineyard

(restaurant, Tunbridge Wells), La Galoche Wine Bar (Tunbridge Wells), Goodhews' Honours Mill Restaurant (Edenbridge).

HARBOURNE VINEYARD
Susan and Laurence Williams
High Halden
Ashford TN 30 7NP
☎ (07977) 420

The vineyard is a member of the Weald and Downland Vineyard Association and covers 3 acres. It is 45ft above sea level on a gentle south-east slope. The soil is a medium loam over Wealden clay and, despite the latter, is naturally well drained. The site was carefully selected to offer protection from the cold north winds, as well as giving an open aspect to the south to maximise penetration of sunlight. Spacing of the vines is 7ft wide rows with 7ft between the plants

A nearby attraction is the Ellen Terry Memorial Museum, Small Hythe

within rows to allow increased air circulation and maximum shading for greater maturity while permitting reasonable cropping levels.

The vines are planted on wires 7ft high using the Single Curtain training system developed at the vineyard to reduce labour. There is annual replacement of vines, no summer pruning and the use of strip herbicide and mowing stops in August. The vines are sprayed by hand.

The vineyard has an average rainfall of 19in a year, and because of the good wind protection, enjoys its own microclimate, about 36°F (2°C) higher than the average for the rest of the area.

A quarter of the production comes from Müller-Thurgau, 20 per cent from Seyval Blanc, 18 per cent from Ortega, 16 per cent from Regner, 8 per cent from Pinot Meunier and Blue Portugese and the remaining 13 per cent from a variety of miscellaneous vines. Madeleine Angevine was 'useless' and replaced by Regner in 1985, and Ortega was planted in the same year to replace Riechensteiner which had been killed off during the preceding severe winter. The winery also produces a medium sweet, low alcohol, apple wine made principally from Kent-grown Bramleys and Cox's.

Harvesting starts in the second week of October on the early varieties and continues over four of five pickings until the first week of November. The wines are made carefully using as little machinery and chemicals as possible, a combination of the old traditional ways with modern knowledge. The grapes are crushed and de-strigged in one action and pressed in old-fashioned manual basket presses, then transferred to glass fibre tanks for fermentation. The reds are not pressed at this stage but fermented on their skins until there is a 50 per cent drop in specific gravity.

No cultured yeasts are used for the fermentation. *Débourbage* is practised only when the must is very turbid. This means allowing it to stand for 24 hours in a cool place so that the solid particles fall to the bottom, and the clear juice can be drawn off.

Fermentation takes place between 46°F (8°C) and 57°F (14°C) and lasts between 14 and 21 days at the lower temperature, and between 36 hours and 5 days at the higher. The wine is racked as soon as fermentation stops and again in the second week of February. The medium dry wines are filtered twice and have 8 per cent *süss* reserve added, the dry wines have a single filtration if needed at all and no *süss* reserve, and the Rosé is filtered three times. Cold sterile bottling takes place at Easter.

The medium dry white 1986 was made from Müller-Thurgau and Seyval Blanc grapes, to produce a light and fruity, well balanced wine. The 1985 was a Müller-Thurgau varietal, very full, rich and grapey with a wonderful bouquet, the result of a long hot summer.

The 1986 dry white was made from late picked and selected Reichensteiner and Müller-Thurgau grapes to produce a dry, crisp wine. It was lightly filtered to retain its full flavour, so may throw a sediment in the bottle.

The 1986 Rosé is a lovely bright English rosé made from Pinot Meunier, Blue Portugese and other red varieties. It is full of depth and flavour with a hint of tannin and aged in English oak.

Although these three styles of wines are made each vintage, the type of grape and blend for each varies from year to year because the weather may favour one variety over another. The aim is to make wines as near to a consistent style as the weather permits. This is done by careful selection of the grapes and detailed analytical and tasting tests of the young wines.

The medium dry is produced to be very fruity with a fine bouquet and long finish. The dry aims to have lovely flowery bouquet, and crisp, clean finish, while the rosé style is elegant in taste and bouquet with a touch of tannin.

The wine is sold at wine festivals and through the winery shop, and some is exported to France and Germany. It is hoped the vineyard will expand to between 6 and 8 acres, and more land is being sought for this purpose.

Visiting times: visits to the vineyard are by appointment only. The winery shop is open Monday to Friday, 3-7pm, Saturday 8.30am-7pm, Sunday 12noon-2pm. These hours can vary according to season, so a telephone call is advisable before you visit. The winery shop sells wine and apple wine, wine vinegar and honey produced by the bees kept in the vineyard. It also sells glasses, corkscrews and grapevines.

How to get there: the Wine Shop is on the B2082 between Rye and Tenterden, just on the Tenterden side of Wittersham. The vineyard is about 6 miles from the shop. Travel north on the B2082 to Tenterden, and turn right on to the A28 staying on the Ashford road until you reach High Halden and the Harbourne Vineyard on the right hand side of the road.

Nearby attractions: Small Hythe Place with an Ellen Terry Memorial Museum, Kent and East Sussex Railway, old town of Rye.

IGHTHAM VINEYARD

Mr and Mrs James Corfe
Ivy Hatch
Nr Sevenoaks TN15 0PG
☎ (0732) 810348

There was a vineyard in Ightham in Roman times. The vineyard is going through a transition period at the moment having established a high reputation for its wines. For 10 years it was the sole supplier of English wine to the Institute of Directors. The Corfes have 20 acres of land, next to the historic Ightham Mote, and they hope the vineyard will prosper and expand in the 1990s.

The vineyard, at the moment, covers 4 acres and is one of the oldest in Kent. The first 300 vines were planted in 1972 as an experiment to test the suitability of the site for a commercial vineyard. A further 3,000 vines were added in 1975 covering about 3 acres facing south and sloping in the direction of Ightham Mote, a beautifully small moated medieval manor house which has remained virtually unaltered for the last 600 years.

The 1975 plantings were 90 per cent Müller-Thurgau with the rest made up by Reichensteiner, Huxelrebe and Schönburger, all trained on the Double Guyot system.

All the vines were grafted on phylloxera resistant American rootstock each variety making a special contribution to the flavour of Ightham wine.

The grapes were harvested during October and into early November and blended together to produce the wine. Although these vines produced high quality, award winning 'Ightham' wines, the yield was small and uneconomic.

The wine was light in style with fresh fruity acidity had the bouquet of Müller-Thurgau and influenced by the slightly muscat flavour of the other varieties. This combination made a pleasant balance of sugar and acidity and a fragrant wine which was refreshing when drunk young and chilled.

In 1982 the vineyard celebrated its tenth anniversary, and its fifth as a commercial wine producer. Production in 1982 was about 8,000 bottles, which increased to more than 10,000 in 1983. In the spring of 1987, an additional acre of Seyval Blanc was planted using the Geneva Double Curtain training system.

In January 1989, after damage from the hurricane and another poor harvest, the original 3 acres were grubbed out. If the Seyval does well, it is intended to replant the old vineyard using the Geneva Double Curtain system, but Ightham wine will not be on the market again before January, 1992.

Visiting times: none at present, but people seriously interested in the development of the vineyard and vines could ask for a visit.

How to get there: the vineyard is in Ivy Hatch, a small hamlet in the parish of Ightham which lies to the east of Sevenoaks and the north of Tonbridge. Ightham has a limited number of shops and restaurants.

KNOWLE HILL VINEYARD

Ian A. Grant
Ulcombe,
Nr Maidstone
☎ (01735) 5135

The vineyard (a member of the EVA and the Weald and Downland Vineyards Association) covers 1.25 acres, with Müller-Thurgau accounting for 60 per cent of production, and Pinot Noir the remainder. Production over the last 5 years has varied between 40 and 600 bottles.

The vineyard is remote, half a mile from the nearest metalled road and is 250ft above sea level, south facing on clay or heavy soil and well protected by a bank of trees. It is part of a fruit farm, and there are no plans to extend the acreage under vines. The varieties have not changed in recent years and there are no new plantings.

Weather conditions can be very variable and pruning takes place each year between April and May, with spraying at four week intervals during the summer. The vines are trained on the Double Guyot system. The harvest starts towards the end of October although there is no regular pattern and all the grapes are picked together. The grapes are sent to the winery where a single white blended wine is produced by a professional winemaker.

Visiting times: it is advisable to write in advance.

How to get there: Ulcombe lies south-east of Maidstone. Take either the A274 Headcorn Road, and turn left just beyond Sutton Valence and follow the signposts to Ulcombe, or take the A20 through Bearsted and turn left at Harrietsham and follow the signs to the village.

Recommended pubs and restaurants in the area: The Pepper Box (restaurant) at Fairbourne Heath.

LAMBERHURST PRIORY VINEYARDS

Kenneth McAlpine
Ridge Farm, Lamberhurst Down
Nr Tunbridge Wells TN3 8ER
☎ (0892) 890286 or 890844

Lamberhurst Priory Vineyard (a member of the EVA and the Weald and Downland Vineyards Association) covers 55 acres, making it one of the largest in the country. It is owned by Kenneth McAlpine, a member of the famous construction family. The vineyards are situated on the Kent and Sussex borders at 250ft above sea level on a predominantly gentle, north facing Weald upland. It is protected by belts of trees from the prevailing south-west winds. The soil is a mixture of well drained Tunbridge Wells sand and pockets of Weald (Wadhurst) clay over sandstone.

The production of Lamberhurst Priory wines began with the planting of 8 acres in 1972 after consultations with Professor Dr Wilhelm Kiefer and his staff at the Geisenheim Wine Research and Training Institute in West Germany. Müller-Thurgau accounted for most of the early plantings but other varieties, such as Seyval Blanc, Reichensteiner, Schönburger and Chasselas then followed. Within 4 years wine production had reached an annual output of 70,000 bottles and the output increased annually until the record 1983 vintage when it reached almost 200,000 bottles from its own vineyards.

In 1980 Lamberhurst Priory Vineyard undertook the planting of 3 acres of vines at Leeds Castle on the site of a vineyard established hundreds of years earlier by monks of the Augustinian Order. This same order of monks built Lamberhurst Priory in the fifteenth century and the re-establishment of the medieval vineyard by today's inhabitants forges an interesting link with the past. The grapes from Leeds Castle vineyard are sent to Lamberhurst for vinification and bottling, as do the grapes from more than thirty other vineyards throughout England.

In 1983 the English Wine of the Year Competition and the Gore-Browne Trophy for the best English wine was won by Lamberhurst's Huxelrebe, and its wines have figured prominently among the list of annual winners ever since. It is one of the few vineyards in England to have won the Gore-Browne Trophy twice, the second time for its 1984 Schönburger. The Gold Seal of the EVA for wines has been awarded to the vineyard every year since 1979 and they have the added distinction of being chosen for serving at Buckingham Palace, the Lord Mayor's Banquet at the Mansion House, and at many British Embassy functions overseas.

Müller-Thurgau is planted on 19 acres and accounts for 34.5 per cent of production, followed by Seyval Blanc 9.5 acres (17 per cent) Reichensteiner 7.5 acres (13.5 per cent) Schönburger 6.5 acres (12.5 per cent) red varieties 6 acres (11 per cent) Kerner 1.5 acres (2.5 per cent) Bacchus an acre (2 per cent), and experimental varieties are planted on 4 acres, accounting for 7 per cent of production. The vineyard also has substantial acreages of vines in other parts of the country contracted to supply Lamberhurst with the grapes. In recent years there have been new plantings of Seyval Blanc, Schönburger, Kerner and Bacchus, as well as the experimental acreage.

Two new acres are being planted in 1989. New but as yet unproductive vines include 3 acres of Schönburger, 2 acres of Seyval Blanc, 1.5 acres of Kerner, an acre of Bacchus and 2.5 acres of experimental varieties.

The vines are pruned between December and March and are trained using a number of different systems — Geneva Double Curtain, Sylvoz and Double Guyot as well as a number of experimental systems. There is a high volume preventative spray programme to control disease and weeds.

The vineyard is doing a lot of experimental work to find the perfect wine producing grape to grow in the unpredictable English climate — rainfall averages about 23in a year. Professor Helmut Becker, from the Geisenheim Institute, has been called in to help with the quest and was a frequent visitor to Lamberhurst. Four years ago he supplied the vineyard with small numbers of various experimental new varieties bred at the institute which he thought would be suitable for commercial wine production in this country. 'There is great potential in the English wine industry and I am convinced that we will find a vine which will thrive in this country. What we are aiming for is constant yield and good site selection, and we have made a good start at Lamberhurst,' he said. He specialises in hybrid varieties, especially crosses between European *Vitis vinifera* and non-European varieties, and the one which shows the most potential is the Russian *Vitis amurensis* and St Laurent, known only at the moment by its code name 6494/5. The *Vitis amurensis* is grown around the river Amur on the border between Russia and China and is early ripening, disease resistant and frost resistant.

Places to visit nearby include Sissinghurst Castle Gardens

Other crossings in the experimental vineyard include a cross between Ehrenfelser and Reichensteiner, and a cross between Rotberger and Reichensteiner, though neither are showing as much promise as the *Vitis amurensis* at the moment. It will be some years before the full potential of each variety can be completely evaluated. Fruit has been harvested from the vines for the last 3 years and has been blended into other wines. For the first time a small quantity of red wine has been produced from the red *Vitis* Amurensis 1988 harvest. A sparkling wine using the Champagne method is also now produced at the winery.

The harvest usually starts about 20 October and lasts for 3 weeks. Reichensteiner is the first variety to be picked, followed by Müller-Thurgau, the reds, Seyval, Schönburger and Kerner. The grapes are picked into steel and fibreglass bins which can be tipped into the Amos crusher and de-stalker. Willmes presses are used and the must is fermented in fibreglass and stainless steel tanks. A Westphalia rotary sieve and separator is also used.

The winery has substantial facilities for processing grapes and can handle up to 50 tons a day. The grapes are crushed, destalked and pressed, and the must allowed to settle before being racked of prior to fermentation. After fermentation the wine is racked off, filtered and bottled. The automatic bottling line can handle 2,200 bottles an hour. Production has been erratic over the last 5 years because of the weather. In 1984 it was 334,000 bottles from home-grown and purchased grapes. It fell to 148,459 bottles in 1985, rose to 204,310 in 1986, crashing back to 82,459 in 1987—the year of the hurricane which struck just before the vintage. Production in 1988, after another terrible year, was 65,000 bottles.

Expansion plans include increasing the acreage of Seyval Blanc and varieties for red wine, and building a miniature steam railway through the vineyard.

Lamberhurst Priory Vineyard is the largest producer of English wines and subject to supplies, distributes them through the trade and sells direct to large customers such as hotel chains, supermarkets, national organisations and major stores, such as

Knole House, near Lamberhurst Priory Vineyard

Harrods. About a third of annual production is sold through the winery shop and there are plans to increase these sales over the next few years. An old oast house is currently being renovated on the vineyard which will increase facilities for guided tours, meals, conferences, reception and the like. The vineyard also attends some twelve shows each year selling its wines. The winery is one of the largest and most modern in private ownership in Europe.

Dry wines produced are: Müller-Thurgau, a delicate wine with a muscat bouquet, attractive fruit and crisp acidity; Seyval Blanc which has fresh green fruit with a clean, crisp acidity; Huxelrebe, a very flowery wine with good fruit, acidity, and a pleasant lingering finish, and the Kerner which is matured in small oak barrels for several months to give it a distinctive taste and character and to increase its ageing potential. It has good fruity acidity, pronounced length of flavour, and is a good accompaniment to most meals.

Medium dry wines: the Müller-Thurgau has a distinct muscat bouquet, lingering fruit and attractive acidity; the Reichensteiner has elegant light fruit, is medium bodied, rich and honeyed with a smooth and elegant finish; the Schönburger, delicately scented, spicy, full bodied, rich and honeyed with a smooth and elegant finish and the Seyval Blanc which has fresh elegant fruit and is well balanced with good length.

The English Rosé, is medium dry, made mainly from Pinot Noir and Seibel grapes. It is a lively highly distinctive wine with a strong fruit character and lingering flavour and a hint of oak on the palate. The Lamberhurst Brut sparkling wine is produced by the traditional *Méthode Champenoise* with bottle fermentation and hand disgorging. Made from a selection of varieties, the flavour is enhanced by more than 2 years ageing on the yeast after its secondary fermentation.

Visiting times: visitors are welcome throughout the year except Christmas Day, Boxing Day and New Year's Day at the following times: summer, Monday to Saturday 9am-6pm, Sunday 10am-5pm, winter, Monday to Saturday 9am-5pm, Sunday 10am-5pm. There is a self-guided vineyard trail, and guided tours take place in July, August and September at 11am and 2.30pm, or by appointment throughout the year.

Conducted group tours of the vineyards, winery and cellar can be made by appointment from 1 May to the end of October. During August guided tours take place twice daily.

Shop opening times: the winery shop is open daily and free wine tastings are available inside. It is well stocked with liqueurs and the staff are knowledgeable and helpful. The shop sells a good selection of specialities — exclusive hand-made Lamberhurst liqueur chocolates, dried flowers, pottery, jams, mustards and so on. The winery produces a range of eight fruit liqueurs and apple wine. The Vineyard Pantry serves home-made lunches, snacks and cream teas, and the oast house conversion will include a restaurant. Vines and herbs are also on sale as well as vineyard and winery equipment. The vineyard runs an advisory service on all aspects of wine production, including site selection, variety selection, planting and managing the vineyard.

How to get there: the vineyard is on the southern outskirts of the village of Lamberhurst (just off the B2162) which straddles the A21 Tonbridge to Hastings road. The vineyard is well signposted. If approaching on the B2169 from Tunbridge Wells, take the right hand turning just past The Swan pub as you enter the outskirts of the village.

Nearby attractions: Scotney Castle Gardens (NT), Sissinghurst Castle Gardens (NT), Knole House and Ightham Mote (NT).

Recommended pubs and restaurants in the area: The Old Vine (pub) Cousley Wood, The Swan (pub) Lamberhurst Down.

LEEDS CASTLE VINEYARD
The Leeds Castle Foundation
Leeds Castle
Maidstone ☎ (0622) 765400

The vineyard was planted in 1980, on the site of a vineyard owned by Bishop Odo of

Leeds Castle near Maidstone, Kent

Bayeaux and recorded in the *Domesday Book* of 1086. It covers 2.75 acres and must have one of the most fabulous locations of any vineyard in the world and is a member of the EVA and the Weald and Downland Vineyards Association. There are no plans at present to expand the vineyard. It is in the grounds of Leeds Castle described by Lord Conway as 'the loveliest castle in the world'.

The vineyard is planted on sandy soil with a southern elevation, and uses Double Guyot pruning methods. It is small and compact and run by the large gardening and grounds staff employed by the castle. Extra casual staff are brought in for busy periods.

The harvest starts in the last week of October, and the duration depends on the size of the crop. The vineyard does not have its own winery and the grapes are taken by road to Lamberhurst Priory Vineyard where the wine is made under contract.

The first vintage was gathered in 1983, produced 1,200 bottles, and rose to 7,000 bottles in 1984. The 1985 vintage was poor and no wine was produced, and a poor summer in 1986 also reduced the vintage with only 3,400 bottles produced. The 1987 crop was totally destroyed by the 16 October hurricane which swept the south-east, creating considerable damage to the vineyard as well.

The varieties grown are Müller-Thurgau 1.5 acres which accounts for 55 per cent of production, and Seyval Blanc 1.25 acres accounting for 45 per cent of production. There have been no changes in the planted varieties in recent years and there are no new, as yet unproductive vines. A single medium white wine is produced, which compares to a good quality Riesling in style, and is light and crisp.

Leeds Castle is one of the most romantic and ancient castles in Britain, and named after Led, chief minister of Ethelbert IV, King of Kent in AD857. The castle is set in 500 acres of parkland, and the wooden Saxon fortress was rebuilt in stone to become a Norman stronghold before being converted into a royal palace by Henry VIII. It was then a royal residence for more than 300 years, and a favourite home of eight of England's medieval kings and queens.

The castle is run by the Leeds Castle Foundation, established in 1975 to preserve the beauty of the castle and its grounds for the enjoyment of the public in perpetuity, to host important conferences, such as the

Wine barrels, Leeds Castle Vineyard

annual Festival of English Wine in May, including those for the advancement of medical research, and to encourage arts.

Visiting times: the vineyard is on view during the castle's opening hours. Summer, April to October daily from 11am-5pm which is the latest time for admission to the grounds. Winter, November to March daily 11am-4pm which is the latest time for admission to the grounds. Group visits can be arranged outside these times. There are special facilities for disabled visitors including limited access for wheelchairs, but groups must pre-book. Facilities include full restaurant, gift shop, parking, toilets and picnic areas. There is no winery at the castle but private wine tastings and dinners can be arranged for private groups and wine societies. Private tours of the castle can also be arranged. For day visitors wine is sold in the restaurant and bar and the wine shop has a wine corner with a range of Lamberhurst wines and fruit liqueurs.

How to get there: Leeds Castle is located 4 miles east of Maidstone at junction 8 of the M20 and A20, mid-way between London and the Channel ports. It is clearly sign-posted and easily reached from all areas of the south-east. The M25 orbital motorway also provides fast, easy access from the north and west, and regular coach and rail services operate from London's Victoria Station to Bearsted Station where road transport meets many of the trains, although it is advisable to check in advance to see which are met.

Recommended pubs, restaurants and hotels in the area: Park Gate Inn pub (on the edge of Leeds Castle estate on the A20), The Great Danes Embassy Hotel, and the Tudor Park Hotel (country club hotel).

MOUNT EPHRAIM VINEYARD

E.S. Dawes
Mount Ephraim Gardens
Hernhill
Faversham ☎ (0227) 751496 or 750940

The vineyard covers 1.5 acres and is planted equally between Müller-Thurgau and Reichensteiner. It is a member of the EVA, the Weald and Downland Vineyards Association and Canterbury Winegrowers. There has been no change in plantings in recent years and there are no new, as yet unproductive vines. It is situated in East Kent, on a north-east facing slope but very sheltered and frost free. The soil is brickearth and the area has low rainfall, about 24in a year and fair sunshine. Main problems are cold east winds in spring and damaging westerlies in the autumn, although the vineyard is specially situated to give maximum protection against both.

The vineyard is integrated with the fruit farm and the alleyways are wide enough to take Massey Ferguson fruit tractors. A wide variety of training systems are used for the vines including Single and Double Guyot, Vertigo, and Geneva Single and Double Curtain, both for experimentation purposes and for wider interest. Spraying takes places at 10-day intervals. Picking takes place over a single day, usually in mid-October when all the farm staff and any extra hands that are needed are drafted in. The entire vineyard is protected, as the grapes ripen, by bird nets which are used on the cherries earlier in the year.

The vineyard does not have its own winery, and all the grapes are sent by road to Christopher Lindlar's High Weald Winery, near Maidstone. Production in 1987 was 400 bottles which doubled in 1988. The first vintage was very encouraging but is not yet available for sale. The bottles are expected to be sold in 1990, and most will be retailed in conjunction with the garden's open days.

The vineyard is set on the edge of the beautiful Mount Ephraim Gardens, looking out onto the 800-acre estate and woodland. There are no plans to extend the vineyard which is seen purely as an added attraction to the gardens. The estate also has 180 acres of fruit, mostly apples, pears, cherries, plums and strawberries. The house, rebuilt in 1870 but the home of the Dawes family for 300 years, commands magnificent views over the wooded park and beyond to the Swale and Thames estuary. Rose terraces enclosed by yew hedges slope down to the lake with the woods as a backdrop.

Visiting times: May, June, August and September, Sundays and bank holiday Mondays 2-6pm. Booked parties are welcome by appointment on any date throughout the week including Sundays, but weekdays are preferred to allow special catering arrangements to be made. There is a crafts centre, orchard walk and vineyard tour. Cream teas are served in the Edwardian kitchen. The gardens have limited access for wheelchairs.

How to get there: from Canterbury take the A2 north towards the M2 and Faversham, through Dunkirk. At Boughton turn right and follow the signs for Hernhill. Mount Ephraim Gardens are well signposted.

Nearby attractions: Canterbury is 6 miles away.

Recommended pubs, restaurants and hotels in the area: White Horse at Houghton (restaurant and hotel), and Three Horse Shoes pub at Hernhill.

PLAXTOL VINEYARD
Jayne and Clive Semple
Periwick Place
The Street, Plaxtol
Sevenoaks TN15 0QF
☎ (0732) 810580

The vineyard covers 2.5 acres and is a member of the EVA and the Weald and Downland Vineyards Association. The varieties are Seyval Blanc (an acre), Schönburger (half an acre), Müller-Thurgau (quarter of an acre) and Seibel (red) quarter of an acre. There has been no change in varieties in recent years and no new plantings.

The vineyard lies on Chartland in the centre of Plaxtol village. It is on greens and over clay at an altitude of 250ft above sea level. The site is sheltered from the north and west by woodland and was the former glebe land of Plaxtol rectory.

It lies on the western slope of the Bourne valley with fine views of typical west Kent farms and hopfields to the east.

All the vines are trained using the Geneva Double Curtain system. Spraying is minimal and the Seibel vines have never been sprayed. All the vines are netted in September to protect them from the birds which come from the surrounding woodlands.

The harvest takes place over one or two days on the last weekend of October. It is a family affair although friends are invited to help out. The crop varies between 2 tons and 6 tons, and there are no plans to expand the vineyard. The grapes are taken by road to the Lamberhurst winery for vinification. The first sales will be in 1989 from the 1988 vintage. Wines currently produced are: Seyval dry, Seyval medium dry, Schönburger, Rosé and Seibel (red).

Visiting times: the vineyard is not open to the public except during wine tastings. Sales are by the case only and mostly through the wine tastings held at the vineyard by invitation or prior arrangement for groups between fifteen and thirty. The tastings take place in the vineyard or the house depending on the weather. The *vigneron* (vine grower) is also an antiques dealer selling Georgian and Victorian furniture and nineteenth- and twentieth-century watercolours.

How to get there: details from owners.

ST NICHOLAS of ASH VINEYARD and WINERY

The Wilkison Family
Moat Lane, Ash
Canterbury CT3 2DG
☎ (0304) 812670

The family-run vineyard covers 2 acres and is a member of the EVA, the Weald and Downland Vineyards Association and Canterbury Winegrowers. Planting started in 1979 but there are plans to extend it by another 17 acres over the next 2 or 3 years. The present acreage is split equally between Müller-Thurgau and Schönburger, about 3,700 vines in all.

The Müller-Thurgau vines were planted in 1979, and the Schönburger added in the spring of 1983. The first crop from these new wines was harvested in the autumn of 1984, made possible because the soil encouraged the speedy development of the plant's root system which stimulate growth.

The Schönburger has some resistance to botrytis and so the grapes can usually be left on the vines until they ripen, often not until mid-November. If the grapes can be left on the vines this long they can produce very high quality wines with good balance and spicy bouquet.

A further 20 acres of land has been earmarked for plantings which will include Schönburger, Seyval Blanc, Baccus and possibly others, but the acreages of each have yet to be decided. New plantings began in 1987 although they will not be productive until 1990.

The vineyard is in the extreme south-east of England, at low altitude, between 30ft and 45ft above sea level, on a sheltered site with south-east facing slopes and good frost drainage. It is on free-draining grade 1 agricultural land, with deep, very fine sandy loam which holds the suns' heat and encourages the vines to establish deep root systems. Rainfall is about 19.5 in a year.

The vines, imported from Germany and grafted on to phylloxera-resistant rootstock, are planted in north-south rows to take full advantage of the sun's heat and light throughout the day. The vineyard is 4 miles from Sandwich on the coast and benefits from a milder climate because of the influence of the sea, but is sufficiently far inland not to be troubled by salt-spray and the worst of the winds.

The vines are pruned in the late winter, and are trained using the Double Guyot system. Budburst occurs in May, and a late frost at this time can reduce the potential crop by two thirds. Flowering takes place in July when the fruit sets. The side shoots and tops of the wine are then cut off to promote the growth of the grapes. All the vines are trained very low, the bottom wire is only 16in off the ground, to take full advantage from the heat of the soil which has to be kept weed free. The close planting and low height also help the vines shelter each other from the wind.

A spray is applied to control weeds in the spring and then the ground is kept clean using mechanical and manual means. Fungicides are used, but every effort is made to keep applications to a minimum,

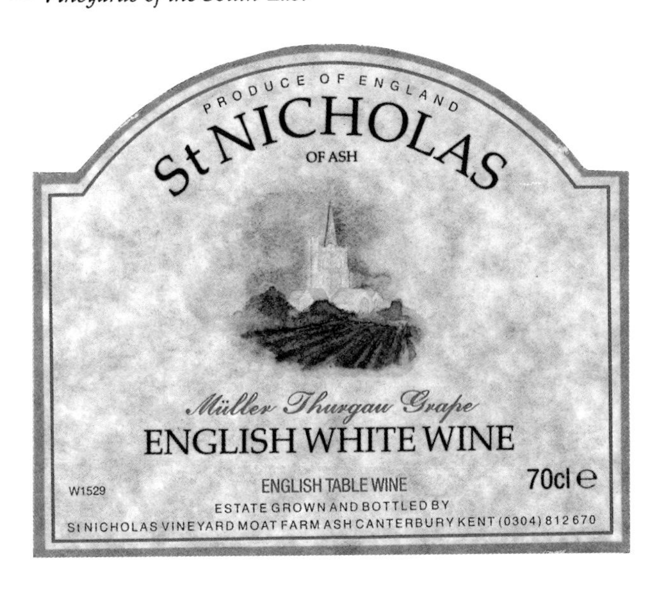

and the last spraying never takes place after early September to give the largest possible interval before picking.

Picking can start at any time between mid-October and mid-November. Müller-Thurgau are the first grapes to be picked. Schönburger with their tinted skin are picked selectively, weather permitting, not to make a separate wine, but to improve overall ripeness. Picking time varies according to the size of the crop, but is usually completed within two or three long weekends.

An average crop should be 3-4,000 bottles (3-4 tons an acre) but varies enormously because of the weather. Since 1983 average production has been about 6,000 bottles a year, although no wine was produced at all in 1986. The grapes are hand picked into buckets and then emptied into a bin behind a tractor which takes them to the winery where they are immediately processed.

The new vineyard is known as Guilton Field, and is another south facing slope with deep sandy loam soil. There are several experimental rows in the vineyard where the progress of different varieties is monitored, including Wrotham Noir, descended from Pinot Meunier, a variety grown in Champagne. It gets its name because an old vine was found growing in the garden of a cottage in Wrotham, Kent. Other varieties being tried are Riesling, Gewürztraminer, Seibel 13053 (also called Cascade), Pinot Noir, Gutedal, Madeleine Sylvaner, Auxerrois and Perlaut, a new white variety which can achieve high sugar levels.

The winery is the former wagon shed, and many of the beams are old ships timbers. The grapes are crushed by machine and then tipped into the press. Each batch of grapes undergoes several pressings and is then pumped into fermentation tanks ranging from 300l to 2,000l. The fibreglass tanks have stainless steel fittings which make them easy to sterilise and keep clean. Fermentation lasts up to 2 weeks, and the wine is then fined and filtered ready for bottling the following spring. The sterilised bottling line can handle up to 600 bottles or 400l of wine an hour.

Visiting times: winery shop, 1 April to 31 October 10am-6pm daily. Winter, every weekend 10am to dusk. Weekday visits can be arranged by appointment. Moat Farm has a sixteenth-century farmhouse, timber-framed winery, thatched vineyard shop and lily pond. The winery shop sells its own wines as well as a limited amount of apple and pear wine, and home-grown vegetables and sweet corn. There are no exports.

Visitors can enjoy self-guided tours of the vineyard and winery with a tasting for a small charge during shop hours. Accompanied children go free. Group tours can also be arranged, and the vineyard is on a well signposted trail linking three local vineyards.

How to get there: the winery is close to the village of Ash about 10 miles east of Canterbury on the A257 Sandwich road. The vineyard is signposted opposite the Lion Hotel in Ash.

STAPLE VINEYARD
Mr William T. Ash
Church Farm, Staple
Canterbury CT3 1LN
☎ (0304) 812571

The vineyard (a member of the EVA, the Weald and Downland Vineyards Association and the Canterbury Winegrowers) covers 7 acres and further plantings are planned. Varieties planted are Müller-Thurgau 4.75 acres, Huxelrebe 1.5 acres and Reichensteiner 0.75 acres. There have been no changes to the varieties planted and there are no new, as yet unproductive vines. Expansion plans include extending the size of the vineyard within the next few years, with plenty of suitable land available for this.

The vineyard is 5 miles from the coast in a traditional fruit and hop growing region on a nearly level site, surrounded by a perimeter windbreak hedge. It is an early growing area with few spring frosts about 75ft above sea level and is on deep sandy loam soil overlying chalk which is naturally free draining.

The vineyard and winery are run by the owner who also farms the rest of the 79-acre holding, mostly with cereals and a break crop of potatoes. He has been the winemaker since 1985. Before that the wine was made under contract at Biddenden or Lamberhurst. It currently has nine commercial members and six non-commercial members.

Almost all the vines are trained and pruned according to the Double Guyot system although there is a small area of Geneva Double Curtain. The canopy is cut at a height of between 5ft and 5.5ft. Preventative spraying is practised as the cropstage and weather conditions dictate, using a 200l airblast Platz sprayer which is tractor mounted.

The start of the harvest varies according to the weather. The earliest picking started was on 23 September in 1982 and the harvest continued until 10 October. The latest finish was on 2 November. The average start is around 18-27 October and 10 clear picking days are usually needed. The Reichensteiner is nearly always the first variety to be picked, then the Müller-Thurgau and finally the Huxelrebe. The grapes are picked into buckets which are emptied into a Chemo harvest trailer. This holds 2,750lb of fruit and includes a self emptying and crushing facility.

A Willmes 1,000l pneumatic press is used which is manually controlled. The grapes are pressed immediately after crushing. All the fermentation and storage vessels are fibreglass with stainless steel fittings. Tank sizes vary from 1,000l to 3,000l and the total current capacity of the winery is 22,000l.

The wine is racked and filtered 3 to 4 weeks after fermentation has stopped, and then further filtrations and treatments take place as the analysis of the wine indicates.

Equipment used includes a forty sheet plate filter with Keiselguhr facility, a twelve-head semi-automatic filter, and a Sprusteller bottler steriliser, all from Seitz. All sterilisation is done with steam. The wine is kept after bottling in the specially insulated bottle store which maintains it at an even temperature and has a capacity of 40,000 bottles.

Production over the last 5 years has been very variable because of the weather. In 1984 both quality and quantity were good and 25 tons of grapes were picked. The 1985 vintage was excellent although the quantity of grapes picked was only average at 13 tons. In 1986 quality was excellent, but only Müller-Thurgau was produced as the other varieties failed completely. Quality was satisfactory in 1987 but quantity very poor at only 3 tons following the hurricane, and the 1988 vintage was good but quantity averaged at 16 tons.

Due to the poor years of 1986 and 1987, the vineyard is very low on stock and will be selling only 1988 wines from June of 1989. The 1988 vintage was not bottled at the time of writing, but the wine was showing very good promise.

Most of the wine produced, about 60 per cent, is sold direct from the winery. It is also distributed to local pubs, restaurants and off-licences. The 1986 Müller-Thurgau was sold by Victoria Wine.

Visiting times: May to September, Monday to Saturday 11am-5pm, Sunday

12noon-4pm. The wine shop is open for sales throughout the year. It is advisable to check opening times in advance of your visit. The winery and shop are both in a large, old brick-built farm barn. The shop sells other goods besides wines, including apple wine made from locally grown fruit. Tours and tastings are available and there is a picnic area. Simple meals as part of the guided tours can be arranged in advance.

How to get there: the vineyard is on the East Kent Vineyard Trail south of Ash which is on the A257 between Canterbury and Sandwich. From Ash take the road signposted to Staple and turn right at the junction and head for the church. The turning to the vineyard is on your left just before you reach the church.

Recommended pubs, restaurants and hotels in the area: The Black Pig (pub, Staple), and The Griffins Head (pub, Chillenden).

SYNDALE VALLEY VINEYARDS
Jonathan Abbs and Partners
Parsonage Farm, Newnham
Nr Sittingbourne ME9 0NSA
☎ (079589) 693/711

Wine production in the Syndale Valley goes back to at least medieval times and there are traces of far earlier habitation. A Roman toga pin has been found on the farm and when the vineyard was being planted a rare Palaeolithic flint working site was discovered, dating back possibly 250,000 years.

Jonathan Abbs has been growing grapes for 26 years — he planted his first vineyard when he was 10 years old. The vineyards at Syndale were first planted in 1977 with 2 acres of Müller-Thurgau. The vineyard now covers 9.25 acres with plans to extend it by another 3 acres. Varieties grown are Pinot Noir, Wrotham Pinot, Seyval Blanc, Marchel Foch, Müller-Thurgau, Ortega, Würzer, Reichensteiner, Pinot Blanc and Zweigeltrebe. The vines are planted on an east facing slope in 6in of flinty loam soil over gravel and chalk — similar to that in Champagne and Chablis. The vineyard is at an altitude of between 200ft and 225ft above sea level and in the valley of Newnham which is a designated area of outstanding natural beauty. The area is mainly concerned with top fruit and enjoys high sunshine amounts although late frosts are a worry.

The vines are pruned and trained according to the Geneva Double Curtain system and are sprayed with wettable sulphur. The vines are planted 6ft apart in rows 11ft apart. Reichensteiner is the first variety to be harvested, followed by Müller-Thurgau, Ortega, Pinot Blanc, Würzer and Zweigeltrebe.

The harvest usually starts in the second week of October. The winery is housed in a new building and the grapes are delivered in a Chemo trailer which crushes them en route. The first vintage vinified in their own winery was in 1986.

After de-stemming the grapes are transferred to a Willmes press and the juice is then pumped into stainless steel tanks for fermentation. The white wines are fermented at as low a temperature as possible to retain the bouquet — usually between 50°F (10°C) and 59°F (15°C). Sulphur levels are also kept as low as possible, and malolactic fermentation is encouraged from during December. The red wines are fermented for about 3 weeks on their skins. Production in 1983 was 40,000 bottles from 4 acres of Müller-Thurgau and the wine, made at Lamberhurst, was awarded the EVA Seal of Quality. Crops since then have only been average but quality has been extremely good.

Wines produced include Müller-Thurgau, an Ortega-Würzer blend, a rosé — which has been described as 'the best English rosé, in fact one of the best rosés anywhere' — and a red wine made from Zweigeltrebe. The winery also produces a very popular apple wine and other fruit wines.

Visiting times: daily from Easter to Christmas. The wine is sold mainly from the winery shop, and through local hotels and restaurants as well as the county and local shows. Booked tours for between twenty and sixty people are catered for. They include guided tour, lunch or supper, a tour of the winery and wine tasting. Container-grown vines are for sale, as well as hand-made earthenware pots, free range eggs and fresh farm fruit in season. There is also a farm trail.

How to get there: the vineyards and farm shop are behind Newnham Church. If travelling on the A2 turn off by the Syndale Valley Motel and follow the road sign-posted to Doddington until you reach Newnham. If travelling on the A20 turn off in the village of Lenham on the Doddington road. Newnham is a further 1.5 miles beyond Doddington.

Nearby attractions: Canterbury city and cathedral, Fleur de Lis Heritage Centre (Faversham).

Recommended pub in the area: The George (Newnham).

THREE CORNERS VINEYARD
Lt Col Charles S. Galbraith
Beacon Lane
Woodnesborough CT13 0PA
☎ (0304) 812025

The vineyard (a member of the EVA, the Weald and Downland Vineyards Association and the Canterbury Winegrowers) covers 1.5 acres and was established in 1980. There are no plans to extend the vineyard which occupies a prime site on sandy, well drained soil in an easily accessible area 2 miles from Sandwich. Charles Galbraith (ex-army) and his wife Jan Galbraith (ex-WRNS) researched diligently before deciding to plant early ripening varieties which would produce fine wines slightly different from those available elsewhere. The vineyard is in the shape of a triangle, thus its name and the tricorne labels (designed by Jan) and is run almost single-handed, with part-time help called in to assist with the harvesting. It is on a slight ridge at the edge of the village with the climate usually mild and dry, but with strong winds in the autumn and winter.

The acreage is divided equally between Siegerrebe, Reichensteiner and Ortega and each variety is grown in its own mini-vineyard. All the vines are grafted on phylloxera-restistant rootstock.

The vines are trained according to the

Double Guyot system with 6ft between rows and 5ft between the vines. The bottom wire is 2ft off the ground, and the top wire 5ft off the ground.

Pruning starts in mid-December and finishes in March. A winter wash is applied in January and a 'cleaning up' spray used in March or April. In order to keep the vines clean, spraying continues at 10- to 14- day intervals after budburst. There are always enough pickers to ensure that the grapes are collected within a day. Picking normally starts at 8.30am with a break for 'a substantial lunch' provided by the vineyard, and then continues to about 4pm.

Siegerrebe is a particularly early grape and is normally harvested during the second half of September with the other varieties gathered about two weeks later.

The vineyard does not have its own winery so therefore the grapes are taken by road to Christopher Lindlar's High Weald Winery, near Maidstone.

The first vintage was in 1984 when 600 bottles of a blended, medium dry white were produced. The 1985 vintage yielded 800 bottles of Siegerrebe dry, and 400 bottles of a blended, medium dry white. The third harvest in 1986 was hit by frost. About 300 bottles of a blended dry, and 850 bottles of a blended medium dry were produced. Production was again hit in 1987 because of a poor set and 200 bottles of blended dry, and 800 bottles of blended medium dry were made. The 1988 crop was also badly hit, first by the October 1987 hurricane and then by a disastrous set. Only 400 bottles of blended white were produced. The vineyard has built up a reputation for its wines and demand exceeds supply. Half the wine produced is sold from the vineyard and 20 per cent by mail order. The remainder is sold through restaurants and hotels, seven local off-licences, two north country off-licenses and a little is exported to Germany.

The vineyard has an off-licence, and is on the Vineyard Trail sponsored by Dover District Council which connects the three vineyards in the area.

The tricorne label consists of: Siegerrebe, a dry wine with distinctive varietal nose and pronounced grapey flavour, described as 'a connoisseur's wine of character'; Trocken, or dry wine, is a blend of Reichensteiner and Siegerrebe. It is a crisp dry wine with an elegant fruity freshness and an ideal accompaniment to any meal, especially fish and white meat dishes and Tricorne Melange, a medium dry blend, fresh and fruity with a delicate bouquet.

Visiting times: visitors, including those walking the vineyard trail are welcome at any time between 10am and 6pm, although guided tours and coaches are by appointment and limited to thirty people. A charge is made for the tours, which includes a talk on the history of English wine, and a glass of the product. There are free tastings, and soft drinks for children. Parking, toilet facilities and picnic areas are provided. The holding also has two small orchards, one of dwarf cherries and the other of mixed apples, pears and plums. There are no plans to extend the vineyard acreage.

How to get there: the vineyard is situated 2 miles south-west of Sandwich. Take the A257 Canterbury to Sandwich road, and turn right in the village of Ash and follow the signs for Woodnesborough. The vineyard is signposted to the west of the village on the Nonington road.

Nearby attractions: Sandwich Cinque Port, Richborough Roman Castle, Dover Castle and Walmer Castle.

Recommended pubs and restaurants in the area: Skippers restaurant at Bridge.

THE VINEYARD TRAIL

This circular route runs for just over 5 miles, mainly on public footpaths, and takes in three vineyards in adjoining villages — St Nicholas of Ash Vineyard (Ash), Staple Vineyard (Staple), and Three Corners Vineyard (Woodnesborough). Allow a good 3 hours if you want to visit the vineyards. There are a number of good pubs along or near the route providing food.

The car park in Ash makes a convenient starting point, but the trail can begin at any of the three wineries. From the car park in Ash turn right and then take the first turning on the right into Puddling Lane. Cross the stile and follow the path to the bridge, or from St Nicholas of Ash Vineyard, walk along the bottom of the vineyard over the style and skirt round the bottom of the graveyard to pick up the path which leads to the bridge. Continue south for about 400ft and then turn right through the double gates. Continue in a westerly direction to the stile next to the gate. Turn right and then left along the top of the dyke to Durlock Road. Turn left for a few yards, and then right into the orchard. Pass through the windbreak and turn right and follow the edge of the orchard to the lane, leaving the hop garden on your right. Turn left over the cattle grid, along a cinder track to a stile next to a white gate. Pass diagonally across the field to a telegraph pole. Cross the stile and follow the line of the telegraph poles to Staple Church. At the road turn left to Staple Vineyard on your right.

Turn right on leaving the vineyard to Buckland Lane, and after about 295ft veer left into Mill Road taking the path opposite the village hall to a gate following the track to the road. Cross the road and follow the cart track, and the line of the hedge and fence, then cross the field diagonally to the post. Turn left over the ditch to the marker post then diagonally across the field to the right hand corner of the hedge, and then right into Claypits. Just before the green rigging, veer right and keep the hedge and telegraph poles on your left. Join the track after the second telegraph pole, and follow the concrete track to the junction. Turn right and proceed to the pumping station, and then turn left after two more pumping stations into Fleming Road.

Cross the road and continue along the

No Through Road and follow the sunken track at the edge of the field. Turn right at the trail sign and follow the headland and track almost to Beacon Hill Road. Turn left up the steep track to Beacon Hill House and follow the track past the house and then bear right to the road with the orchard on your left. Cross the road and through the kissing gates to Three Corners Vineyard.

Leave the vineyard through the kissing gates, cross the road and follow the track, with the orchard and underground reservoir on your left, admiring the magnificent views as you go. At the T-junction turn left, with the radar station on your right, and just before the metalled road cross the stile on your right. Follow the footpath signs across parkland, skirting the wood, and over the stiles to the white gate. Turn left down the track to Coombe Lane and then straight on to Mount Ephraim. At the top of the rise go left down the hill to St Nicholas of Ash Vineyard, which you leave via Moat Lane to the village and left to the car park.

Sussex

ARUNDEL VINEYARDS

John and Valerie Rankin
Church Lane
Lyminster
West Sussex BN17 7QF
☎ (0903) 883393

This vineyard is a family business which also includes goats, bees and sheep. The vineyard covers 1.5 acres divided equally between Reichensteiner, Schönburger and Spätburgunder. It is a member of the EVA and the Weald and Downland Vineyards Association. There have been no changes in the varieties planted in recent years and no new, as yet unproductive vines. The vineyard is about a mile south of Arundel, on flat fertile, deep sandy loam. It is 2 miles from the sea which exercises a moderate influence, and is in a sheltered, warm well drained site. The climate is sunny, warm and dry.

The vines are trained according to the Guyot high trellis system, and spraying starts in March and continues until October. The harvest normally starts in the second week of October and takes about six days to complete. Reichensteiner is harvested first, followed by Spätburgunder, both which take about two days to collect. The Schönburger is usually gathered about a week to ten days later, and again picking takes about two days.

Most of the wine is made by traditional manual methods to produce a clean and fruity, not too dry wine sold from the winery. This is a fifteenth-century barn saved from demolition and carefully rebuilt on the site for the purpose.

Visiting times: May to October 12noon-5pm (closed Monday and Friday), open at weekends all year round 12noon-5pm. Conducted tours and tastings, and parties of ten or more can be arranged outside regular opening hours. The vineyard also offers bed and breakfast facilities.

How to get there: the vineyard is in Lyminster which lies between Arundel and Littlehampton on the coast. Take the A284 south out of Arundel and after about a mile the vineyard is signposted at Lyminster Church corner.

Nearby attractions: sandy beaches, Arundel Castle, Wildfowl Trust, Fontwell and Goodwood racing.

BARKHAM MANOR VINEYARD

Mark de Gruchy Lambert
Piltdown
Uckfield
East Sussex TN 22 3XE
☎ (082572) 2103

Mentioned in the *Domesday Book*, Barkham Manor was given to Earl Goodwin by King Edward and was valued, before 1066, at 20s. In 1409 it was held by Thomas Skelton and his wife Johan. In 1723 it passed to Thomas Maryon-Wilson whose family held the title Lords of Netherall, Barkham and Tarring Chamois. By the mid-1830s the Maryon-Wilsons demolished the earlier

Barkham Manor Vineyard, the vineyard (above) and house (below)

house and built the majority of the present house on the site. It was extended by the Kerr family in the 1920s.

The vineyard is a member of the EVA, the Weald and Downland Vineyards Association, the Country Landowners Association and the East Sussex Tourist Attractions Association. It covers 33.9 acres of which 3.7 acres are productive Huxelrebe. The majority of the vines were planted in 1985. There have been no changes to varieties planted in recent years, but new, as yet unproductive varieties are: Schönburger 13.8 acres, Müller-Thurgau 5.1 acres, Bacchus 5.1 acres, Kerner 4.8 acres, and Pinot Noir 1.4 acres. There are plans to produce apple wine and a number of other products.

The vineyard is at Piltdown and Barkham Manor is situated entirely on the uppermost sub-division of the Hastings Bed-Tunbridge Wells sand. This is a variable geological formation which comprises yellow or white fine grained sand, much of it cemented together into sandstone rock. The vineyard is situated at 120ft above sea level and 15 miles from the south coast. It gets above average sunshine — about 1,700 hours a year, and below average rainfall at 31in a year.

Pruning starts in December and continues through the winter and early spring until April. Training the vines takes place between May and August and picking starts in September, depending on the weather, and can continue until November. All the vines are trained on the Geneva Double Curtain system, the High Wire trellis system, because of the danger from frequent spring frosts. The rows are 12ft apart and the vines 8ft apart within the rows. Windbreaks of *Alnus Incana* and *Alnus Rubra* have been planted every fifteen to twenty rows.

The first harvest was picked in 1988 and 1,200lb of Huxelrebe grapes were gathered. The grapes are crushed and de-strigged, then pressed in a Willmes press. The must is fermented in stainless steel tanks. The winemaker is Karl Heinz Jöhner.

The vineyard has a modern winery including press, de-stalker, filtration equipment, bottling plant and laboratory. It is housed in a 106ft long thatched barn which dates back to 1750.

Visiting times: 1 April to 24 December, Tuesday to Saturday 10am-5pm, Sunday and bank holiday 11am-5pm. Closed all day Monday. Latest admission for trails 4pm. Groups and school parties can book at other times by arrangement. There is a wine and souvenir shop, a vineyard trail, guided tours, tutored wine tastings and lectures on wine and the Piltdown Man excavations, one of the greatest archaeological hoaxes this century, which can also be visited. Piltdown Man (*Eoanthropus dawsoni*) was thought to be the missing link in man's evolution from the apes. The remains found enabled the scientists to build up a picture of what the skull of the Piltdown Man must have looked like. They can still be seen in the Natural History Museum.

Catering facilities for up to 200 can be provided in the thatched Great Barn on request. A tea room is to be opened later.

How to get there: the vineyard is south of the A272 between Newick and Uckfield. It is well signposted from the Barcombe road.

Nearby attractions: Bluebell Railway (Sheffield Park), Bentley Wildfowl Park and Motor Museum (Halland), Barbican House Museum (Lewes), Bridge Cottage (Uckfield) Lewes Castle (Lewes) and Newick Park Gardens (Newick).

Recommended pubs and restaurants in the area: Sussex Barn (restaurant) Uckfield.

BERWICK GLEBE VINEYARD

Christopher Lindlar
Berwick
Polegate
East Sussex
☎ (05806) 4996

Correspondence to: 1 Golden Square, Tenterden, Kent.

The vineyard is a member of the EVA and the Weald and Downland Vineyard Association. It covers 2 acres and there is no scope for expansion. Müller-Thurgau vines account for 75 per cent of production and Reichensteiner the remainder. The vineyard is on a fairly open site, behind the

South Downs on heavy clay, and the weather can be very varied. The vines are trained and pruned under the Double Guyot system.

Harvest starts in mid-October and usually lasts for 2 days. The wine is made at the High Weald Winery, near Maidstone, where Christopher Lindlar is the winemaker. He has been involved in English wine since 1976 when he started working with the pioneering Merrydown Vineyards under Jack Ward, having been trained in Germany.

He has worked for some years as an independent consulting winemaker and the success of this led him to establish High Weald Winery, a new purpose-built winery which is worth a detour for a visit. He acquired Berwick Glebe in January 1989, having been technical adviser to the previous owners since the vineyard was planted.

Production has averaged about 45 hectolitres an acre and the aim is to produce a dry, fragrant style. The single wine is marketed as Berwick Glebe. About 30 per cent of sales are private or direct, about 40 per cent to the on trade, and 40 per cent to the off trade.

Visiting times: by arrangement only and there are limited tasting facilities available.

How to get there: the vineyard is at Berwick, to the west of Alfriston on the A27 between Polegate and Lewes.

Recommended pub in the area: The Cricketers.

BURWASH WEALD VINEYARD

P.F. Valpy
Burnt House Farm
Burwash
East Sussex TN19 7LA
☎ (0435) 882739

The vineyard (a member of the EVA) covers 3 acres, divided equally between Huxelrebe and Bacchus. There have been no changes to varieties planted in recent years, no new plantings, and no schemes to expand the vineyard acreage.

The vineyard is 300ft above sea level, on a gentle, south-east facing slope on Tunbridge Wells in the valley of the river Dudwell. It is on clay and Ashurst sand which gives reasonable drainage. Climatic conditions are good.

The vines are trained on the Double Geneva Curtain system, and there is a regular spraying programme during the growing season. The harvest starts in late October and picking normally takes about 3 days. The vineyard does not have its own winery and so the grapes are taken away for vinification under contract nearby. The wine is bottled the following March. The first crop was picked following the devastating hurricane which hit the south-east in October 1987. The vines produced a small but quality crop and the wine was bottled the following spring. The wine, a blend of Huxelrebe and Bacchus, was slightly sweet, rounded and fresh and won the EVA's Seal of Approval. Limited sales to date have been to friends.

The vineyard, surrounded by hedges, is in an area designated as one of outstanding natural beauty, and is part of a 100-acre farm enterprise with sheep. The vineyard is worked by the family and friends under the guidance of a management service contract, and casual labour is brought in when necessary, especially during the harvest.

Visiting times: by arrangement.

How to get there: take the A265 which runs between Heathfield and Hawkhurst and turn off at Burwash Weald. Almost opposite The Wheel pub is a lane which leads directly to the vineyard.

Nearby attractions: Batemans (a National Trust property within a mile).

Recommended pub in the area: The Bell Inn, Burwash.

BYLSBOROUGH VINEYARDS

Mrs S.J. Clark
Oldfields
Woodmancote
West Sussex BN5 9AE
☎ (0273) 494444

This new vineyard covers 2.5 acres, with half an acre each of Triomphe D'Alsace, Müller-Thurgau, Madeleine Angevine and

Seyval Blanc. The remaining half an acre is planted with various varieties. It is a member of the EVA and the Weald and Downland Vineyards Association and run by Mrs Clark and her husband. The vines have still to yield their first grapes and the vineyards will not open to the public until production has started. It is on the edge of the Weald, 10 miles from the south coast on a gentle south, south-west facing slope on greensand, about 150ft above sea level. The climate is quite mild although a little exposed to north-easterly winds. The vines are all trained using the Lenz- Moser system.

CARR TAYLOR VINEYARDS
David and Linda Carr Taylor
Carr Taylor Vineyards
Westfield
Hastings
East Sussex TN35 4SG
☎ (0424) 752501

The vineyard covers 21 acres of established wines and the Carr Taylors are among the most progressive English wine producers. It is a member of the EVA and the Weald and Downland Vineyards Association of which David Carr Taylor is chairman.

Established in 1971, the present plantings consist of Reichensteiner 7 acres, Guttenborner 4 acres, Kerner 2 acres, Huxelrebe 2 acres, Schönburger 4 acres, and Pinot Noir 2 acres. There have been no changes to the varieties planted in recent years although there are considerable expansion plans including encouraging local farmers to establish their own vineyards with the Carr Taylors advising them and buying the grapes. It also provides contract winemaking and bottling for eighteen other vineyards.

The vineyard is 6 miles north of Hastings, and a mile north of the village of Westfield. The gentle southerly slopes are well protected by woodland and a 600ft high ridge. The surrounding areas are well known for apple and soft fruit production and are more influenced by the continental weather. The vineyard is on a bed of Ashdown sand which affords good drainage,

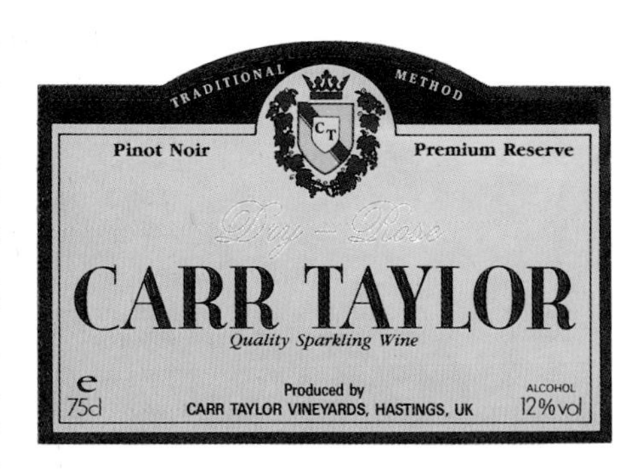

overlying a sub-strata of ironstone and clay shale. The vineyard enjoys a general maritime climate with warm winter conditions and mild summer temperatures. The vineyard area develops its own microclimate due to extensive wind breaks and high hedging.

Pruning starts early in January and it takes three people to complete the 21 acres by the end of March. Training of all vines is on the Geneva Double Curtain system with long cane-spur pruning to renew cordons every 4 years. David Carr Taylor is one of the pioneers in growing grapes on thisHigh Wire trellis system.

Spraying takes place every 10 to 15 days with ten summer sprays and two winter sprays. The spraying machine is an airblast unit which takes 7 hours to treat the 21 acres.

When the vineyard was first in production between 1976 and 1982 harvesting always started about 21-4 October. Since then the harvest has been getting progressively earlier, and in 1988 picking started on 7 October.

A twenty-five strong band of pickers is used and it takes them between 18 and 25 days to harvest the whole vineyard.

The vineyard was specially planned and laid out so that varieties ripened in rotation making it easier for picking and controlling supplies to the winery. The Reichensteiner is usually the first variety to be picked, followed by Guttenborner, Huxelrebe, Kerner, Schönburger and so on.

The grapes are hand picked with secateurs into buckets which are emptied into 110lb bins. The bins are collected by tractor and then taken to a collecting point where the grapes are emptied into a 2-ton transporter which takes them to the press house. The transporter is reversed up to either of the two presses, one of which can take 2 tons of grapes and the other 5 tons. The transporter pumps the grapes and stalks straight into the presses, or into holding tanks if the presses are occupied.

Pressing lasts from 3 to 5 hours. The juice is pumped into holding settling tanks before being racked off and inoculated with special wine yeast. Average crush is 300 tons and this capacity will increase substantially in the next few years. First fermentation lasts for 8 to 10 days and the wine is then kept on the lees for a further 8 weeks. The first racking usually takes place in early January, and at one week intervals the wine is centrifuged, coarse filtered, fine filtered and then sterile filtered.

At the end of January the wine is stabilised and samples are sent off for independent analysis. At the end of February bottling starts for other wineries and about 25 per cent of their own production is also bottled to fill the bonded warehouse ready for the early spring market.

The *Méthode Champenoise* is also bottled for the second fermentation and laid down

to rest for the next 18 months. The previous year's *Méthode Champenoise* is disgorged, re-corked and dressed for the coming year. At present, production of Champagne method sparkling wine tops 30,000 bottles of vintage, rosé and non-vintage.

Production in 1983 was 189,000 bottles but the quality of vintage was poor. In 1984 the quality of the vintage was still poor and production was 125,000 bottles. There was

Attractions near the vineyard include Rye (above) and Battle Abbey (left)

some improvement in 1985 when 100,000 bottles were produced, and by 1986, when production was 87,000 bottles the wine had achieved 'good sound quality'. In 1987 85,000 bottles of very good wine were produced, and the 95,000 bottles produced in 1988 are the best yet. Wines produced currently are: dry 1988 Schönburger, with high fruit and well balanced good acidity; dry 1988 Kerner-Huxelrebe, strong fruity dryness and full flavour; medium dry 1988 Guttenborner, full flavoured, spicy and honeyed and well balanced, and medium 1988 Reichensteiner with strong fruit, good bouquet and good alcohol. Other wines include a medium dry Pinot Noir rosé with very good fruit which must be served chilled, a medium dry Sussex county, and medium Hastings table wine, both blended wines made from the vineyard's grapes. The vintage sparkling wine is rested on the lees with a special yeast for more than 3 years and has a full, mature flavour with a subtle fragrance and soft finish. The sparkling rosé has a delicate pink colouring which comes from the Pinot Noir grapes having been crushed and fermented on the skins for 6 days. The 1985 vintage was the first commercial English pink quality sparkling wine. The non-vintage sparkling wine is a blend of Kerner grapes for acidity and Reichensteiner for fruit and bouquet. It is rested on its lees for a year, and is young, lively and full of fruit finish.

The Gold Seal Certification Trade Mark is awarded to all David Carr Taylor's wines, and they regularly win awards. The Carr Taylor 1986 Reichensteiner was judged by a panel of experts at the 1988 Bristol World Wine Fair as the English wine of the year. The vintage sparkling wine won the gold medal, and the 1986 Guttenborner received a silver. The Concours National Des Grand Vins de France also awarded Carr Taylor a gold medal for his vintage sparkling wine at its international meeting in 1988.

There is a balanced sales programme for the wines, split between direct vineyard sales, directly into hotels and restaurant and postal sales, specialist wine shops, wholesale into supermarkets and exports to sixteen countries including France, Germany and Canada.

The vineyard has a modern winery and automatic bottling plant. There is storage capacity for a third of a million litres in tanks and bottles, and a bottling line which can handle 1,200 bottles an hour.

The traditional *Méthode Champenoise* production and storage is kept separate. The vineyard is operated with the minimum of staff because the latest techniques are used and the modern equipment in the winery. There is a foreman for the vineyard, and one member of staff runs the winery and bottling hall, while another looks after the mechanical services. David Carr Taylor is the winemaker.

Visiting times: Christmas to Easter, Monday to Friday 10am-5pm, Easter to Christmas, daily 10am-5pm. The wine shop and tasting area is in an attractive old barn which has catering facilities. There are also facilities for meetings and lunches and dinners. There is a vineyard trail for individuals for which a charge is made and vineyard and winery tours with tastings can be arranged for groups of twenty or more. Talks, lectures and comparative wine tastings can be arranged.

How to get there: the vineyard lies a mile north of the village of Westfield which is on the A28 Hastings to Ashford Road. From Hastings, drive for about 6 miles and take the right hand turn at the New Inn pub towards Seddlescombe. The vineyard is well signposted by the brown tourist signs. From London follow the A21 towards Hastings, and turn left on the A28 and follow the signs.

Nearby attractions: Battle Abbey, Great Dixter, a timber framed manor house and gardens, Batemans (a 1630 Ironmaster's house at Burwash now owned by the NT), Hastings Castle and old town, Pevensey Castle, Bodiam Castle, Rye old town and the Royal Greenwich Observatory (Herstmonceux Castle).

DOWNERS VINEYARD

Commander and Mrs E.G. Downer
Clappers Lane
Fulking
Henfield
Sussex BN5 9NH
☎ (079 156) 484

The vineyard covers 7 acres exclusively planted with Müller-Thurgau and a further 6 acres are to be planted. There have been no changes to varietals grown in recent years, and all the vines planted are productive. It is a member of the EVA, the Weald and Downland Vineyards Association, the Country Landowners' Association and the National Farmers Union.

The vineyard borders a narrow lane and is three-quarters of a mile from the small village of Fulking which nestles at the foot of the South Downs. The vineyard gently slopes to the south, with panoramic views of the Downs from Wolstonbury Hill in the east to Chanctonbury Ring in the west. The vineyard is on the greensands and the soil is sandy loam.

All the vines are grafted onto American phylloxera-resistant rootstock and were originally trained on the Lenz-Moser High Culture system, with the bottom wire 3ft and the top 6.5ft from the ground. In 1983 a start was made to change to the Geneva Double Curtain system.

The grapes ripen slowly during the mild summers and are normally harvested during the last week of October. Picking usually takes about a week. The grapes are picked into stackable, stowable containers and sent to a contract winery for vinification. The wine is then kept in a bonded store on the vineyard at a controlled temperature of 50°F (10°C) which retains the quality of the wine over a long period.

Production has fluctuated enormously over the last few years because of weather. In 1984 production was 6,000l, which fell to 4,000l the following year, and down again to 2,500l in 1986. The vineyard was particularly badly hit by the October 1987 hurricane and production was only 700l. The 1988 production was 1,500l but in all recent years, a very good, dry fruity wine has been produced. The 1985 and 1986 vintages are still being marketed, with the 1987 and 1988 not ready for drinking. The wine is sold through the vineyard shop, wholesalers, restaurants and pubs.

Visiting times: the vineyard is open daily from June to early October, and there is an admission charge. Conducted tours including tasting are available for groups of fifteen to thirty people, but must be prebooked. The vineyard also has a Caravan Club approved site. The vineyard shop is open daily throughout the year for the sale of wine by the bottle or case.

How to get there: from the north either travel south on the A2037 and turn left on to the A281 at Henfield, or use the A23 and turn on to the A281 about a mile after the Hurstpierpoint turn off. The vineyard is signposted down Clappers Lane which is south of the A281.

Recommended pubs, restaurants and hotels in the area: Tottington Manor Hotel and Restaurant, Golding Barn Restaurant, Shepherd and Dog pub, and Royal Oak pub.

FLEXERNE VINEYARD

Peter and Brenda Smith
Fletching Common
Newick
East Sussex
BN8 4JJ
☎ (082 572) 2548

The vineyard covers 5 acres, exclusively Müller-Thurgau, which includes an acre of new, as yet unproductive vines and is a member of the EVA. The area is a well known soft fruit growing locality, and the vineyard was formerly run as a commercial fruit farm.

The vineyard is on site which slopes gently to the south, and is well sheltered by tall hedges and mature trees on the north, east and west boundaries. The soil is free-draining Tunbridge Wells sand and combines to make the site warm, sheltered and very well suited to the cultivation of vines.

The original planting of vines started in 1963 with cuttings obtained from the Viticultural Research Station at Oxted. All further stock has been propagated by the previous owners from these original vines. The vines are trained on the Double Guyot system with rows 8ft apart and 4ft spacings between vines. There are 78 vines to each 105yd long row, and 60 rows altogether in the vineyard.

As one of the first vineyards involved in the current revival, Flexerne has enjoyed a great deal of publicity over the years and won a number of prizes in English wine competitions.

For a number of years, Flexerne was the venue for the Agricultural Training Board's instructional classes in all aspects of viticulture, and many of today's vineyard owners worked in and became familiar with vineyard management from their visits to Flexerne.

The vineyard was purchased in 1984 by the present owners who have continued the developments. Good yields have been obtained and a steady improvement in the quality of the wine has been achieved over the years. Pruning starts early in the new year and is completed by the end of March. Spraying starts in late May or early June depending on the weather and is carried out at 10- day intervals until the end of September. The harvest usually starts in the last week of October and takes 2 to 3 days to complete with fifteen to twenty pickers. The vineyard does not have its own winery and the grapes are sold to the English Wine Centre where vinification takes place.

Visiting times: by appointment between June and October.

How to get there: the vineyard is half a mile north of the A272 in Newick.

Nearby attractions: Bluebell Railway at Sheffield Park and Sheffield Park Gardens (NT).

HIDDEN SPRING VINEYARD
M.J. Doubleday and C.R. Crammell
Vines Cross Road
Horam
East Sussex
☎ (04353) 2640

The vineyard is part of an agricultural enterprise which also involves top fruit. It is a member of the EVA, the Weald and Downland Vineyards Association, and the Rother Valley Farmers Co-op, covering 8.5 acres with a further half an acre planting planned. There is an acre of Faber and 1.5 acres each of Ortega and Müller-Thurgau which should all crop for the first time this year. Other varieties planted but not yet in production are: Dunkelfelder half an acre, Pinot Noir half an acre, Reichensteiner 2 acres and Seyval Blanc 1.5 acres. The new half acre planting will be to Chardonnay.

The vineyard is on the northern, south facing slope of a small valley formed by the Waldren Gill. It is about 150ft above sea level, with a slope of about 15°. The soil is medium loam over Tunbridge Wells sand. The vines are trained on the Double Guyot, Single Guyot or Pendelbogen systems.

The vineyard plans to open a wine shop for sale of its first vintage in 1990 (made from the 1989 harvest). There is already an orchard shop open from October to December, and sells apples, pears, apple wine, vines and honey produced from their own apiary. When the winery shop opens there will be tasting facilities and picnic sites. Other facilities offered include tours, farm trails, and a self-catering holiday cottage.

Visiting times: from 1990 April to Christmas, Wednesday to Sunday 11am-5pm.

How to get there: Horam is on the A267 between Heathfield and Hailsham. From Horam take the B2203 Heathfield Road and then turn right into Vines Cross Road, the vineyard is a short way down on your left.

Nearby attractions: Farm Museum (Horam), Batemans (NT), Royal Observatory, Herstmonceux Castle, Merrydown Cider Co (Horam) and Michelam Priory.

Recommended pubs, restaurants and hotels in the area: Horam Inn (Horam), May Garland (restaurant, Horam), Gunn Inn (Chiddingly), Brewers (pub, Vine Cross) and The Star (pub, Old Heathfield).

NYETIMBER VINEYARD
Nyetimber Ltd
Gay Street
West Chiltington
West Sussex RH20 2HH
☎ (07983) 2235

The vineyard covers 30 acres, consisting of 2 acres of Gewürztraminer and 28 acres of Chardonnay. The first 2 acres were planted in 1988 and the remainder in 1989. None of the vines are yet in production. The vineyard is south facing on greensand and a member of the EVA and the Weald and Downland Vineyards Association. A new winery is to be established in 1990-1 in time for the first vintage.

Visiting times: none at present but serious visitors interested in seeing the establishment of a young vineyard could write or phone for an appointment and ask for directions from the owners.

ROCK LODGE VINEYARD
Norman Cowderoy
Scaynes Hill
Nr Haywards Heath
West Sussex RH17 7NG
☎ (044486) 224/567

Rock Lodge Vineyard, the harvest

The vineyard (a member of the EVA and the Weald and Downland Vineyards Association) covers 10 acres, which includes Ditchling Vineyard, and there are plans to expand it to 26 acres during 1989. It is in mid-Sussex, on a south facing slope and well sheltered. It is on sandy clay loam and clay loam, partly land drained.

Müller-Thurgau, Reichensteiner and Ortega account for 80 per cent of production, and the remainder is made up by Pinot Noir, Triomphe D'Alsace and Zweigeltrebe. In addition to the varieties listed above, there are another forty or so clones and varieties under trial. The experimental plot covers about 2 acres, and trials include different pruning methods and trellising systems. Some vines are being grown under polythene and all the different varieties are being evaluated for suitability.

The first vines were planted in 1961 when English viticulture was still in its infancy. There were only six English vineyards in the country and knowledge about suitable grape varieties was small. More than fifty different varieties were tested and evaluated, and as a result of these experiments, Müller-Thurgau was selected as the most suitable, and 1,000 vines were planted in 1965. The first commercial crop was achieved in 1970 and for the next 5 years, the wine was made by a co-operative. In 1976 in order to achieve an individual character, and to ensure quality control, the Cowderoy family established their own vineyard. It was a challenging year with a huge harvest, and the winery and equipment was installed only just in time before the vintage started. The wine produced by the family in that first year won a silver medal in the English wine of the year competition.

Although Müller-Thurgau has proved successful on this vineyard, it has not stopped the family from continuing with their trials and experimentation. Almost every year new varieties are planted, both white and red, including early ripening clones of Chardonnay and Pinot Noir.

The vines are mainly trained according to the Pendle Bogen system, but this is being switched to the Ruakura, Twin Tiro, Tier and Lyre systems. Spraying takes place at intervals of 10 to 20 days, and the mix of sprays depends on the weather. Pruning starts in January and different methods are used and evaluated. The harvest starts usually in the second week of October with the Müller-Thurgau being picked, followed a week later by the Reichensteiner, and the others in the last week of the month.

The grapes are dosed with sulphur dioxide and ascorbic acid and de-stemmed and crushed under a carpet of carbon dioxide for protection. There is some skin contact. The grapes are then pressed and pectolytic enzymes added. The must is allowed to settle overnight and then clarified using an earth filter. Sugar is added and de-acidification takes place to 3-4oz per quarter gallon. The 'Intek' yeast is then added and fermentation starts within 36 hours. The fermentation temperature is kept at a constant 59°F (15°C) by either heating or cooling the tanks.

Some wines have the fermentation stopped before all the sugar has been converted to alcohol to produce a medium dry style. Others are fermented to dryness. The tartrates are stabilised by the contact process, the wines are then earth filtered, and then membrane filtered prior to bottling. Sparkling wines made according to the *Méthode Champenoise* are also produced.

Production in 1984 was 18,000 bottles and the vintage was good. In 1985 production was 10,000 bottles and the vintage average. It was bad in 1986 when 8,000 bottles were made, and worse in 1987 when production fell to only 4,000 bottles. In 1988 although the vintage was still described as bad, production had increased to 8,000 bottles.

The vineyard is very much a family business headed by Norman Cowderoy. Jo Cowderoy is marketing manager and the winemaker is David Cowderoy who graduated from Wye College, London University, with a degree in soil science and plant nutrition, and then studied at Australia's top wine college, Roseworthy, for his post graduate diploma in viticulture and viniculture. Bob Bryant joined the vineyard in 1967 as vine dresser and has been with the family business ever since. His care and devotion of the vines has ensured the winery has grapes of high quality to vinify each year.

Wines produced include various vintages of Müller-Thurgau, a special reserve, a *Méthode Champenoise* sparkling wine and some oak aged reds and whites.

It is interesting to see how the vintages develop. The 1987 Müller-Thurgau has a pale straw colour with strong green hues. The nose has an intense fruity, pear-drop character typical of Müller-Thurgau. The palate is full, with the same pear-drop, lychee character and has a long finish. It is medium dry. The 1986 Müller-Thurgau was described as spice and peaches in the 1988 International Wine Challenge, organised by *Wine* magazine. It is a light wine with structure. Dark straw in colour, the palate is medium dry, fruity and quite full with a soft finish. The 1985 Müller-Thurgau is mid-straw in colour with slight green hues. The nose is fresh and floral showing a slight estery character. The palate is dry and crisp with a lemony zest. The 1984 Müller-Thurgau is mid-straw in colour with strong green hues. The nose is fresh and grapey, as is the palate which is medium, making it smooth and ideal as an apéritif. The Special Reserve 1985 is matured in new small French oak barrels from the Limousin and Aliers regions. It has a light gold colour with some pale green hues. The nose has adopted a vanilla-wood character but still retains fruit. The palate is very full with smooth wood characters balanced by soft fruit. It is dry.

The wines are sold at the cellar door, to local off-licences and exported to Germany, Denmark and Japan.

Visiting times: the winery shop is open Monday to Saturday 9am-5pm. Tours including a tasting can be arranged by appointment. The vineyard also produces cider which is sold in the winery shop, together with pottery (made by another member of the family) and vines and other vineyard goods are for sale. It also runs a business selling equipment and other supplies to vineyards.

There is a restaurant providing lunches and supper for groups giving advance notice.

How to get there: the vineyard is situated just to the east of Scaynes Hill on the A272 between Haywards Heath and its junction with the A275.

Nearby attractions: Sheffield Park, Bluebell Railway and Nymans Gardens.

Recommended pubs and restaurants in the area: The Sloop (pub, Scaynes Hill), The Farmers (pub, Scaynes Hill).

SEYMOURS VINEYARD

Hector and Beryl McMullen
Forest Road
Horsham
Sussex RH12 4NL
☎ (0403) 52397

The vineyard (a member of the EVA and the Weald and Downland Vineyard Association) covers just over 5 acres of which Seyval Blanc accounts for 4.8 acres and 90 per cent of production. The other varieties are Kerner 0.2 acres with 7 per cent of production, and Schönburger 0.1 acres and 3 per cent of production.

There has been no change in the varieties planted in recent years, and there are no new, as yet, unproductive vines.

The vineyard is 2 miles from the centre of Horsham, on the edge of St Leonards Forest in an area of outstanding natural beauty. It is 300ft above sea level on very fine sandy loam over shale. The vineyard is sheltered from the east and north-east by stands of beech, oak and spruce, and to the south-west by beech and hawthorn.

The vineyard is worked by Hector McMullen, who is also the winemaker, assisted by his wife. Casuals are employed when necessary. Mr McMullen's occupation of winemaker is a far cry from his previous job as a Concorde captain. He commanded the world record flight to Sydney and back just before his retirement in 1985, celebrating the achievement at Sydney Airport with a bottle of Seymours Seyval.

That is the reason why one of the shields used on the wine labels depicts a Concorde. The other label shows a deer, symbolic of the wild herds roaming the adjacent forest and surrounding land since the sixteenth century. The records show a case brought to court by the Duchess of Norfolk in 1545 against deer poachers in the forest.

The McMullens began planting the vines in 1981 with Seyval Blanc, with later plantings of Kerner and Schönburger. All the vines are trained on the Double Guyot system, and spraying takes place at 10 to 14 day intervals through the growing season. There are two 50ft long plastic tunnels planted with Kerner and Schönburger. These are spur pruned and the grapes used for *süss* reserve. The outdoor grapes ripen slowly in the English summer to produce a bright crisp wine with a delicate bouquet and hint of grapes on the palate, unobtainable in hotter climates.

The harvest takes 2 days to gather and the starting date is usually around the middle of October but depends on the weather. Seyval is the first variety to be picked. The winery is in the vineyard and the grapes are taken straight to the crusher de-strigger and then into the hydraulic press. Fermentation takes place in stainless steel vats.

Average production is about 5,000 to 6,000 bottles a year, and the wine is cellar stored to keep it in prime condition. Wines currently produced are Seyval Blanc, dry and medium dry, and Seymours Select which is medium dry. All are crisp, delicate wines with good bouquet. The dry is excellent with fish, while the medium dry is good with almost any dish and also for drinking on its own.

Visiting times: July to mid-October, Thursdays, Fridays and Saturdays 10am-6pm. Dogs are not allowed. There is a vineyard walk which is a good opportunity to see an estate in miniature. An explanatory leaflet is available from the winery to allow visitors to follow a route round the different types of vines in the open, and the experimental vines under cover in the tunnels. People can enjoy a walk through the vineyard, inspect the winemaking equipment and then taste the wines.

The winery sells wine by the bottle or case. Guided tours of the vineyard and winery with tastings can be arranged from July to October for groups between ten and thirty.

How to get there: the vineyard is signposted on the lane which runs from Horsham eastwards to Pease Pottage, at the southern end of the M23, Exit 11.

Nearby attractions: Leonardslee Gardens, Wakehurst Place, Petworth House, Parham House and Park.

Recommended pubs, restaurants and hotels in the area: James King (Pease Pottage, a pub and restaurant) and South Lodge (Lower Beeding, an hotel and restaurant).

STEYNING VINEYARD

Miss S.R. Elsden
Steyning Vineyard
Nash Hotel
Horsham Road
Steyning
West Sussex BN4 3AA
☎ (0903) 814988

The vineyard and its wine is named after Nash House, now a hotel. At one time Nash was a farmhouse and parts of the building date back to medieval times.

The vineyard covers 3 acres, divided equally between Müller-Thurgau and Schönburger. Only half an acre is currently productive. There are no plans to expand the vineyard which is a member of the EVA and the Weald and Downland Vineyards Association. It is situated on upper greensand and sandy loam and is south facing on a gentle slope of the South Downs. Climatic conditions are mild, influenced by the proximity of the sea. The vineyard was planted in 1984 and 1985 on the Double Guyot system, with wide rows to allow maximum use of mechanisation.

The first harvest was picked on the 16 October 1988, and the grapes were sent to Lamberhurst Priory Vineyard in Kent for vinification.

Visiting times: daily 10.30am-6pm. Group visits with wine tastings and video of English wine production can be arranged. The winery shop and tasting room are at the rear of the hotel.

How to get there: the vineyard is off the B2135 Partridge Green road, which heads north from the A283 at Steyning.

A selection of wines from St George's Vineyard

Nearby attractions: Steyning — museum, twelfth-century church, and medieval timber-framed houses. Bramber Castle and Chanctonbury Ring (a Roman hill fort).

Recommended pubs, restaurants and hotels in the area: Nash Hotel, White Horse pub and Springwells Hotel.

ST GEORGE'S VINEYARD
Peter and Gay Biddlecombe
Waldron
Nr Heathfield
East Sussex
TN21 0RA
☎ (04353) 2156

The vineyard (a member of the EVA and the Weald and Downland Vineyard Association) covers 20 acres and there are plans to plant a further 30 acres. Varieties planted and their acreages are Müller-Thurgau 5, Reichensteiner 5, Pinot Noir 3, Seyval Blanc 3, Schönburger 3 and Ortega 1. There have been no changes in the varieties planted in recent years and there are no new, as yet, unproductive vines.

The vineyard is 15 miles from the south coast and 45 miles south of London. It is in the centre of Waldron village in the Sussex Weald standing at 300ft above sea level.

Because of good natural protection and a particularly good microclimate, there are no frost pockets. The soil is Tunbridge Wells sand and Wadhurst clay, although part of the vineyard is planted on sandstone rock. Because of the microclimate the vineyard is able to harvest later than most others.

The vineyard is divided between three

Picking the grapes at St George's

fields. The microclimates are especially good in two of the fields. The whole vineyard usually escapes late spring and early autumn frosts. Average temperatures are always slightly higher than those in neighbouring Kent, and because of the natural wind protection and the ability to pick later, higher sugar concentrations in the grapes are achieved.

The vineyard was planted on an ancient estate mentioned in the *Domesday Book* in 1086, and on which vines were grown hundreds of years ago. St George's claims to be the prettiest vineyard in England lying as it does amid landscaped gardens. There is a fountain and rose garden set in the middle of the vineyard and its aim is 'to become the Château Petrus of England, producing top quality wine on a small scale to the highest standards for a selected clientele.' The first vines were planted in 1979 on 4 acres.

Expansion plans include more plantings and the purchasing of top quality fruit only from other vineyards.

Gay Biddlecombe is winemaker and Karl Heinz Jöhner, consultant. The vineyard year starts in January with pruning. All the vines are trained on the Double Guyot system and during January and February manure is spread throughout the vineyard. In March the first spraying against weeds takes place on the non-organic vines only, and soil analysis is carried out.

The spraying programme against disease starts after budburst in April and continues as necessary throughout the summer. Fertiliser is also added as required. In late August the leaves around the fruit are removed by hand to expose the grapes to the sunlight and in late September the vines are covered with nets to protect the grapes from birds. Harvesting starts at the end of October or into November, and the vines then usually receive a winter spray. Harvesting in 1988 began on 29 October, considerably later than most other vineyards, and took almost three weeks to complete. The varieties are usually picked in the following order: Müller-Thurgau, Seyval, Ortega, Reichensteiner, Schönburger and Pinot Noir.

Six experienced pickers are used, two to a row and one on each side of the vines. The grapes are taken by a Chemo grape picking trailer to the winery which only uses stainless steel equipment. The grapes are pressed in a Willmes rotary press, 4 tons in each press, and the must is then transferred to stainless steel tanks of various sizes for fermentation. The vineyard was the first in England to buy the revolutionary new Romicon hollow fibre filtration system. It filters just once and results in a clearer wine without any loss of flavour. It is unique in that it is a complete one step crossflow filtration system which sterilises as it filters and removes tanins in white wine — often the cause of headaches. It allows continuous filtration round the clock if necessary, and is capable of handling 500l an hour.

The Pinot Noir is matured in new oak barrels, and from the 1988 harvest a sparkling wine using the *Méthode Champenoise* is being produced. A new bottling plant is being added to the winery, which has always aimed for quality rather than maximum production. Before 1987 not all the 20 acres were in production but the best vintages produced were undoubtedly from 1984 and 1985. In 1988 they began an expansion programme to boost production by buying in grapes from other producers. They only buy in the same varieties that they grow themselves and only top quality grapes. The 1988 production was about 70,000 bottles which followed just 2,400 bottles in 1987 made from grapes gathered just after the hurricane had struck. The vineyard hopes to reach a production of about 120,000 bottles a year from its own acreage.

The wines produced are: Müller-Thurgau, a dry, elegant, very fruity wine, with good variety nose and a little of the Riesling character showing (it keeps well); Reichensteiner, a medium dry, complex wine, with a fruity and refreshing bouquet; Tudor Rosé, made from Pinot Noir and matured in oak. It is medium dry, oaky and has good colour; Domesday, a blended sweeter wine, specially produced for the National Domesday Committee and the Public Record Office to celebrate the 900th anniversary of the *Domesday Book*; Seyval Organic, a very dry wine, earthy and with a fruity, French style and Hurricane Harvest, made from grapes rescued after the storms, dry and complex. Profits went towards a tree planting programme on nearby Ashdown Forest.

Gay Biddlecombe is one of the great champions of English wine and a formidable marketeer. She does all her own public relations, promotion and selling, preferring to deal directly with her customers rather than use an agent. The vineyard was the first in England to introduce own labelling and clients include the House of Commons, Tower of London, Trusthouse Forte, the Lord Chancellors Office and Herstmonceux Castle. Other special commissions have included producing an English wine to commemorate the 400th anniversary of the Spanish Armada, and to celebrate the world conference of the Esperanto Society in Britain, with suitably translated label. She exports to Japan, Canada, Australia, West Africa, Germany, Hong Kong, Luxembourg and the USA. A St George's wine was the first English wine to be served on an American airline.

The winery is purpose-built and lays claim to being the most modern in England. The exterior was designed to stay in keeping with the estate's listed buildings and the interior is modern with special insulation and tiles.

Other products available from the vineyard include apple wine, a Tudor Rosé sorbet (made with their own pink wine), vines, vine prunings for barbecues, baskets and decorative wall hangings from vine clippings, mustard made with their own wines, and honey from their own bees.

There are free tastings during opening hours and more formal wine tastings are organised. Wine is available for sale by the glass or bottle for drinking on the premises, in the restaurant, or with a picnic in the gardens. The winery received more than 20,000 visitors a year, at least 10 per cent of them from overseas. The vineyard also organises wine mastermind evenings, arranges conducted vineyard and winery tours with tastings, walkabouts and audio tours. It runs an advisory service for growers and organises a full summer programme of events including art exhibitions, concerts, recitals, craft fairs and medieval banquets. An unusual feature is the 'adopt a vine' scheme. People taking part 'buying' their own vine and in return receive their own personalised bottle of wine.

There is a large winery shop in a converted 300-year-old barn selling wines and wine associated gifts as well as up-market crafts and food produce, all from Sussex. These include willow baskets, dried flowers, cheeses and so on. There is also a restaurant in the conservatory which overlooks the vineyard, and with large windows looking down into the winery itself. A magnificent eleventh-century tithe barn, reputed to be the oldest in Sussex, a permanent exhibition on English wine and a giant chess set laid out in the vineyard gardens is also here.

Visiting times: summer from 23 April (St George's Day) to 31 October. 11am-5pm every day. Winter, 1 November to 24 December, weekends 1-4pm. January and February closed. 1 March to 22 April, weekends 1-4pm.

How to get there: the vineyard is well signposted in the centre of Waldron village, 3 miles off the A2 London to Eastbourne road or 3 miles off the A267 Heathfield to Tunbridge Wells road.

Nearby attractions: the vineyard is opposite a twelfth-century church. Batemans, Rudyard Kipling's home (NT) is 5 miles away, Bentley Wildfowl Park, 7 miles away, Ashdown Forest, and Merrydown Winery (wine and cider) 3 miles away.

Recommended pubs, restaurants and hotels in the area: Horsted Place Hotel, Halland Forge Motel, The Priory (restaurant), The Star Inn pub (Waldron) and Blackboys Inn (Blackboys).

Surrey

THORNCROFT VINEYARDS

Guy Woodall and Shiela Smith
Highlands Farm
Leatherhead
Surrey KT 22 8QE
☎ (0372) 372558

The vineyard (a member of the EVA and the Weald and Downland Vineyards Association) covers 10.3 acres of which 4 acres are in production. Varieties planted are Reichensteiner 4 acres, Schönburger 2.5 acres, Ortega 2.5 acres, and Pinot Noir 1.3 acres. New but as yet unproductive plantings are Reichensteiner 2.8 acres and 1.3 acres each of Schönburger, Ortega and Pinot Noir.

The vineyard is on a south-easterly slope which runs down to the river Mole in the Dorking Gap in the North Downs. It enjoys an excellent microclimate due to its low altitude — between 90ft and 120ft above sea level — and is well sheltered by the Downs. The soil is free draining alluvial sand with some chalky outcrops.

The vines are trained on the Geneva Double Curtain system. Pruning is delayed as long as possible to minimise the risk from frost. In the spring careful attention is paid to controlling growth to maximise fruit quality and to curb excess vigour. Weeds are controlled by cultivating between the rows. The use of chemical weed control is avoided where possible. A full spray programme to combat disease (botrytis and mildew) is used with sprayings at approximately two week intervals throughout the growing season.

The first vintage was in 1988 and the three main varieties ripen in convenient order, starting with Ortega, then Reichensteiner about ten days later, and the Schönburger a week after that. Presently only a small proportion of the grapes grown are vinified at the vineyard, although expansion plans include a fully equipped winery within the next 2 or 3 years. The vineyard also makes elderflower cordial, which has helped produce income while the newly planted vines reach maturity.

Current winemaking equipment includes a Kieselguhr filtration system, a vacuum assisted bottling machine, stainless steel and fibreglass tanks, a crusher and small bladder press. This equipment is also used to produce a small quantity of excellent sloe gin every year. The aim of the winery is to produce as dry a wine as possible avoiding malolactic fermentation, and more in the Loire style rather than the Germanic.

The 1988 vintage produced very low quantity but very high quality. About 150 bottles were produced. There are no plans at present to extend the vineyard acreage and the major work will involve the new winery. It is planned to continue producing elderflower cordial and sloe gin and to extend the range by introducing other compounded spirits. Other agricultural enterprises include some free range and additive free pork, and half or whole porkers are sold ready for the freezer.

Visiting times: by appointment only at present.

How to get there: details provided by owners who do not yet live on site.

Nearby attractions: Box Hill, Norbury Park and Chessington World of Adventures.

Chapter 6
Vineyards in Southern England

Hampshire

ALDERMOOR VINEYARDS
M.F. and W.A. Baerselman
Poulner Hill
Ringwood
Hants BH24 3HR
☎ (0425) 472912

The vineyard (a member of the EVA and the Wessex Vineyards Association) covers 4 acres, three-quarters of which is planted with Müller-Thurgau and the rest with Reichensteiner.

There have been no changes to the varieties planted in recent years and there are no new, as yet unproductive vines. The vineyard is 194ft above sea level on a light sandy loam over clay and gravel. Climatic conditions are described by the owners as 'bloody awful'. The vines are all trained using the Double Guyot system and there is a regular machine spraying programme through the growing period to combat disease.

The harvest can start as early as the first week of October or be late as 24 October. The vineyard does not have its own winery and vinification is carried out under contract. Production over the last 5 years is described as 'lousy'. Wines currently produced are the 1985 Müller-Thurgau, both dry and medium dry. Sales are direct from the vineyard.

There are no plans to expand the vineyard at present, but it is worth a visit to see how grapes should be grown. The vineyard also has a labelling equipment agency.

Visiting times: by appointment only. There are full tasting facilities and tours for groups of between fourteen and thirty-five can be arranged.

How to get there: the vineyard lies south of the A31 Bournemouth to Cadnam road, a short way out of Ringwood. From Ringwood follow the A31 and take a right turning into Noual Lane, and then the first left which leads to the vineyard.

BEAULIEU ABBEY VINEYARD
Montagu Ventures
John Montagu Building
Brockenhurst
Hants SO43 7ZN
☎ (0590) 612345

The vineyard covers 4.6 acres, 50 per cent of which is Müller-Thurgau, together with Reichensteiner, Huxelrebe and Seyval Blanc and the red varieties Seibel and Zweigeltrebe. It is about 50ft above sea level, just over a quarter of a mile north of the Beaulieu river, and some 8 miles from The Solent. The vineyard is planted on a fairly heavy gravelly, clay loam. The vines are trained on the Geneva Double Curtain system, planted on a grid 12ft by 6.5ft.

Beaulieu Abbey was founded in 1204 by the Cistercians and records show that a vineyard was quickly established. Legend has it that a royal visitor of that time on tasting the wine thought them so good that he was sure they came from France. In 1736, the second Duke of Montagu ordered the vineyard to be replanted on its original site.

The grapes, however, were fermented and distilled into brandy. The vineyard holds a special place in English wine history because the first four rows of vines — Müller-Thurgau and Seyve Villard — were planted in 1958 by the Gore-Browne's who did much to fuel the post-war revival and were founder members of the EVA. The association's first meeting took place at Beaulieu. They engaged Archangelo Lanza, a cousin of Mario Lanza, from Italy, to look after the vineyard and make the wine.

Lieutenant Colonel and Mrs Gore-Browne had recently returned from duty in Africa and in 1956 they chose a house called The Vineyards next to the Beaulieu estate — Ralph Montagu was Margaret Gore-Browne's godson and decided to establish a vineyard. By 1960, 5 acres had been planted and the first vintage was gathered the following year.

The vineyard was known as Beaulieu Abbey and the wines, produced in their small winery, received a number of awards during the 1960s. In 1966 production topped 7,000 bottles, and 8,000 the following year. The old winery is still at Beaulieu but now used as a wine store. The vineyard transferred to Montagu Ventures in 1974 with the wine being made first at Merrydown, then Lamberhurst and recently at Lymington. It continues to win awards in national and international tastings. The 1987 Beaulieu won a silver medal at the 1988 English Wine of the Year Competition.

Margaret Gore-Browne played a leading role in the winemaking revival. She was also a great supporter of Welsh viticulture and Lord Montagu tells how she donated cuttings to people wanting to establish their own vineyards in the Principality. She planted vines in a number of plots in Wales but what happened to them is not recorded. The Welsh Vineyards Association was formed with her backing in 1966, although it did not flourish, and a year later she wrote *Let's Plant a Vineyard*, which inspired many people. When Margaret Gore-Browne died in 1976 she left the vineyard to Ralph Douglas Scott-Montagu, Lord Montagu's son, and it is now a major attraction within the National Motor Museum complex. Apart from helping set up the EVA, the Gore-Browne's are also remembered by the trophy donated by them and which carries their name. It is the EVA's top award and presented annually to the maker of the judged best English wine.

The Montagus have also been staunch supporters of English winemaking. The first English Wine Festival was held at Beaulieu in 1975. Belinda, Lady Montagu, was the EVA's vice-president for 10 years from its founding in 1967, and Lord Montagu has been president since 1981. Most of the wine is sold through the National Motor Museum shop.

Visiting times: the museum shop is open daily from 10am-5pm. The vineyard is open by appointment only. Guided tours for up to thirty can be arranged.

How to get there: the vineyard is part of the National Motor Museum and is well signposted. Take the B3056 Beaulieu to Lyndhurst road.

BISHOPS WALTHAM VINEYARD

John and Leslie Youles
Tangier Lane
Bishops Waltham
Hants SO3 1BU
☎ (04893) 6803

The vineyard (a member of the EVA and the Wessex Vineyards Association) covers 11.5 acres with a further half an acre still to be planted. The varieties are Schönburger 5 acres, Würzer 4 acres and Madeleine Angevine 1.5 acres. There have been no changes to the varieties planted in recent years but there is an acre of new Reichensteiner vines which are not yet productive. The vineyard is located in the Southampton basin, about 90ft above sea level. It is slightly sloping to the south-west with a soil of loam on clay and is situated in one of the warmer areas of Britain with an annual rainfall of 29in.

The search for the vineyard started in 1981 with the aim of producing high quality, distinctive English wines. The following year the 13-acre site was acquired, and by 1983 10 acres of vines were planted. The winery was completed in time to process the 1986 vintage.

All the vines are trained on the Geneva

Double Curtain system. Pruning starts in January and usually continues until early April. Spraying against mildew takes place at two week intervals from May until September.

The Madeleine Angevine is the earliest variety to ripen and on one occasion had to be harvested at the end of September. The Würzer normally ripens around the middle of October, and takes 2 to 3 days to pick. The Schönburger ripens at the end of the month and picking usually takes 3 days, although obviously this is dependent on the size of the crop. The grapes are picked into plastic boxes and these are collected on a tractor-drawn harvest trailer which crushes the grapes. At the winery the crushed grapes are pumped into a stainless steel press which exerts pressure via an air bag. The grape must is settled overnight in fibreglass tanks and then bentonite is added to clarify it. The following day sugar and yeast is added to start fermentation which generally takes between 2 and 3 weeks, and the wine is then racked into tanks, and held for about 4 months. It is then filtered before being sterile bottled on the premises.

The aim of the winery is to achieve a good balance between sugar and acidity levels. A slightly high acid at bottling times allows the wine time to mature in the bottle and gain complexity.

The first vintage was harvested in 1985 when 3,000 bottles were produced. In 1986 production reached 5,000 bottles, and increased again in 1987 to 8,000 although the vineyard lost half its crop in the October hurricane. The 1988 harvest was also hit by bad weather and production was only 5,500 bottles. The very wet weather in July affected the fruit setting and reduced yields.

Wines produced are: Würzer, a medium dry, fruity wine; Schönburger, medium dry, fruity and spicy, with good balancing acidity and dry wine, a blend with a particularly attractive bouquet. The wines are not German in style nor French. 'They are distinctively English and a new tradition has been started,' said the Youles. The wine is sold direct to shops, restaurants and wine bars, and from the winery by the case if people ring first. It is also sold by mail order.

There are no plans to extend the present vineyard acreage, and all the work at the vineyard is undertaken by the owners. No staff are employed except to help out at busy times.

Visiting times: the vineyard is not open to the public at this stage, but the situation is being reviewed. Serious visitors may be able to arrange an appointment, and wine can be purchased from the vineyard shop if arranged in advance.

How to get there: the vineyard is in Tangier Lane, which is on the outskirts of Bishops Waltham, travelling towards Twyford and Winchester on the B2177.

COURT LANE VINEYARD

Stephen A. Flook
Ropley
Alresford
Hants SO24 0DE
☎ (0962) 773391

The vineyard (a member of the EVA and the Wessex Vineyards Association) covers 1.3 acres, comprising Müller-Thurgau, which accounts for 38 per cent of plantings, Reichensteiner 46 per cent and Huxelrebe 16 per cent. Seyval Blanc is now being introduced although it is not expected to be in significant production until 1992.

The vineyard was planted in 1979, pro-

duced its first commercial vintage in 1983 and is in rolling countryside, 4 miles east of Alresford on a south-west sloping site which encourages its own microclimate. The slope also helps prevent the collection of any potentially damaging late spring frosts. The soil is well drained being a light clay loam overlying chalk. It also contains many flints which are allowed to collect on the surface in the rows to help reflect the warmth of the sun. At present there are two small vineyards and these will eventually be extended when trials with new varieties have been completed. Pruning is by the traditional Double Guyot replacement cane method. This means that the grapes hang low on the vines, making it difficult for the pickers at vintage time, but it does have the advantage of allowing the bunches to benefit more fully from the heat which is radiated from the ground. Winter pruning usually starts in December and is normally completed in February. Summer pruning takes place in August. The vines are spaced 4ft apart in rows running from north to south, spaced 6.5ft apart.

Spraying is carried out at approximately fortnightly intervals during the growing season using approved fungicides. A small vineyard tractor is used for this work and cultivation. The harvest usually takes place in mid- to late October and all the grapes are picked over two consecutive days.

The vineyard does not have its own winery and the grapes are taken by road to Meon Valley Vineyard for vinification.

The first vintage in 1983 yielded 2,600 bottles which increased to 3,200 in 1984. The 1985 harvest was a disaster with no wine produced and the 1986 and 1987 vintages were much reduced because of bad weather.

Two white wines are produced. The Müller-Thurgau-Reichensteiner blend is completely dry, light and fragrant in style with good fruit and well balanced acidity. The Huxelrebe-Reichensteiner is a medium dry blend, still quite dry but with a hint of sweetness. It is well balanced with full flavour and light, fruity nose. The wines are sold direct from the vineyard by the case, and through local outlets. It is stocked by Peter Dominic and the Mid-Hants Railway Company.

The vineyard is a small, family run business with no additional staff employed, although enthusiastic help is received from the village at harvest time. Expansion plans include the planting of a further acre of vines and the construction of their own winery.

Visiting times: the vineyard is not open to the general public, but interested individuals are welcome by appointment.

How to get there: the vineyard is in Ropley, 4 miles east of New Alresford just off the A31 to Alton road.

Nearby attractions: Mid- Hants Railway (Watercress line).

Recommended pubs and restaurants in the area: The Chequers at Ropley on the A31.

DANEBURY HOUSE VINEYARD

C.A.F. Dunning
Danebury House
Stockbridge
Hampshire SO20 6JX
☎ (0264) 781240

The vineyard (a member of the EVA) covers 6.3 acres of which half has been planted to date. Varieties of new, but as yet unproductive wines are Auxerrois 2.1 acres, Schönburger 0.88 acres and Pinot Gris 0.25 acres. The vineyard is by the Danebury Hill fortress on a south facing slope at 280ft above sea level on a light loam soil overlying chalk. The site enjoys a mild climate with average rainfall.

Plantings took place in April last year using the Double Guyot method of training. There was no spraying at all during the first year, and only a light spray programme during the second year. There is continuous cultivation to control weeds together with the use of Mynox plastic mulch although no chemical weed killer is used.

The vineyard is run with the help of a gardener and under-gardener when required, and advice is sought from the Ministry of Agriculture's ADAS (Advisory and Scientific Service) when needed. The vineyards are developing well and the growth looks good, but the vines need feeding as the soil is inclined to take nutrients from the surface into the chalk sub-strata.

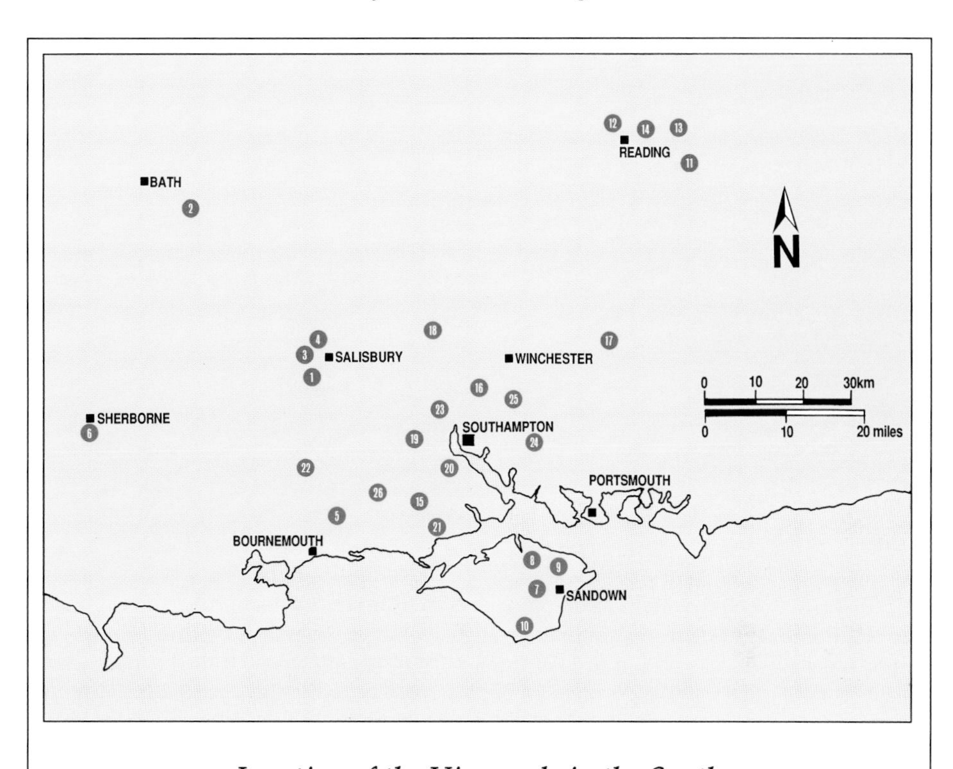

— *Location of the Vineyards in the South* —

Wiltshire
1 **Chalkhill**
2 **Elms Cross**
3 **Fonthill**
4 **Jesses**

Dorset
5 **Horton Estate**
6 **Wake Court**

The Isle of Wight
7 **Adgestone**
8 **Barton Manor**
9 **Rosemary**
10 **St Catherines**

Berkshire
11 **Ascot**
12 **Cane End**
13 **Lillibrooke Manor**
14 **Thames Valley**

Hampshire
15 **Aldermoor**
16 **Bishops Waltham**
17 **Court Lane**
18 **Danebury House**
19 **Flaxfields**
20 **Holly Bush**
21 **Lymington**
22 **Rockbourne**
23 **Wellow**
24 **Wickham**
25 **Meon Valley**
26 **Beaulieu Abbey**

Expansion plans include the planting of an additional 3 acres in 1990 and a further 2 acres in 1991.

Visiting times: none at present but interested individuals can contact the owner.

How to get there: the vineyard lies to the north of the A30 Salisbury to Stockbridge road. Turn left off the A30 just to the west of Stockbridge at the signpost for The Wallops. Head for Nether Wallop and then take the lane on your right which will take you past Danebury Place to Danebury House and the vineyard.

Nearby attractions: Danebury Hill fortress, Stockbridge.

Recommended pubs, restaurants and hotels in the area: The Grosvenor (Stockbridge), and Firehead Manor (Wallop).

Here is a cautionary tale concerning Efford Experimental Horticultural Station, Lymington, Hants. The following information was sent by the director of this Ministry of Agriculture-owned research establishment, dated 19 January 1989: 'Owing to lack of interest in, or recognition of the need for experimental work on vine growing by UK producers all experimental work at Efford has been terminated and the vines grubbed'.

FLAXFIELDS VINEYARD

Mr and Mrs N. Daniel
Hyde Farm
Hyde Lane
Stuckton
Fordingbridge
Hants SP6 2HD
☎ (0425) 54504

The vineyard (a member of the EVA) covers 1.5 acres of Kernling which were planted in April 1989 while a further 1.5 acres will be planted in 1991. It is on the edge of the New Forest, in the Avon Valley, on a soil of greensand over gravel, and is part of an agricultural enterprise which also has commercial sheep, beef cattle and Christmas geese.

Visiting times: there are no visiting times at present but people seriously interested in viticulture or seeing the development of a young vineyard could contact the owners.

How to get there: instructions from the owners.

HOLLY BUSH VINEYARD

C. and E. Landells
Holly Bush Farm Ltd
Brockenhurst
Hants SO4 27UF
☎ (0590) 23054

The vineyard (a member of the EVA and a local horticulture co-operative) covers 5 acres and there are plans to expand it by a further acre in the near future and then considerably if things work out well. The present acreage is split equally between Seyval Blanc, Schönburger, Pinot Blanc, Reichensteiner and Huxelrebe.

The first vines were planted in 1982 and since then there have been small changes in the varieties planted with a shift towards more Seyval Blanc. All the acreage is as yet unproductive except for some Reichensteiner. A small crop is expected in 1989 from the Seyval, Schönburger and Pinot as well.

The vineyard is in the New Forest area surrounded by woodland and private grazing with the open forest to the south-west and outside the village of Brockenhurst. The soil is poor and variable and some of the ground is typical forest heathland, almost podsol. It makes the early establishment of a vineyard extremely difficult but once the vines are over a certain size, they start to prosper.

The vineyard enjoys a typical south coast climate, with slightly less rain than surrounding areas. It is part of the 'Banana belt' which runs across from France and curls round and inland from the coast, which is associated with particularly good weather. It is rather windswept from the south-west and windbreaks are extensively planted, but are yet to become effective.

The vines are pruned and trained according to the High Wire replacement system, a sort of inverted Guyot system. There is also an acre trained using the Geneva Double Curtain method. The main plantings are 5ft between vines and 7ft between rows. There is a regular routine of weed and pest control, and the pathways are mown.

The first harvest was picked in 1988 by three people in a single day. The vineyard will aim to pick as late as possible, taking the ripest or most diseased crop first. Overhead nets and wire base nets are essential to combat birds, badgers, squirrels, hedgehogs, foxes and other pests.

The vineyard has little winery equipment so far and uses a hand operated press, mill and small vats. More equipment will be acquired as the crop demands. The vineyard is a family run horticultural holding.

A garden centre operates on the site with some buildings, a large car park and main road frontage. The vineyard plans to install its own processing plant, together with wine shop and bar with other tourist facilities. The vineyard already sells a small number of vines to the public, and produce grown on the horticultural enterprise.

Visiting times: May to October 10am-5.30pm. It may be possible for people with a serious interest to arrange visits outside these times.

How to get there: on the main A337 Lyndhurst, Brockenhurst, Lymington road. It is a mile south of Brockenhurst with a large pull-in and car park. If approaching from the M3 and M27, take the Cadnam-New Forest turn off, and then directly on to the A337.

Nearby attractions: New Forest, Beaulieu, Lymington, Isle of Wight, Brockenhurst Park and the Lyndhurst New Forest Museum.

Recommended pubs, restaurants and hotels in the area: The Filly Inn and Hobler Inn, both on the A337 within three-quarters of a mile. The Cloud Hotel, and Careys Manor Hotel in Brockenhurst and Limpets Restaurant in Lymington.

LYMINGTON VINEYARD

C.W. and M.M. Sentance
Wainsford Road
Pennington
Lymington
Hants SO4 8LB
☎ (0590) 672112

The vineyard (a member of the EVA and the Wessex Vineyards Association) covers 6.5 acres. Müller-Thurgau cover 1.3 acres, Seyval Blanc an acre, Würzer an acre, Regner an acre, Reichensteiner 0.5 acres, Guttenborner 0.5 acres, Schönburger 0.5 acres, Huxelrebe 0.3 acres and Triomphe D'Alsace 0.3 acres. This last variety is not as yet in production. It is on the outskirts of Lymington between the New Forest and the sea and is on a gentle south facing slope only 50ft above sea level, with a mild, sheltered, protected maritime climate. It is on gravel overlying clay. There is very little frost because of the proximity of the sea and the prevailing south-westerly winds.

The vineyard is part of what used to be the Efford estate, and the house used to be the gamekeeper's cottage. The land was used to rear more than 800 pheasants a year. Before planting vines the present owners grew soft fruits while preparing the land. The first vines were planted in 1979 on the field near the winery called the 'Donkey Field' by the previous owners who rescued old and sick donkeys and nursed them back to health.

Pruning takes place between December and March each year, and all the vines are trained on the Double Guyot or Pendelbogen system. Spraying includes a winter wash in January and the application of fungicides at approximately two week intervals through the growing season. Weed control is mainly by hoeing and during the winter there is post and wire maintenance.

The harvest usually starts around 10 October and lasts for 2 or 3 weeks. The Reichensteiner is normally the first variety to be picked, followed by Huxelrebe, Guttenborner, Müller-Thurgau, Regner, Würzer, Schönburger and Seyval Blanc.

The grapes are crushed, pressed and fermented, and the wine is then racked, filtered, balanced, blended and bottled.

Every vintage since 1984 has won an award, and the vineyard produces single (varietal) and blended wines, both dry and medium dry. Most of the sales are from the farm gate to holiday visitors. The enterprise is a family run business, including the wine making and small snail farm, although casual labour is brought in to help with the harvest. There are no plans to expand the vineyard at present.

Other products on sale include vines, herbs, mustard, cookies and snacks.

Visiting times: the vineyard is open from 1 May to 30 September. The wine shop is open 10.30am-4.30pm each day except Saturdays for the sale of wine by the glass during licensing hours, and by the bottle at other times. There is an unguided vineyard walk, with a map and free wine. Special tours for groups of twenty or more can be arranged outside normal visiting hours. Light catering can also be arranged if required. The fully equipped winery is on display, and there is a fully stocked wine and gift shop and tasting room. There is a car park, picnic sites as well as a herb garden and farm livestock.

How to get there: the vineyard is off Wainsford Road, Pennington, on the western outskirts of Lymington. Take the A337 to Pennington if travelling south from Brockenhurst, Lyndhurst or Southampton, or north from New Milton and Bournemouth.

Nearby attractions: New Forest, Beaulieu, Bournemouth, Hurst Castle and the Isle of Wight.

Recommended pubs, restaurants and hotels in the area: Chewton Glen, Elmers Court and Rhinefield House Hotel.

MEON VALLEY VINEYARD
C.J. and K. Hartley
Hill Grove
Swanmore
Southampton
Hants SO3 2PZ
☎ (0489) 877435

The vineyard (a member of the EVA and the Wessex Vineyards Association) was established in 1977 on a site previously used for strawberry production. Christopher Hartley, the owner, is also the winemaker and was trained as a cidermaker at the Government's Long Ashton Research Station. There are no plans to extend the vineyard which covers 8.75 acres planted with Müller-Thurgau, Seyval Blanc, Madeleine Angevine, Zweigeltrebe and Pinot Meunier. Some Müller-Thurgau has been grubbed out and some new varieties from Geisenheim have been planted on an experimental basis.

The vineyard is in the Meon Valley in south Hampshire, 6 miles from the coast. The soil is well drained medium loam, just off chalk. It is planted on a gentle southerly slope. The area enjoys a better than average climate with good sunshine, and not excessive rainfall, although it is exposed to westerly winds. The vines are trained on the Geneva Double Curtain system. Pruning starts in December and continues until March or April depending on the weather conditions. Spraying includes a winter wash followed by regular applications against mildew and phomopsis during the growing season.

Madeleine Angevine is the first variety to be picked, usually at the end of September or beginning of October. Müller-Thurgau is harvested next, normally in early to mid-October, followed by Seyval Blanc and Zweigeltrebe in the second half of the month. Pinot Meunier is harvested last, usually at the beginning of November. The grapes are picked by hand and passed through a tractor drawn crusher and then taken to the winery. The grapes are transferred to a rotary press and the juice is then allowed to settle in barrels before being pumped off into the fermentation tanks where yeast is added. Fermentation normally takes between 2 and 3 weeks. After fermentation, the wine is allowed to stabilise and is then racked once or twice. It is filtered before bottling.

Production in 1984 — 'a super year' — was more than 20,000 bottles from 5 acres then in production. Some wine from the vintage is still stocked. The 1985 vintage yielded about 10,000 bottles, a third red and two-thirds white which was produced as a medium wine. Quality was good. A similar yield was obtained in 1986 and 1987, and similar proportions of wine produced. All the 1986 red sold out, and the 1987 stock has just been released. A white *Méthode Champenoise* was produced in 1987 for the first time.

The 1988 vintage was 'the worst yet'. Quality was good but yields were low. The red is recommended, as is the dry white Madeleine Angevine, and medium Seyval Blanc. Wines produced include, Red Meonwara which is dark red, fruity and satisfying; White Hill Grove Madeleine Angevine, a dry, fruity and spicy young wine; Hill Grove Müller-Thurgau-Seyval Blanc, medium dry, fresh and fruity; Hill Grove Seyval Blanc, a medium wine, very fruity for those who prefer sweeter wines and Sparkling, a medium dry *Méthode Champenoise*, made from Seyval Blanc, Pinot Meunier and Chardonnay. The wine is sold direct from the vineyard, retailed to selected off-licences and restaurants and some is exported.

Visiting times: by appointment at all times of the year. During the growing season — May to 30 September — open on most days between 2-5pm. The winery is open to visitors by appointment, and there are open days throughout the year. The wine shop also sells vines, country wines, mead farmhouse cyder and fudge, all produced on the premises. There are tasting facilities and tours are available.

How to get there: the vineyard is off the A32 Wickham to Droxford road. Follow the signposts for Swanmore and the vineyard is on the right hand side of the road.

Nearby attractions: Bishops Waltham Palace, Hamble Manor Farm Museum and Meon Valley.

Recommended pubs, restaurants and hotels in the area: Hunters Inn, next door.

ROCKBOURNE VINEYARDS

John Cain
Rockbourne Road
Sandleheath
Nr Fordingbridge
Hants SP6 1QG
☎ (07253) 603

The vineyard (a member of the EVA) covers 12 acres and a further 5 acres are fenced ready to be planted in 1990 although the varieties to be used have not yet been decided. Varieties planted are Müller-Thurgau 3.5 acres, Seyval Blanc 2 acres, Siegerrebe 2.5 acres, Kerner 2 acres, Bacchus 1.5 acres, and Chardonnay half an acre. All the vines are trained according to the Geneva Double Curtain and all, except the Chardonnay, will crop for the first time in 1989 although samples from the 3-year-old vines were taken in 1988. The Chardonnay were not planted until 1987.

The vineyard is on a soil of sandy clay loam over gravel and is well drained. It is on a south-east facing slope in the valley of Sweatford Water, a tributary of the river Avon.

The vineyard enjoys a generally mild climate although wind coming down the valley can be a problem. Two windbreaks of mixed hardwoods have recently been planted to try to tackle this problem.

The vineyard year starts in January with pruning which continues through into February. The vineyard gets a treatment of fertiliser in March, and the winery gets a spring clean. In April there is bud rubbing and May is spent tying the sprouting vines down and spraying. Between June and August there is a continuous programme of spraying to combat disease and mowing to keep weeds down. The final spraying takes place in September and the vineyard and the winery gear up for the harvest which starts in October. The action moves to the winery in November, while December is spent planning for the coming year.

The harvest can start at the end of September and continue until the last day of October. Siegerrebe is the first variety picked, followed by Müller-Thurgau and Seyval Blanc, Bacchus, and then Kerner. It is expected that the Chardonnay when in production will also be late ripening and can be picked at the same time as Kerner.

The grapes are picked by hand and then loaded on to a harvest trailer which has an integral crusher. The crushed grapes are then tipped into a one-ton Vaslin press. German pumps and fittings will be capable of handling 10,000l of must or wine an hour. Fermentation will take place in fibreglass tanks ranging in size from 1,500l to 2,600l.

In 1988, 300l of red and white samples were made. The reds were produced from small quantities of bought-in red hybrid grapes. The winery is 60ft by 40ft, with concrete coated floor, tanks, pressing and other equipment, office and storage space. It obtained a beer and wine licence in March 1989 for sales in the on-site shop and refreshment facility, also used by anglers.

The vineyard-winery manager is Guy Gibson who does almost all of the vineyard work and winery maintenance, as well as the winemaking, with occasional help from the owner and his wife, Jenny Cain.

Visiting times: Tuesday to Thursday 10am-4pm and prior notification is preferred. The vineyard also sells rooted vine cuttings, and locally produced smoked trout. Light meals and drinks are available. There is trout fishing on the site with six spring-fed trout lakes which are stocked daily. Anglers can obtain day tickets and the fishery can accommodate twenty-eight rods.

Booking is advisable.

How to get there: the vineyard lies on the Rockbourne to Alderholt road, half a mile north of Sandleheath and its junction with the B3078.

Nearby attractions: Roman villa at Rockbourne, half a mile away.

Recommended pubs, restaurants and hotels in the area: The Cartwheel (Whitbury), Victoria Guesthouse (Sandleheath), Ashburn Hotel (Fordingbridge) and Compasses Inn (Damerham).

WELLOW VINEYARD LTD

Andy Vining
Wellow Vineyards Ltd
Merryhill Farm
Tanners Lane
East Wellow
Romsey
Hants SO51 6DP
☎ (0794) 522860 or 522431

The vineyard (a member of the EVA) covers 80 acres making it the largest viticulture enterprise in the UK. In 1987 Andy Vining, who has traced both French and German winemakers among his ancestors, planted more than 30,000 vines on 45 acres of gently rolling farmland in East Wellow, near Romsey, in the heart of the Test Valley.

He already had 5,500 vines growing on another 5 acres of land next to his house in Tanners Lane. In 1988 a further 30 acres were planted, increasing the total acreage to 80.

When the vineyard is in full production by the early 1990s, between 300,000 and 500,000 bottles of dry, medium dry and possibly single grape wine will be bottled annually.

The vineyard venture began in April 1985 with the trial planting of 5,500 vines made up of Müller-Thurgau, Bacchus, Auxerrois and Reichensteiner. The success rate among the vines was high, reflecting the quality of the vine and root stock bought and despite a poor summer they established themselves well.

Surprisingly, these first vines produced twenty-seven bottles of wine in the autumn of 1986, two years earlier than is usually the case. The success of that first 5-acre planting however, led to an expansion plan certainly greater than anything yet seen in the UK.

The statistics are large, even on a continental scale. In the Wellow vineyards there are 3,280 Auxerrois vines, 8,192 Bacchus, 10,220 Chardonnay, 2,280 Faber, 875 Huxelrebe, 1,820 Kerner, 130 Kernling, 7,219 Müller-Thurgau, 3,226 Ortega, 295 Pinot Noir, 4,260 Reichensteiner, 210 Riesling, 8,728 Seyval Blanc, and 859 Siegerrebe. On two nearby vineyards — Tytherley and Awbridge, which cover 15 acres, and are managed by Wellow — there are an additional 850 Bacchus, 3,345 Chardonnay, 33 Madeleine Angevine, 2,399 Müller-Thurgau, 1,490 Reichensteiner, 1,680 Seyval Blanc, and 1,128 Triomphe D'Alsace.

A network of underground pipes had to be laid to drain the 80 acres of land before the vineyard could be planted. More than 12,500 posts were erected, and 550 miles of wire attached to them, held in place by over 62,500 staples. Almost 5 miles of 8ft high fencing was erected to keep out the deer with rabbit fencing attached to the base. There are 1,254 rows of vines and the distance up and down the rows measures 110 miles.

Six weather stations are situated round the vineyard to monitor temperature and humidity. The vineyard is on undulating land, between 145ft and 260ft above sea level, south facing in the main on loamy soils and generating its own warm microclimate. It seems to be one or two degrees warmer than the rest of the Romsey area, and the frosts are not so severe. When Andy Vining was seeking advice on viticulture, he was told to think big if he wanted to make money out of wine.

'Small vineyards appear to have great difficulty in attaining commercial viability, but once you exceed the 15- to 20-acre size threshold, the cost per vine, in direct proportion to the labour and equipment used, is much lower. This is because the labour and equipment required for a 15-acre vineyard could quite easily manage a 50- to 100-acre estate,' he said.

A computer software programme has

been developed which enables the life history of each vine to be recorded and analysed, where it came from, when it was planted, when it was sprayed and so on.

More than 10,000 bottles of wine were produced from the 1988 harvest which was considerably better than 1987 which produced 1.5 tons of grapes — enough for 2,000 bottles. More than 8 tons of grapes were picked during October and the crop was of very high quality. The classic Chardonnay vines produced their first crop even though they had been planted on an experimental basis only 18 months before.

Picking was carried out by a small team of workers supported by three generations of Vinings. Grapes harvested were Müller-Thurgau, Reichensteiner, Bacchus, Chardonnay and Triomphe D'Alsace, the last of which was used to produce 400 or so bottles of red wine.

Visiting times: early May to mid-October but because so much work is going on it is best to ring for precise dates and times. The vineyard, which opened to the public in the spring of 1989, plans a wide range of attractions under the banner of The Wellow World of Wine. There are guided tours of the estate, a reception centre where Wellow and other English wines can be tasted, a wine bar selling all English food, an off-licence selling Wellow wine by the bottle or case, and Wellow's own spring water. There will also be exhibitions on Florence Nightingale, who lived at nearby Embley Park and is buried locally, and the history of English wine. There is also a woodland walk and nature trail, picnic areas and a play area for children.

Wellow also offers a vineyard consultancy and management service. Andy Vining is not only looking for more land on which to grow vines, but is also prepared to run established vineyards for other people. Expansion plans include winery and restaurant and further acreages of vines.

How to get there: the vineyard lies a couple of miles to the west of Romsey on the A27 Salisbury road. The vineyard is well signposted to the south of the A27, almost opposite Dunwood Manor.

WICKHAM VINEYARD

John and Caroline Charnley
Botley Road
Shedfield
Hants SO3 2HL
☎ (0329) 834042

The vineyard (a member of the EVA and Wessex Vineyards Association) covers 11 acres comprising 2.4 acres of Schönburger (23 per cent of production), 2.2 acres of Seyval Blanc (21 per cent), 2.1 acres of Faber (20 per cent), 1.3 acres of Würzer (12 per cent), 1.2 acres of Reichensteiner (11 per cent), 1.2 acres of Kerner (11 per cent), and 0.3 acres of Bacchus (0.3 per cent). The original planting included Huxelrebe which was taken out in 1988, the planting of Bacchus was reduced in 1988 and 1989 and the area under Seyval Blanc extended in 1989. Acreages of new, as yet unproductive vines, are Seyval Blanc 2.2 acres, Faber 1.6 acres and Würzer 0.6 acres.

The vineyard is on a gently south facing slope about 60ft above sea level. It is well sheltered from the prevailing south-west winds, and benefits from being in the Hampshire or Solent Basin which enjoys its own microclimate. The soil is mainly a fairly heavy clay, which was extensively drained before the vineyard was planted. It rarely gets winter temperatures below 18°F (8°C) and hardly ever gets spring frosts after the end of March, so damage to young buds in April is rare.

The vineyard is entirely trained on the Geneva Double Curtain system with rows 12ft apart. In the main part of the vineyard, planted in 1984, the vines are 8ft apart in the rows, and in the 1989 plantings the vines are placed at 6ft intervals in the rows. In the winter the vines are spur pruned 2 years out of 4 years while cane replacement is used on the alternate years. Each vine is trained with four arms.

Weed control is mechanical and herbicides are avoided. The vines are sprayed with a mist blower against the usual fungal diseases, and a foliar fertiliser (organic) is applied several times a year.

Harvesting takes place in the second or third week of October and is usually spread over 7 to 10 days. The Reichensteiner, Sch-

Grapes ripening in the sun at Wickham Vineyard

önburger and Würzer are ready first, followed by the Faber and Bacchus with the Kerner last.

Because the fruit bearing canes are trained along wire 5ft above the ground, harvesting is easy. The bunches are snipped with secateurs and dropped into clean plastic buckets or boxes, before being tipped into the stainless steel harvest trailer. The harvest trailer holds up to 2 tons of grapes and as these are pumped out by a stainless steel auger, the skin of every grape is broken by rollers, ready for pressing. Two tons are pumped out in about five minutes, and the crushed grapes go straight into the press, one of the new Howard pneumatic presses which again holds some 2 tons of crushed grapes. It is made entirely of stainless steel, and has a computer controlled programme that provides a very gentle pressing cycle to ensure maximum juice quality. The press programme takes between 2 and 6 hours and a small amount of sulphur is added in the juice tray to prevent spoilage. The juice is then pumped into stainless steel or fibreglass tanks to settle for 25 hours. After settling, the must is racked off into clean tanks, the yeast added, and the tank topped up with carbon dioxide to keep air contact to a minimum until fermentation begins.

A cool fermentation yeast is used to allow a slow but steady fermentation at 41°F (5°C) to 46°F (8°C). A slower fermentation is preferred to preserve the wine's fresh, fruity flavours that might otherwise be lost if fermentation was faster. When fermentation is complete, the wine is left to settle for a few days and is then racked off into sterile tanks and allowed to rest and clear until February or March. Sulphur levels are carefully checked, and the air space in the tank above the wine is kept topped up with carbon dioxide.

The careful back-blending of *süss* reserve (sweet, unfermented grape juice), is usually done in early April, and the wine is immediately sterile filtered and bottled. It then spends at least 2 to 3 months in bottle before being offered for sale.

The 1987 vintage was the first and yielded 2,500 bottles. In 1988 the anticipated yield was almost halved by cold, wet weather at flowering time at the end of June and early in July. Total production was only 4,000 bottles. The vineyard expects production to reach about 20,000 bottles a year by 1990, and 30,000 bottles annually by 1993. Although from 1989 most of the wine produced will be from single varieties, the 1987 and 1988 harvests were blended to produce a clean, fruity medium dry white.

For most of the year the vineyard is worked by the owners with the help of one worker from April to October. Up to thirty pickers are brought in for the harvest. There has been considerable expansion of the vineyard in 1989 and future plans include contract winemaking for other growers and providing management services to nearby vineyards.

Visiting times: by telephone appointment until 1990 when the shop will be open 10am-5pm Tuesday to Sunday. Closed Mondays. Guided group tours can be arranged. The wine is sold from the vineyard and through local retailers, restaurants and hotels. The vineyard also sells vines and oak barrel products and other wine related goods will be available for the shop from mid-1990 onwards. The winery is in a restored 200-year-old timber-framed barn and will also be open to the public from 1990. Free tastings are available, and a picnic site is being provided.

How to get there: the vineyard is on the A334 exactly 2.2 miles from either Botley or Wickham, on the north side of the road.

Nearby attractions: Wickham (eighteenth-century town square), Portsmouth (*HMS Victory*, *Mary Rose*), Winchester (old town and cathedral) and the New Forest.

Berkshire

ASCOT VINEYARD

Col A. R. Robertson
Ascot Farm
Winkfield Road
Ascot
Berkshire SL5 7LJ
☎ (0990) 23563

The vineyard (a member of the EVA, the Thames and Chilterns Vineyards Association, Thames and Chilterns Chamber of Commerce and the Thames and Chilterns Tourist Board) covers 10.5 acres, of which 7 acres were planted with new vines in 1989. The original varieties were Müller-Thurgau 1.5 acres (45 per cent of production), Pinot Noir 0.5 acres (15 per cent), Reichensteiner 0.75 acres (20 per cent), Madeleine Angevine 0.5 acres (15 per cent) and others about 0.5 acres (5 per cent).

The new plantings were 3 acres of Müller-Thurgau, 2 acres of Seyval Blanc and 2 acres of Pinot Noir. These three varieties will account for almost all production in future years. There have been no changes to the varieties planted in recent years.

The vineyard is on the verge of the Bagshot sand area. It is very light and free draining on a slight, south facing slope, sheltered from the prevailing south-west winds approximately 200ft above sea level.

The vineyard is situated on Crown Lands adjacent to the Royal Ascot Racecourse, and was planted in 1979. It is the first vineyard planted on Crown Lands since the reign of Henry II, who after marrying Eleanor of Aquitaine (and Bordeaux) actively discouraged the planting of English vineyards so that he could import French wine, and gain the import revenue as well!

The longer days and lower average temperature of the English summer give that slower maturity and added character and quality that makes English wines so special.

Pruning starts in January and continues through until February followed by light summer thinning and topping. All the original vines were trained according to the Guyot system but the latest plantings are using the Geneva Double Curtain method.

Spraying takes place at two weekly intervals from mid-May to within 10 days of the harvest, with constant changes in the types of spray depending on the conditions. The sprays are mainly sulphur based. There is one winter spraying of tar oil, usually in November.

The harvest starts as soon as the sugar in the grape has risen to satisfactory levels, usually in the first week of October for early varieties, but it can be as late as the last week in the month. The harvest usually takes about ten days and the picking is done entirely by members of the family and friends, and volunteers recruited from visitors to the vineyard. The order of picking is usually Madeleine Angevine, Reichensteiner, Müller-Thurgau and Pinot Noir.

The vineyard does not have its own winery and vinification takes place under contract at a nearby vineyard. The grapes are transported by road and crushed and pressed on the same day. Each variety is crushed, pressed and fermented separately.

When the whole 10 acres are in production the vineyard will install its own winery and bottling plant. It insists on very high standards of filtering, racking and bottling as it sells to 'a highly discriminating sector of the market, and the product must both look and be right.'

The first vintage was gathered in 1983 when about a ton of grapes were picked. A white and red wine were made, both of outstanding quality. This doubled in 1984 and rose to 3 tons in 1985. The 1986 harvest reached 3.5 tons, and the last two harvests have been disappointing. The 1987 vintage was hit by bad weather, and the 1988 by poor pollination. Experience suggests that there are eight satisfactory years out of ten in England for vines.

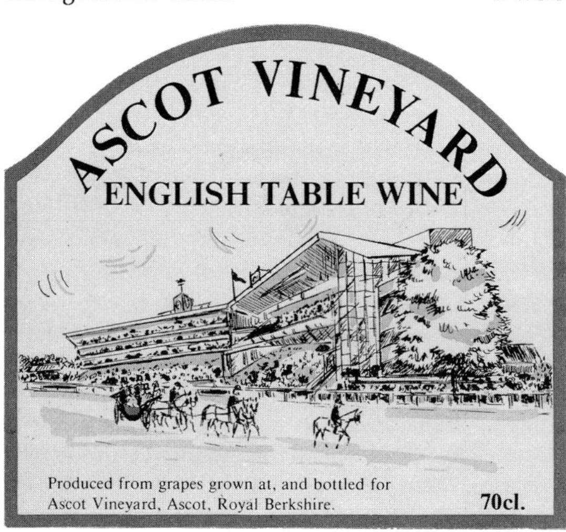

The vineyard produces three whites, a dry, medium and sweet. There are Müller-Thurgau and Seyval varieties, and a Müller-Thurgau-Seyval blend. A red is produced from Pinot Noir.

The owners market their own wines and promote the vineyard, especially throughout the Thames Valley trying to ensure that every hotel, restaurant, club and business is aware of it and its products. The vineyard has also developed a special connection with a number of leading West End hotels and the wine is also exported in small quantities to Switzerland, West Germany, Denmark and Sweden.

Vineyard sales are restricted exclusively to wines, but there is a flourishing business in the run up to Christmas packaging wines in gift boxes for use by commerce and industry as presents to staff and customers.

The vineyard won the Mars Award for environmental improvement in 1986 and 1987, and was awarded a 'Come to Britain' certificate of merit by the British Tourist Authority in 1987.

Visiting times: 12noon-dusk daily for visitors, and by prior arrangement for organised parties of up to thirty-five. The vineyard actively encourages visits by organised parties, and attaches great importance to them as a way of introducing its wines to an ever widening public both from home and overseas. Organised tours can include a welcome drink, a conducted tour of the vineyard, a wine tasting and talk on English wines and the Ascot vineyard, and a farm supper, if an evening visit. There is ample car and coach parking. All individual visitors are welcomed, given a wine tasting and if required, shown round the vineyard. During the summer a student is employed to handle the growing number of visitors from home and abroad. Talks on English viticulture and wine tastings are also held. The vineyard is also part of an agricultural enterprise that includes horses and sheep.

How to get there: the vineyard is opposite the race course. It lies on the road which skirts the eastern boundary of the race course, which connects the A329 and A332 north of Ascot. If travelling from London, approach on the A30 Camberley road and turn right on to the A329 which takes you to the race course and the turn off.

Nearby attractions: Royal Ascot Racecourse, Windsor Castle and Park, Windsor Safari Park, Eton, and Saville Gardens.

Recommended pubs, restaurants and hotels in the area: Royal Hotel, Berystede

Hotel, Thatched Tavern Pub, Cottage Inn and The Hatchet (Ascot). Castle Hotel and Oakleigh Court Hotel (Windsor).

CANE END VINEYARD
Mr L. Hordern
Cane End
Reading
Berks RG4 9HG
☎ (0734) 722244

The vineyard (part of a 1,000-acre cereal, beef and woodland agricultural enterprise) covers 12.15 acres, consisting of 2 acres each of Madeleine Angevine, Reichensteiner and Bacchus in production, and about 1.5 acres each of Madeleine Angevine, Huxelrebe, Reichensteiner and Bacchus not yet in production.

The vineyard rises from the Thames Valley at about 350ft above sea level. It is on gravel overlaying clay and flint. Average rainfall is 27in and the prevailing winds are from the south-east.

Pruning starts each year in January, and there is disbudding and general pruning throughout the growing season.

All the vines are trained on the Geneva Double Curtain system. There is total weed control along the rows, and a complete fungicide regime throughout the growing season as well as a winter wash. Insecticides are applied if necessary.

The harvest normally starts between 22 and 30 October and picking is usually completed within a day. All the varieties are picked together to make a blended wine as individual varieties at present do not produce sufficient quantities to warrant being picked separately and made into varietals.

The vineyard does not have its own winery and the grapes are taken by road to Old Luxters Vineyard, Hambledon, Henley-on-Thames where they are vinified under contract.

Production in 1985 was 0.4 tons, which increased to 1.5 tons in 1986 and 4. 25 tons in 1987. The harvest was hit by bad weather in 1988 and 2.25 tons of grapes were picked.

The blended wine currently being produced is medium sweet, very fruity and described as a refreshing, quality wine. The wine is sold from the vineyard, in village shops and at wine tasting evenings.

Visiting times: the vineyard is not open to the public at present but serious visitors interested in the development of the vineyard could contact the owners. Expansion plans include building a winery and possibly a farm shop and opening to the public for special viewing and tasting days.

How to get there: directions from the owners.

LILLIBROOKE MANOR VINEYARD
U.M. and D.C. P. Wheeler
Cox Green
Maidenhead
Berks SL6 3LP
☎ (0628) 32131

The vineyards (members of the EVA and the Thames and Chilterns Vineyards Association) cover 7 acres on two sites. There is a one-acre walled garden, half of which was planted with Müller-Thurgau, Schönburger and Ehrenfelser. The remaining half acre was more recently planted with Schönburger and Bacchus, and should produce its first light harvest this year. The further 6 acres were acquired when they bought a vineyard in Windsor Forest planted with a variety of one to three old vines.

Varieties include Müller-Thurgau, Schönburger, Ehrenfelser, Bacchus, Pinot Noir, Triomphe D'Alsace, Seyval Blanc, Madeleine Angevine, Seyve Villard and Optima.

Varieties of new, as yet unproductive vines, are Bacchus, Pinot Noir, Triomphe D' Alsace, Seyval Blanc, Madeleine Angevine, Seyve Villard and Optima.

The vineyard is 100ft above sea level in the Thames Valley with an acre in a walled garden grown in a clay soil on a slight southerly slope. The Thames Valley tends to be less wet than further west and the walled garden helps create a microclimate, retaining the heat and reducing the strength of the winds.

The vines are trained according to the

Harvest at Cane End Vineyard

Geneva Double Curtain method, with a slight variation developed by the owners. The vines are sprayed with fungicides at approximately two week intervals depending on the weather and time available, because this has to be fitted in with other farm activities. The weeds are sprayed at the beginning of the year and the soil then remains clear all year.

The vineyard has had three harvests so far from the first half acre planted. The harvest starts in late October with the Sch-

Lillibrooke Manor

önburger and Müller-Thurgau while the Ehrenfelser is left on the vines for as long as the weather and the birds allow. It usually takes four people about a day to pick the grapes.

The grapes are delivered to the wine maker in a mini skip lined with plastic.

Production in 1986 was 332 bottles and the wine was described as 'pleasant and nice'. About 530 bottles were produced in 1987 when the wine had 'excellent flowery flavour which improves all the time. Very more-ish.' The 1988 production was 330 bottles equivalent. A single medium dry white wine is produced, a blend of Müller-Thurgau, Schönburger and Ehrenfelser.

Visiting times: Monday to Saturday 10am-5pm, Sunday 12noon-3pm. The wine is sold at the door by the bottle or case. The vineyard does hold tastings in the wine shop, a former Carter's room, next to the Elizabethan manor house. The shop also sells some other farm produce, and there are tours of the vineyard. It is run with the aid of a farm worker and is part of an arable farm and woodland estate, which also has 5 acres of asparagus, and horses.

How to get there: Exit from junction 8/9 from the M4 and take the Maidenhead west road. After half a mile, turn left towards Cox Green and White Waltham. At the T-junction turn right and continue straight on past the first small roundabout and then take the left turning at the second small roundabout. Almost immediately turn right into Lillibrooke Manor Vineyard.

Nearby attractions: Boulters Lock, Maidenhead, Windsor Castle and Great Park, Windsor Safari Park, Clivedon House and Taplow.

Recommended pubs, restaurants and hotels in the area: The Plough (pub, Waltham St Lawrence), The Waterside (the only three star Michelin restaurant outside London, Bray on Thames), The Hindshead (pub and restaurant, Bray), The Old Bell (pub, Hurley), The Compleat Angler (pub and restaurant, Marlow), Oakley Court Hotel (Windsor).

THAMES VALLEY VINEYARD

Jon Leighton
Stanlake Park
Twyford
Reading
Berks RE10 0BN
☎ (0734) 340176

The vineyard (a member of the EVA and the Chiltern Vineyards Association) covers 17 acres and can be expanded to 32 acres.

Varieties in production are Kerner 1.2 acres, Scheurebe 1.2 acres, Schönburger 3.2 acres, Regner an acre, Triomphe D'Alsace 0.4 acres, Seyval Blanc an acre, Black Pinot 0.4 acres, Millers Pinot 0.2 acres, Müller-Thurgau 0.6 acres, Reichensteiner 1.6 acres, Ortega 1.6 acres, Würzer 0.8 acres, Bacchus 0.7 acres, Gray Pinot 0.3 acres, Chardonnay 0.2 acres, Gewürztraminer 0.3 acres, Siegerrebe 0.1 acres, Optima 0.1 acres, Chasselas 0.3 acres and Ehrenfelser 0.8 acres.

In recent years more Kerner, Scheurebe, Triomphe D'Alsace, Black Pinot, Ortega, Würzer, Ehrenfelser, Gewürztraminer, Siegerrebe, Optima and Chasselas has been added. It is thought the Chardonnay is too late ripening, and the Riesling and Muscadet have been grubbed out.

New, as yet unproductive acreages, include half an acre each of Ortega, Ehrenfelser and Kerner, and a quarter of an acre each of Siegerrebe, Optima, Chasselas and Black Pinot, and an eighth of an acre of Gewürztraminer.

The vineyard is in the rain shadow of the Berkshire Downs in one of the driest parts of south-east England. It has an average rainfall of about 25in and the maximum sunshine hours in the locality, low incidence of frost and moderate winds. It is a site which stays sunny when surrounding countryside is in shadow.

It produces grapes that consistently have the highest sugar values in England and is on old alluvial flats. The soils are very mixed but well drained, and the location is well sheltered from the prevailing winds.

Pruning starts in December and continues until May. Herbicides are used during March and April, and tucking up of the vines continues from May until August, while vine hedging takes place from July until September. Budburst occurs in early May, flowering in the first week of July, and veraison in the last week of August. A spraying programme is carried out between June and October and leaf removal takes place from July to September.

There are eight different training systems for the vines in use on three types of trellis. Most of the vineyard is under grass. The wires which carry the fruit are at either 3ft or 6.5ft to keep out of the frost and keep the vines well ventilated. Fruit exposure is of prime importance. Much of the vineyard is sloping to the south-east so the vines are orientated up and down the slope. The vines are spaced 6.5ft by 4ft or 11ft by 6.5ft.

The harvest usually starts in the middle of September and continues until the middle of November. The vines are usually picked in the following order: Siegerrebe, Ortega, Optima, Reichensteiner, Regner, Schönburger (first pick), Müller-Thurgau, Würzer, Seyval Blanc, Bacchus, Schönburger (second pick), Pinot Gris, Kerner, Scheurebe, Pinot Noir, Triomphe D'Alsace, Pinot Meunier, Gerwürztraminer, Chasselas, Ehrenfelser and Chardonnay.

The grapes are crushed and de-stalked, although sometimes whole berry pressing is used. The grapes are then transferred either to a horizontal screw press, which is used for most varieties, or to a vertical Zambelli, which is good for the phenolic varieties. The free run and heavy pressing are kept separate, and a lees filter is used to collect the quality lees must.

Most of the must ferments through on low solids between 5 and 10 days. There is now some new barrel fermentation, and the Pinot varieties are initially fermented on their skins. Most wines are clarified as soon as possible although for some wines, lees contact is used, and there is some barrel maturation.

As little de-acidification as possible is used and care is taken to preserve the flavour components. Bottling can take place at any time from the December of the vintage to May, 2 years later, depending on the wine.

The wine is clarified using an earth filter if necessary, then two sheet filters and a membrane filter before being bottled under carbon dioxide cover.

The 1984 vintage has been the best yet for quality. About 4,000l of wine was made from grapes picked on 2.5 acres. The 1985 vintage was the worst yield but marvellous quality. About 2,500l of wine was made from 4.5 acres. In 1986 production hit 15,000l from 8 acres, it was good quality from a medium size crop. In 1987 10 acres were in production and yielded 15,500l of wine of reasonable quiet, while in 1988 12 acres were in production but poor yields meant production of only 10,500l.

The wines made include: Müller-Thurgau 87, a dry but low acid wine, made with lees contact to increase the complexity; Reichensteiner 87, dry and fruity, a pleasant easy drinking wine; Regner-Seyval Blanc 87, has Bordeaux like austerity, complex and interesting; Ortega 87, a big, fruity zestful wine demands to be drunk with food. Schönburger 86, quite sweet, mouth filling, with some Alsace characteristics; non vintage medium sweet, a blend bringing together the interest of older wines, and the freshness of younger ones and Siegerrebe-Gewürztraminer, spicy Alsace style, and winner of the President's Trophy for small batch winemaking in 1988. Jon Leighton the winemaker uses a mixture of Australian, American and traditional techniques. Guest winemakers are taken on in some seasons.

The vineyard expects to expand to around 32 acres eventually. The winery will be extended to include all the buildings in the complex with very much extended bottle storage, bottling line and stock holding facilities. The winery, workshop, fermenting room and fruit reception area will also be increased. A restaurant and tasting room-lecture theatre are also planned.

Visiting times: by appointment. Wine (including wine vinegar, mustard and cider) are sold from the cellar door, through off-licences and local outlets. Cellar door sales and tastings are on weekdays 11am-6.30pm in winter and until 7pm in summer; Saturdays and Sundays 12noon-5.30pm. The winery is in a seventeenth-century barn with a purpose built viewing area adjacent to the tasting and sales area. There is a barbecue for hire in the vineyard, and tastings and functions are organised. Tours and tastings can be arranged by appointment, and ploughman's lunches can be provided.

How to get there: the vineyard is three-quarters of a mile south of Twyford on the B3018. You can approach on either the A4 and turn off at the sign for Twyford, or leave the M4 at either junctions 9 or 10 and follow the signs for Twyford.

Nearby attractions: Royal Ascot, Henley, Windsor Castle and Great Park, Windsor Safari Park, Thames, Chilterns, Sonning, Cookham and Bray.

Recommended pubs, restaurants and hotels in the area: The Farriers Restaurant (Littlewick Green), The White Hart (pub, Sonning), and The Bottle and Glass (pub and restaurant, Binfield Heath).

Wiltshire

CHALKHILL VINEYARD

Douglas Mann and Son
Chalkhill
Knowle Farm
Bowerchalke
Salisbury
Wiltshire SP5 5BP
☎ (0722) 780041

The vineyard (a member of the EVA and the Wessex Vineyard Association) covers 6.5 acres with Bacchus and Müller-Thurgau each accounting for 35 per cent of production, and Kerner the remaining 30 per cent. There has been no change in varieties planted and there are no new, as yet unproductive vines. The vineyard is set in the Chalke Valley on the outskirts of Bowerchalke, in southern Wiltshire. The soil is greensand and chalk and the area receives about 29in of rain a year.

The vineyard was planted between 1980 and 1982. All the vines are German in origin, grafted on to phylloxera-restistant rootstock and trained on the Single Guyot system to ensure maximum quality and flavour. Pruning takes place between December and March and the aim in cutting back is to allow growth from ten to twelve buds only.

There is a programme of systematic and preventative spraying against fungal disease. Herbicides are used to control weeds under the vines and the rows are planted to grass.

The harvest usually takes place between

the beginning and middle of October. The Müller-Thurgau is the first variety to ripen and is normally picked during the second week of the month. Bacchus follows a week later with the Kerner being gathered in the fourth week. The grapes are crushed and pressed using a Vaslin press, and the must transferred to stainless steel or fibreglass tanks for fermentation.

The winery adopts a policy of minimum handling of the wine after fermentation to preserve flavour characteristics, although there is a racking in the middle of December, and a second followed by filtration in the middle of February. The wine is normally bottled between April and May.

Average production over the last 5 years has been about 2 tons an acre. The 1984 vintage yielded a large crop of good quality, and the vintages since have produced small crops of medium quality because of adverse weather conditions.

Wines produced are: Chalkhill Müller-Thurgau, a light well balanced wine with clean aromatic nose, fresh, fruity taste and dry finish. It is an ideal summer wine to be drunk by itself or with fish or light meat dishes. Chalkhill Bacchus which has a strong Sauvignon-like bouquet, a sharp gooseberry flavour and a rich fullness. The underlying acidity will allow the wine to improve with keeping over 2 or 3 years. Chalkhill, a blend of Müller-Thurgau and Bacchus producing a rich, complex wine with a buttery nose and fresh, appley taste and Chalkhill 'Chalke Valley', a soft fruit wine for everyday drinking, light, fresh and medium dry.

Visiting times: visitors are welcome to the winery and vineyard at all times but an appointment is recommended. The wine is sold from the vineyard by the case only, and through independent off-licences, wine merchants, hotels and restaurants. The vineyard is part of a 1,100-acre farm and there are no plans to expand it at present.

How to get there: the vineyard is 8 miles south-west of Salisbury off the A354. Take the A354 Salisbury to Blandford road, turn right at Coombe Bissett for Broad Chalke, and then left for Bowerchalke and Chalkhill.

Nearby attractions: Cranbourne Chase, Salisbury.

ELMS CROSS VINEYARD

Rowland Dunkley and Gurli Klingenberg-Dunkley
Bradford-on-Avon
Wiltshire BA15 2AL
☎ (02216) 6917

The vineyard (a member of the EVA and the South West Vineyards Association) covers 3.5 acres, of which half an acre was planted in the spring of 1989. The main varieties are Müller-Thurgau which accounts for 2 acres and Auxerrois. Reichensteiner, Cabernet Sauvignon and Merlot were planted in the spring of 1989. The vineyard is 150ft above sea level on loam over broken limestone. There is excellent drainage on the gentle south facing slope and rainfall is between 27in and 29in annually. All the vines are trained and pruned according to the Double Guyot system. There is a regular spraying programme during the growing season against fungal diseases and botrytis.

The harvest normally starts about the middle of October, and takes between 3 and 4 days with a band of 12 to 15 pickers. The grapes are crushed in a berry mill, and then transferred to a vertical press. The must is then allowed to settle in a holding tank for 24 hours, before fermentation takes place in 700l tanks. After fermentation the wine is racked three or four times. It is generally held in tanks for 12 months or so to mature before bottling. It is sterile filtered immediately before being bottled and labelled by hand. Average production over the last 5 years has been between 3,500 and 5,000 bottles. No wine was made in 1986 when the previous owners sold the grapes under contract. Their first vintage in 1987 saw poor yields and only about 2,000 bottles were produced although quality was good. In 1988 no wine at all was made. There was a poor yield and then an attack of botrytis. Between 20 per cent and 30 per cent were mouldy and the owners did not think it worth the cost of bringing in labour to pick them.

The wine is sold from the vineyard and locally to residents, restaurants and hotels. There is a considerable sale of wine from the vineyard during the summer as

Bradford-on-Avon is a major tourist area.

The vineyard is run with the aid of a part-time worker. The owner formerly had a vineyard in north-west London which he planted in 1967 and ran until he moved in 1976. There are no immediate expansion plans but the owners hope to enlarge the vineyard by low density plantings of vines, about 700 to 800 an acre. The site covers 10 acres so there is considerable scope for expansion.

Visiting times: Friday, Saturday and Monday 9am-6pm. There are tasting facilities and group tours for between fifteen and twenty-five can be arranged for a small charge. They include a tasting and slide lecture on vine cultivation and winemaking.

How to get there: take the B3109 Frome road out of Bradford-on-Avon and after about three-quarters of a mile turn right on the road signposted to Westwood. The vineyard is about 300yd from the junction on the left hand side.

Nearby attractions: Bradford-on-Avon and Bath, 8 miles away.

Recommended pubs, restaurants and hotels in the area: Highfield House (hotel, Semington, near Trowbridge), Ancient Fowl (pub, Bradford-on-Avon), Spindles (restaurant, Bradford-on-Avon) and Leigh Park Hotel.

FONTHILL VINEYARD

C.P.M. Craig-McFeely and
J.F. Edgington
Fonthill Gifford
Tisbury
Salisbury
Wiltshire SP3 6QH
☎ (0747) 870231 or 871230

The vineyard (a member of the EVA, Wessex Vineyards Association, South West Vineyards Association and Wiltshire Larder) covers 13.5 acres although it is not fully planted with vines. Productive varieties are all white grapes — Müller-Thurgau, 1.6 acres which accounts for 20 per cent of production, Reichensteiner 2.2 acres (30 per cent), and Seyval Blanc 2 acres (50 per cent).

In 1982 Seibel, a red grape, was planted on a trial basis on 0.2 acres and as a result of its success 2 acres of red varieties were planted in 1986. These as yet unproductive varieties are Dunkelfelder an acre, Leon Millot 0.3 acres, Zweigeltrebe 0.25 acres, and Marechal Foch 0.2 acres. There is also a further 2 acres of new, as yet unproductive Seyval Blanc.

The vineyard is about 15 miles west of Salisbury and 1.5 miles north of Tisbury in hilly and well wooded countryside. It is at an altitude of about 450ft above sea level on well drained greensand over limestone. It is on a gentle slope, well sheltered and enjoys excellent natural protection from adverse weather conditions. The vineyard has about 34in of rain a year and is protected by 2,000 acres of woodland so is generally free of severe frost. The vineyard is run by two family partnerships with assistance as required from labour employed on the farm owned by one of the partners. There are no immediate plans to extend the acreage of the vintage or plant more vines.

Grapes have been grown in the area certainly since the eleventh century and local vineyards were recorded in the *Domesday Book*. In the Middle Ages the Benedictines had monasteries at Shaftesbury and Tisbury and there is evidence that they had vines. Fonthill has been planted on a regular basis since the first acre was established in 1979. The first vintage was harvested in

1982. There are about 8,200 vines of which 7,000 are white grapes and 1,200 red varieties. Winter pruning starts at the end of December or early in January, and most of the vines are trained on either the Double Guyot or Geneva Double Curtain systems. The rows are 8ft apart for the Double Guyot system, and 12ft apart for the Geneva Double Curtain. The Double Guyot area is cultivated between rows, while a combination of grass and cultivation is practised in the rows of the Geneva Double Curtain. The vineyard is also conducting a number of trials with other varieties such as Madeleine Angevine, Huxelrebe, Kernling and Siegerrebe, and different training systems are also being tested.

There is a regular programme of machine spraying at intervals of between 10 and 14 days against fungal diseases and mildews which starts at budburst and continues until 4 weeks before harvesting, although spraying is suspended during flowering. There is also winter spraying during the dormant season. The use of herbicides is kept to a minimum and weed control is generally by mechanical cultivation. Fertiliser is applied annually in the spring and is based on soil and leaf analysis.

Budburst is in May followed by flowering in July. Harvesting usually starts in the second half of October, normally about the third week of the month. Reichensteiner is usually the first variety to ripen and be picked, followed a week later by Müller-Thurgau and Seyval Blanc, with Seibel last.

A poor summer usually delays the harvest until the end of the month and sometimes into November so therefore annual production is very variable according to the weather and can vary from under a ton to the acre to more than 7 tons.

Wines produced are: Fonthill Dry, a fruity Seyval varietal; Fonthill Medium Dry and Medium, a blend of Müller-Thurgau, Reichensteiner and Seyval Blanc; and Fonthill Rosé, a medium dry blend of red and white grapes. It is made from Seibel, Müller-Thurgau, Reichensteiner and Seyval Blanc and is semi-sparkling. Wine is sold from the vineyard and retailed through wine merchants, supermarkets, restaurants and hotels.

Visiting times: June to September by appointment. Tastings, as well as group and family tours, can be arranged and special annual vineyard open days are held which include scenic and farm tours. There is a certified caravan and camping site.

How to get there: the vineyard is to the north of the village of Tisbury on a minor road which runs between the A30 and the A303. If travelling on the A30 take the turning for Tisbury in either Ansty or Swallowcliffe. Go through Tisbury and the vineyard is on your left just past a crossroads. If travelling on the A303 turn south at Chicklade and follow the road to Hindon and Fonthill Bishop. The vineyard is on your right a little way out of Fonthill Bishop.

Nearby attractions: Wilton House, Longleat, Stourhead, Old Wardour Castle, Stonehenge and Salisbury Cathedral.

Recommended pubs, restaurants and hotels in the area: The Lamb (pub, Hinton), King's Arms (pub, Fonthill Bishop) and Howard House restaurant (Teffont).

JESSES VINEYARD

Major Roger Beck
Jesses
Snow Hill
Diton
Nr Salisbury
Wiltshire SP3 5HN
☎ (072276) 220

The vineyard is a member of the EVA and the South West Vineyards Association, but because of its size is not open to the public. This is an acre vineyard with half an acre of Madeleine Angevine, and a quarter of an acre each of Müller-Thurgau and Triomphe D'Alsace. No further plantings are envisaged although a further 7 acres could be made available.

The vineyard is 300ft above sea level, on a gentle south facing slope protected by an escarpment and woods from the north. It is on greensand overlying clay and in places, chalk. The area can experience hard frosts.

The vineyard was first planted 11 years ago and the first vintages won a large number of accolades for their quality. The wine from the 1985, 1986 and 1987 vintages was not marketable and in 1988 agreement was reached with Fonthill for them to take the grapes.

Dorset

HORTON ESTATE VINEYARD

Brian and Jane Burch
Horton
Wimborne
Dorset BH21 7JG
☎ (0258) 840258

The vineyard (a member of the EVA and the Wessex Vineyards Association) covers 10 acres and there are plans to extend it to 25 acres. Varieties planted are Reichensteiner 3 acres, Bacchus 4.25 acres, Würzer 1.25 acres, Kerner 0.75 acres, and various red varieties 0.5 acres.

All the vines have been planted in the last 4 years and the first commercial crop will be harvested in 1989, although small quantities of wine were made in 1987 and 1988.

The vineyard is about 150ft above sea level, on a gentle south-west slope with shelter from the surrounding land. The soil is sandy loam 6ft to 12ft deep overlying chalk. It is in an area of above average sunshine and temperatures for southern England. The site was very carefully selected for its ideal (within the UK) climate and soil conditions for the production of quality white wine.

Pruning starts in January and continues until March. There is short cane pruning following the Geneva Double Curtain system of training. There is training of the young vines only throughout the growing season. Spraying is kept to a minimum, mainly 'organic' wettable sulphur, but some chemicals have to be used at times to combat fungal diseases and botrytis. Spraying is carried out using a tractor-mounted Hardi airblast sprayer.

Although no commercial crops have yet been harvested, the last two vintages have shown that the reds ripen first about the end of September. Bacchus, Reichensteiner and Würzer are harvested in the second half of October, while the Kerner is left on the vines as late as possible.

The grapes are hand picked into tubs and when full, these are transferred to a harvest trailer and taken to the winery, where they are gently transferred into a Willmes pneumatic press. The whole uncrushed bunches are pressed and the must transferred directly to tanks. There is no addition of sulphur dioxide, and fermentation is encouraged by some aeration and the addition of the yeast culture. Fermentation proceeds naturally in tanks in the purpose-built winery which was specially designed to retain the autumn warmth well into December.

The wine is cold-stabilised over the winter and receives its first racking in March. Air is excluded and sulphur dioxide avoided, with carbon dioxide being used to blanket the wine and prevent oxidation. Malolactic fermentation takes place in May and June and the wine is left on light lees to clarify naturally with very low sulphur addition (about 40 parts per million).

The wine is left to clarify before its final racking. The free sulphur dioxide is increased to 20 parts per million and the carbon dioxide blanket replenished for final settling in the winter of its second year.

So far, the vineyard has avoided fining and filtration and has bottled a minimal sulphur dioxide biologically stable wine with minimal residual sugar. Their aim is to make low sulphur dioxide wines without de-acidification and minimal fining and filtration.

The vineyard is not in full production but in 1987 about 300l of Würzer dry was produced, which was commended in *Wine* magazine's international challenge. It was dry, honeyed, spicy, with citrus flavours and a long finish. Sales at present are by the case only to regular customers.

Expansion plans include the planting of 15 more acres of vines over the next 5 or 6 years. As production increases, a bonded store-cellar will be added to the existing building complex.

Visiting times: by appointment only for individuals or small groups of between six and twelve people. The vineyard has its own purpose-built winery and tasting room. Tours of the vineyard and winery can be arranged.

How to get there: the vineyard lies just to the east of Horton on the Horton to Ringwood road. It can be approached on the A31 and turning off on the minor road signposted to Ashley Heath and Horton, or from the A354 and turning off onto the minor road at Cashmoor.

Nearby attractions: Bournemouth and Poole Harbour.

Recommended pubs, restaurants and hotels: La Belle Alliance (restaurant, Blandford), Northill House, Horton Inn and Drusilla's Inn (Horton).

WAKE COURT VINEYARD

Mr J.K. Wingfield Digby
Wake Court
Bishops Caundle
Sherborne
Dorset
☎ (096 323) 249

The vineyard (a member of the EVA and the South West Vineyards Association) covers just over 3 acres. There is an acre each of Schönburger and Seyval Blanc, and an acre of Bacchus and Reichensteiner. There is some Pinot Noir for sparkling wine production, and a few vines of Leon Millot for red wine.

The vineyard is on a south facing slope between 150ft and 200ft above sea level. It has good shelter from the north and some from the west. The soil is loam overlying clay with some limestone. It enjoys a good microclimate.

Vines have been grown in the area for hundreds of years and it was one of the places favoured by the Normans in the eleventh century to plant their vineyards.

All the vines are trained and pruned according to the Geneva Double Curtain system. There is a regular spraying programme every 2 weeks between June and September for protection against powdery and downy mildew. There is also spraying for protection against botrytis.

The Bacchus and Reichensteiner are normally the first grapes to be harvested and picking starts generally in the middle of October. The second picking takes place at the end of the month to harvest the Schönburger and Seyval Blanc.

Each picking takes a good morning's work by a gang of twenty-five casual workers. The vineyard does not have its own winery and the grapes are transported by lorry in the afternoon to Wootton Vineyard, near Shepton Mallet, in Somerset for vinification.

Average annual production over the last 5 years has been about 5,700 bottles and wines produced are: Bacchus Reichensteiner, a blend, a dry, fruity wine which has been compared in taste to a Loire Sauvignon, presumably due to the Bacchus grapes and Schönburger, a full bodied, fruity, dry wine with characteristics similar to those of Gewürztraminer. The Seyval grapes harvested are sold to Wootton.

The vineyard is part of an 800-acre arable and dairy farm and is part of a farm diversification scheme to counter falling profits from corn growing and dairy quotas. The spraying is done by the arable staff and the pruning by the farmer with some assistance from contract pruners. Local women are recruited for the harvesting.

Visiting times: by appointment.The wine is sold by the case at the vineyard by appointment, to individuals, wine merchants, restaurants and hotels.

How to get there: take the A3030 from Sherborne heading towards Blandford Forum. About 6 miles from Sherborne you enter the village of Bishops Caundle. Take the second turning on the right down Ryalls Lane, and Wake Court Farm is down the drive by the white gates.

The Isle of Wight

ADGESTONE VINEYARD

Ken Barlow
Sandown
PO36 0ES
☎ (0983) 402503

The vineyard (a member of the EVA, Wessex Vineyard Association and Isle of Wight Fine Foods) covers 8 acres with Reichensteiner, Seyval Blanc and Müller-Thurgau the main white varieties grown together with a hybrid cross with *Vitis amurensis* for the Adgestone red wine.

The vineyard was established in 1968 and the site was specially chosen for its suitability for growing vines. Ken Barlow had spent the previous 20 years devoted to agricultural crop research and development overseas and with his wife Anne Barlow runs the vineyard and winery and makes the wine.

The first commercial harvest was picked in 1970 and by the time the vines had started to mature in 1974, the wines were winning awards and medals, and are still doing so today, consistently gaining the EVA quality mark.

The vineyard has a southerly aspect between 150ft and 250ft above sea level, and is set on south facing slopes to catch the sun from dawn to dusk. It is surrounded by trees on the hill tops which afford protection against cold winds. The soil consists of a chalky loam mixed with flints over greensand and is well drained.

The vineyard enjoys a cool winter allowing the vines to lie dormant and conserve their energy and has a high summer sunshine rate. The vineyard is rather exposed to the prevailing south-westerly winds. There are few problems with frost, and sunshine levels at more than 1,850 hours a year are remarkable, especially compared with the Moselle which gets 1,400 hours and the Rhinegau which receives 1,600 hours on average. The vineyard also benefits from the warmer summer period which comes later than is usual on the continent, and temperatures in early November can still be as high as 44°F (17°C).

This long, cool growing season with high sunshine is an essential factor in quality wine production in England. It is because of this that the Müller-Thurgau has so much freshness, fruit and is better balanced with greater acidity.

It is this special climate that has allowed the vineyard to produce a very acceptable red wine, although production is very small and quickly snapped up. It has a good rich colour and is concentrated and with a good combination of fruit and oak. The vines have the advantage that they flower early so the fruit has time to mature, and yields are good even in poor summers.

Pruning starts each year in December and continues until March. The vines are trained using high cordons with canes. There is routine spraying against powdery and downy mildew, and weed control is by mowing and rotavating throughout the summer. There is foliage trimming by machine during the summer and the harvest for the white varieties takes place towards 23 October and can run into November. It takes between 2 and 4 weeks and Reichensteiner is the first variety picked, followed by Müller-Thurgau and then Seyval Blanc.

The grapes are milled and de-stalked by passing through an Amos mill then emptied into 500l tubs and left to stand for an hour before they are pressed. Each batch is pressed three times in either a Vaslin 700l, or Howard 700l press. The must is collected in tanks, left overnight, and then racked, and the lees filtered the following day into 6,000l fibreglass tanks. The yeast is added and the must is chaptalised once fermentation has started. Fermentation takes between 10 days and 3 weeks.

After fermentation the wine is racked about the middle of January through a lees filter, and then blending takes place. The wine is fined, racked a second time again through a lees filter, and then sterile filtered. *Süss* reserve is added and the wine is bottled on a twelve-head Fredrich filler, usually in May or June. The wine is then corked and binned before labelling and packing.

The Adgestone Estate bottled wine is a blend of all three white varieties which is light, fragrant and not too dry.

Production in 1984 was 2,000 cases of a record breaking wine. It was a full bodied botrytis wine which won the *Sunday Times* Wine Club gold medal. The 1985 harvest produced 1,000 cases of a similar wine but slightly lighter in style. The 1986 production was 2,000 cases. It was a large crop, late ripening, and produced a distinctly buttery wine. The 1987 crop was small, yielding 900 cases of a fresh, fragrant, fruity wine while the 1988 vintage was a slight improvement at 1,000 cases. It was a very ripe crop and its potential is excellent. The Adgestone 1987 was a quite dry medium dry, with good balancing acidity which becomes very smooth with bottle age.

The wine is sold from the winery shop and is served in top restaurants and hotels, locally and nationally such as the Savoy. It is available in the palace of Westminster and exported. Expansion plans include red wine production and an Adgestone sparkling wine, already being produced on an experimental basis.

Visiting times: the vineyard shop is open all year round Monday to Friday 9am-4.30pm, Saturday 10am-12.30pm.

How to get there: the vineyard is close to Brading near to the east coast of the island on the Ryde to Sandown road. As you enter Brading take the Lower Adgestone road which runs inland, then right into Sheep Lane, and left into Upper Adgestone road and the vineyard.

Nearby attractions: Brading Wax Museum, Brading Roman Villa, Morton Manor and Nunwell House.

Recommended pubs, restaurants and hotels in the area: Anglers Inn (Brading), A La Carte (restaurant, Brading), and Seaview Hotel (Seaview).

BARTON MANOR VINEYARD

Anthony and Alix Goddard
Whippingham
East Cowes
Isle of Wight PO32 6LB
☎ (0983) 292835

The vineyard (a member of the EVA and Wessex Vineyards Association) covers 10.5 acres with a further 5.5 acres to be planted in 1990 and 1991. Varieties planted are: Seyval Blanc, 3,002 vines planted between 1977 and 1988 on 2.95 acres and accounting for 28.8 per cent of total production; Müller-Thurgau, 1,272 vines planted in 1977 on 1.57 acres and accounting for 15.37 per cent of production; Huxelrebe, 1,204 vines planted in 1977 (522 vines on 0.645 acres) and 1987 (682 vines on 0.569 acres) now covering just over 1.2 acres and accounting for 11.87 per cent of production; Reichensteiner, 499 vines planted in 1977 on 0.6 acres and a further 682 planted in 1987 on 0.569 acres, giving a total acreage of 1.186 acres and 11.6 per cent of production Gewürztraminer, 1,477 vines planted in 1982 on 0.9 acres and accounting for 8.92 per cent of production; Schönburger, 204 vines planted in 1979 on 0.126 acres, and a further 682 vines planted in 1987 on 0.569 acres, a total acreage of 0.695 acres and 6.8 per cent of production; Bacchus, 682 vines planted in 1987 on 0.569 acres and accounting for 5.56 per cent of production; Ortega, 682 vines planted in 1987 on 0.569 acres and accounting for 5.56 per cent of production and Zweigeltrebe, 456 vines planted in 1979 on 0.56 acres accounting for 5.5 per cent of production.

The vineyard is on a gentle south-south-east facing slope less than 90ft above sea level and well sheltered. It is on silty clay loam soil. It enjoys a milder climate than the mainland and has high light intensity, and often does better than the mainland when flowering is difficult, and can be up to 2 weeks earlier than elsewhere.

The first 5 acres of vines were planted in 1977, the year after the Goddard's moved into the historic manor house, set in 20 acres of gardens laid out by Prince Albert and Queen Victoria and later extended by King Edward VII.

The main variety was Müller-Thurgau with lesser quantities of Seyval Blanc, Huxelrebe, Reichensteiner and Schönburger. An acre of red Zweigeltrebe vines was planted in 1979 in place of trial varieties that were grubbed up. A further acre of Gewürztraminer was planted in 1982.

The three summers of 1979, 1980 and 1981 were terrible and production was only 2,300, 1,000 and 4,750 bottles respectively. In 1982, the first decent summer since 1976, production reached more than 17,000 bottles. Production in 1983 hit 20,000 bottles, about as much as the winery can cope with, and it has averaged about 16,000 bottles over the last 5 years. The 1987 vintage was badly hit by the production and up to 20 per cent of the crop was lost as well as a number of trees, including one planted by Prince Albert on his twenty-seventh birthday.

Winter pruning takes place between December and February. Because only shoots growing from one-year-old wood are capable of bearing grapes in the following season, the mass of growth left over from the summer is cut back to two or more canes tied to the bottom wire, from which the new shoots grow.

Budburst is in late spring and flowering takes place in July. There is a regular spraying programme to control mildew and the vines are treated about ten times during the growing season. There is also weed control and summer pruning to tidy up the vines.

The harvest usually starts around the middle of October and is spread over 3 weeks, with picking taking place on 5 to 7 days. The grapes are handpicked into buckets which are then emptied into a trailer and taken to the winery.

They are then weighed before being tipped into the grape mill hopper and destrigged. After the grapes have been crushed, they are transferred into 550l bins, and after up to 12 hours maceration, are tipped into the 700l Howard rotapress.

The press takes about two bin loads at a time and has three automatic pressing programmes. The pressing takes about 2 hours. The must is collected in a stainless steel tray and then pumped into tanks.

The dry residue of grape skins and pips in the press is removed and used as a fertiliser on the vineyard. The must is left to settle for up to 36 hours and then the clear must is pumped off, tested for total acidity and any adjustments made, the yeast is added and fermentation starts. Fermentation continues for about 4 weeks and the wine is then allowed to settle again for between 2 and 4 weeks before being pumped off the yeast lees in the bottom of the tanks. The wine is then carefully analysed and checked for stability, acidity and alcohol content. Any necessary finings and filtrations are done, although these are kept to a minimum as is the handling of the wine. The analysis also includes a series of testings to achieve the right balance, and *süss* reserve is added. The wine is then sterile filtered before bottling.

The wine is cold sterile bottled on a six-headed Velox bottling machine which inserts long filler tubes into the bottles to allow them to be filled gently. A Bertolasso semi-automatic corking machine is then used. To help maintain the sterility of the corks, they are, with the machine, periodically sprayed with a solution of sulphur dioxide. The capsules are then spun on, and the bottles taken into the bonded store.

Wines produced are: Barton Manor medium white, a light crisp fruity, slightly sparkling wine with pleasant nose and aftertaste. The 1987 vintage was a blend of 46 per cent Seyval Blanc, 31 per cent Reichensteiner, 16 per cent Müller-Thurgau and 7 per cent Huxelrebe; Barton Manor dry white, a fuller style, un-chaptalised and bone dry. A blend of 85 per cent Gewürztraminer and 15 per cent Schönburger in 1987 and at its best from 1989 onwards and able to last for 10 years; Barton Manor medium rosé, made from Zweigeltrebe and lightened in colour by the addition of an equal quantity of Seyval. A fairly soft wine with typical varietal 'raspberry' flavour and medium 'Wight Wine', an Isle of Wight vineyard wine produced and bottled by Barton Manor, medium dry and fruity; Barton Manor medium apple wine, different from cider in that it is made from the unoxidised juice of exclusively English dessert and cooking apples. The apple wine was first made in 1980 and proved so popular that 8,000 bottles were made the following year. It has been going strong ever since.

The aim of the vineyard is to produce the best wine it can, and it has an outstanding record in the English Wine of the Year competitions. In the last 16 years, it has entered sixteen of its wines and been the outright winner once, runner up once and won six gold medals, six silvers and a bronze.

The vineyard and winery is run by three full-time staff who also look after the 20-acre gardens as well. Anthony Goddard is the winemaker.

The wines have been served at Buckingham Palace and aboard the royal yacht, and are available at many top restaurants and hotels, including the Ritz. Most of the sales, however, are direct to vineyard visitors.

Visiting times: 10.30am-5.30pm daily from the beginning of May to the second Sunday in October plus weekends in April and Good Friday to Easter Monday. A ninety-seater wine bar and café opened in 1989 and expansion plans include increasing the present vineyard acreage to 15.5, a new winery and bonded store in converted Victorian buildings, which were originally part of the home farm to Osborne House designed by Prince Albert. There is also a gift shop specialising in products made by the island's craftsmen. Vines and plants grown in the vineyard and gardens are on sale. Other attractions include a display of winemaking equipment and a video made at Barton Manor on the winegrowers year, a beautiful wooded walk with 250,000 daffodils in the spring, azaleas and rhododendrons in the early summer and roses and herbaceous borders during the summer, a magical water garden, once the royal skating rink, a lake with wildfowl, a scented garden, and thatched boathouse.

Barton Manor is mentioned in the *Domesday Book* and from 1439 to 1845 were annexed to Winchester College as an agricultural estate, before being bought by Queen Victoria to form part of the Osborne House estate. After 80 years of royal ownership during which it played host to many of the crowned heads of Europe, it was sold and it has been in private ownership since.

How to get there: Barton Manor Vineyard and gardens are well signposted at Whippingham on the outskirts of East Cowes on the north of the island. It is close to the ferry terminal and an hour's boat ride from the mainland.

Nearby attractions: Osbourne House.

ISLE OF WIGHT WINE CO-OPERATIVE

c/o ROSEMARY VINEYARD
Rosemary Lane
Ashey Road
Ryde
PO33 2UX
☎ (0983) 616005

This includes Whitfield Vineyard, Ashey Vineyard and Smallbrooke Vineyard. Members are Messrs C. Gauntlett, P. Godber, R. Sopar and N. Gauntlett.

The vineyard (a member of the EVA) covers 45 acres and further plantings are planned. Varieties planted are Reichensteiner 8 acres, Madeleine Angevine 8 acres, Schönburger 7 acres, Seyval Blanc 6 acres, Müller-Thurgau 4 acres, Bacchus 3 acres, Kerner 3 acres, Pinot Gris 2 acres, Chardonnay an acre and Triomphe D'Alsace an acre. All the vines are between one and four years old and none are yet productive.

The vineyard is about 60ft above sea level and has the highest sun hours a day of anywhere in the UK. There is about 9in of top soil on green sand and clay. The vineyard is valley-based and south facing. The site is warm and windy with the prevailing winds from the west, and rain often misses the vineyard but hits the mainland.

All the vines are pruned and trained according to the Geneva Double Curtain system. The rows are planted 10ft to 12ft apart with 6ft and 8ft between vines. All the lanes are grassed. There is normal annual pruning and so far it has not been found necessary to spray the vines. The first harvest is expected in 1990.

A new 2,000sq ft winery has been built and a wine shop will open in 1990. The winemaker will be Conrad Gauntlett. Four other part-time staff are employed in the vineyard. The vineyard will be expanded as and when good land adjacent to it comes on the market.

Visiting times: telephone to arrange a visit. The vineyard can be visited at present and from 1990 there will be the wine shop, vineyard trails and a number of other attractions.

St Catherines Vineyard

How to get there: the vineyard is a quarter of a mile from Ryde hospital on the main Ryde to Sandown road.

ST CATHERINES VINEYARD

Marion and Tony Aldridge
St Catherines House
St Catherines Road
Niton
Isle of Wight
☎ (0983) 730465

The vineyard (a member of the EVA) covers 3 acres and a further acre is being planted. Varieties planted are Madeleine Angevine, Madeleine Sylvaner, Pinot Blanc, Sauvignon, Gamay, Schönburger and Reichensteiner. All the vines have been planted since 1986.

The vineyard is close to the southernmost tip of the Isle of Wight, facing the sea and about 250ft above sea level, on well drained sandstone. The vineyard enjoys a warm climate with the heat reflected from the sea. All the vines are trained and pruned on either the Guyot or Double Guyot system, although the Mosel loop will be used on new plantings. The first spraying programme was introduced in 1989. The first harvest of Madeleine Angevine and Sylvaner only was gathered in 1988 and picking started on 25 September. The first commercial harvest will be gathered in 1989. It is planned to market the wines on the Isle of Wight and in France. Expansion plans include increasing the acreage if further land nearby can be purchased.

Visiting times: by appointment at present. The vineyard can be visited and there is a picnic site as well as two self contained flats for holiday lets.

How to get there: the vineyard is in Niton, about 4 miles west of Ventnor on the southernmost tip of the island. As you enter Niton from Ventnor turn left into Undercliffe Drive and then left again into St Catherines Road.

Nearby attractions: St Catherines lighthouse, Blackgang.

Recommended pubs, restaurants and hotels in the area: Buddle Inn.

Chapter 7
Vineyards of the South-West

Somerset

Many of the vineyards in the county are on the Somerset Wine Trail which was established to introduce visitors to a number of vineyards of different sizes in different settings. All are licensed to sell their wine and most offer light meals or refreshments. The trail was established by a Taste of Somerset, a producers' marketing co-operative set up to promote quality food and drink produced in the county. Further details can be obtained from A Taste of Somerset, Agriculture House, 31 Trull Road, Taunton, Somerset, ☎ (0823) 337873.

There are now twelve vineyards in the county all of which have been established in the last 20 years. Both the number of vineyards and the acreage planted is now increasing annually. There is evidence of vines being grown since before the Norman Conquest. In AD955 King Edwy presented a vineyard to the monks of Glastonbury Abbey, and the *Domesday Book* of 1086 recorded seven vineyards in Somerset — at Glastonbury, Mere, Panborough, North Curry, Muchelney, Midelney and Thorney. The winemaking traditions of the county are also recorded in the stone carvings at Wells Cathedral and Muchelney Abbey, and in many other wood and stone carvings in churches and historic houses in the county.

AVALON VINEYARD
Dr H.R.H. Tripp
The Drove
East Pennard
Shepton Mallet BA4 6UA
☎ (074986) 393

The vineyard (a member of the EVA, the Soil Association and the South West Vineyards Association) extends to 2.5 acres of which 2 acres are in production. A further 2 acres are to be planted. Varieties planted are Seyval 1.5 acres, Schönburger an acre and a few Reichensteiner. This acreage includes 0.5 acres of newly planted but as yet unproductive Seyval Blanc. The vineyard is at an altitude of between 250ft and 300ft above sea level on a south-south-east facing slope. The soil is silt, sand and clay loam overlying clay sub-soil. There is reasonable drainage, and some of the vineyard has old, clay land drains. No new drainage has been undertaken.

Most of the vineyards are trained on the Guyot system although there is some Lyre trellising, and some Lenz-Moser on Lyre.

All the vines are organically grown and chemicals are not used. The Seyval Blanc vines are treated with foliar feed for any deficiencies, but are not sprayed at all otherwise. The Schönburger and Reichensteiner are sprayed with Bordeaux mixture and sulphur when appropriate to protect against fungal diseases, mildew and botrytis. All the vines are grown and treated according to the Soil Association's standards for organic cultivation.

The harvest for the last few years has not started until early November and as there has been a succession of very poor crops, the grapes have been picked very quickly. They are picked into plastic dustbins and then tipped into a roller mill. The pulp is pressed on an old hand-turned cider press in a 'cheese' of straw as traditionally used in cider making. The grapes are then fermented in polythene or stainless steel vats. The wine is then racked and coarse filtered in early spring, and sterile filtered just before bottling in late spring. The winery uses a four-head syphon bottle filler and a hand corker.

The 1984 vintage was excellent and 2,200 bottles of wine were produced. The wine subsequently won the President's Cup in the English Wine of the Year competition.

In 1985 and 1986 poor weather reduced the crop and only about 500 bottles were produced in both years, although quality was good. Production in 1987 was hit by bad weather again, only 200 bottles were produced and quality was poor. The 1988 vintage suffered even more from the weather, only 100 bottles of wine were produced, and at the time of writing, it was too early to determine the quality. The wine currently produced is Avalon Seyval, which is dry, fresh and clean.

The vineyard and winery is run by the owner with the help of an apprentice, although volunteers are drafted in to help at harvest time. The vineyard runs alongside the family's cider making interests. They have planted their own cider apple orchard, and the new plantings of vines are interplanted with strawberries, garlic, onions and beans. Everything is planted under black plastic mulch. There are a number of expansion plans and the acreage of the vineyard will be increased.

Visiting times: the vineyard and 'pick your own' operation is open in June, July and August from 2-6pm daily. The vineyard sells its own wine, rooted vine cuttings, cider — still and sparkling — apple wine, fruit wines and fresh organic fruit. There are free tastings and a picnic site. The wine is sold from the winery, in local shops and restaurants and is now being retailed further afield through shops, restaurants, wine merchants and special organic wine merchants. The vineyard has its own purpose built winery with underground wine cellar. There is also a 'pick your own' organic vegetable and fruit enterprise, specialising in strawberries, raspberries and tayberries, garlic, onions and beans.

How to get there: follow the A37 for 5 miles south of Shepton Mallet, then turn right at the cross roads in Wraxall, opposite the Queen's Arms pub, for East Pennard. After 1.5 miles, turn right at the vineyard sign and Avalon is about a quarter of a mile along the rough track.

Nearby attractions: Wells with its cathedral, Glastonbury Tor and Abbey ruins.

Recommended pubs, restaurants and hotels in the area: Bowlish House Hotel (Shepton Mallet) and George and Pilgrim (Glastonbury).

BATHSPRINGS VINEYARD

Christopher and Debbie Davey
The Wine House
Bailbrook Lane
Bath BA1 7AB
☎ (0225) 852131

The owners are 'fairly certain' that this vineyard is on the site of a former Roman vineyard, and it takes its name from the springs which feed it from the hillsides. Christopher Davey retired as a major after spending 19 years in a tank regiment, and it was perhaps his time spent in the Rhine that developed his love of wine. It may be the reason why so many other ex-army officers are now involved in viticulture. The vineyard (a member of the EVA) covers 1.5 acres and is planted with an acre of Madeleine Angevine for white wine, and half an acre of Leon Millot for red. The vineyard could be expanded to cover 7 acres but there are no immediate plans to do so. None of the vines are yet commercially productive.

The vineyard is in a tourist area on a south facing slope in hilly country on clay and sand overlying limestone. The vineyard enjoys a mild, rainy, warm climate and trees shield it and protect it from the worst of the winter frosts.

The vines are all trained on the Double Guyot system, but the Madeleine Angevine are planted in rows north to south, while the Leon Millot are planted in rows running east to west.

Pruning starts in January and continues until March. Spraying to protect the Made-

The George at Bathampton, near Bathsprings Vineyard

leine Angevine starts at the beginning of June and continues through the growing season, but spraying for the Leon Millot is negligible. There is summer pruning, mostly of the Leon Millot which is very prolific. The Madeleine Angevine ripens first and is usually harvested at the beginning of October, while the Leon Millot is picked at the end of the month. The winemaker is Tony Cox of Bannerdown, Batheaston. He plans to make a medium dry white, and has not yet decided on the style for the red. A few bottles of red have been produced so far for home consumption, but the vineyard does not have its own winery at present.

Visiting times: open at all times because of the public footpath to the vineyard but serious visitors interested in the vineyard can ring for an appointment.

How to get there: directions supplied by the owner.

Nearby attractions: Bath.

Recommended pubs, restaurants and hotels in the area: The George, Bathampton.

BRYMPTON VINEYARD
Charles Clive-Ponsonby-Fane
Brympton d'Evercy
Yeovil
Somerset BA 22 8TD
☎ (093586) 3528

The vineyard (a member of the EVA and the Somerset Pick Your Own Group) is run by Roy Scrivens, a viticulturist and covers an acre, planted equally between Müller-Thurgau and Reichensteiner. There have been no changes to the varieties planted in recent years, and no new, as yet unproductive vines.

The vineyard is on a south facing slope alongside the house, on well drained loamy topsoil, about 12ft deep and is frequently overcast. The major problem is mildew exacerbated by the mild, moist climate, and this is tackled by a regular spraying programme.

The harvest is gathered in a single day and the grapes are taken to Wraxall Vineyard, at Shepton Mallet, where they are processed under contract. Production was 2,500 bottles in 1983 and 2,800 in 1984 but

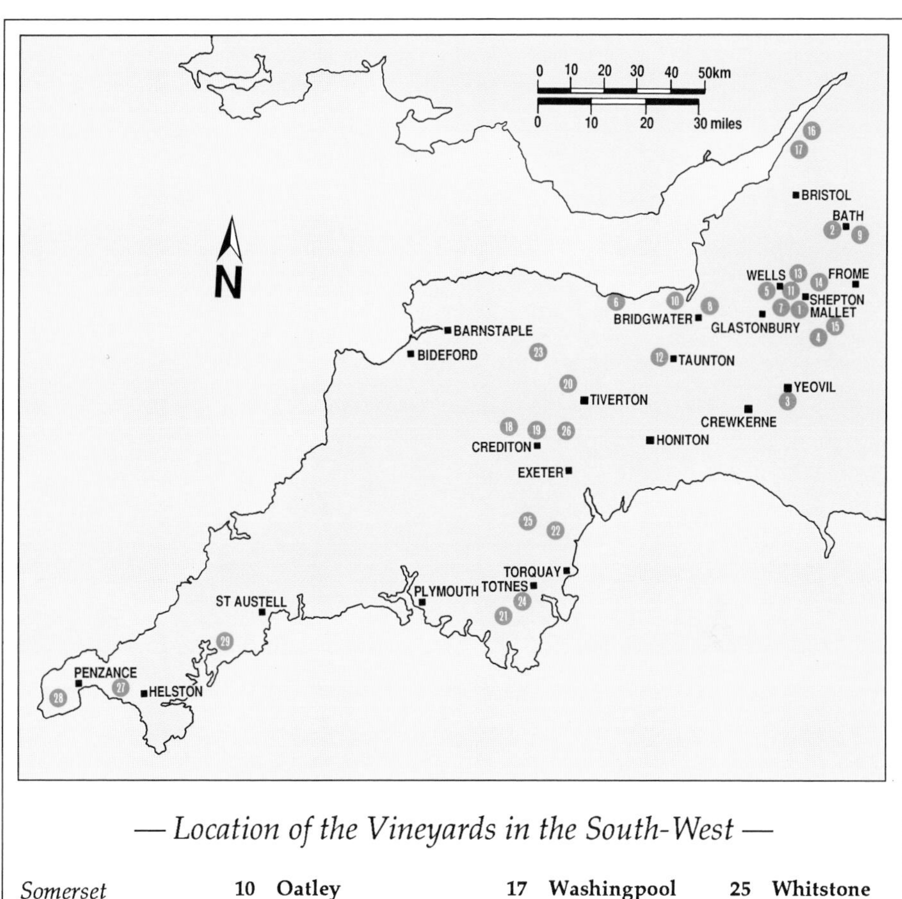

— *Location of the Vineyards in the South-West* —

Somerset
1 Avalon
2 Bathsprings
3 Brympton
4 Castle Cary
5 Coxley
6 Dunkery
7 Monk's
8 Moorlynch
9 Mumfords
10 Oatley
11 Pilton Manor
12 Staplegrove & Coombe
13 Wootton
14 Whatley
15 Wraxall

Avon
16 Thornbury Castle
17 Washingpool

Devon
18 Down St Mary
19 Follymoor
20 Highfield
21 Loddiswell
22 Manstree
23 Saul's
24 Sharpham
25 Whitstone
26 Yearlstone

Cornwall
27 Mounts Bay
28 Penberth
29 Polmassick

has been poor for the last 4 years averaging under 500 bottles. The wine produced is a blend and the total production is sold through the estate shop. It also sells Brympton home produce, including cider.

Visiting times: Easter Friday to Easter Monday 2-6pm. 1 May to 28 September, every afternoon except Thursday and Friday, 2-6pm. Other attractions include the state rooms in the house, an antique collection of coopering equipment, a country life museum, extensive gardens, a fourteenth-century parish church, the Brympton distillery in the Priest House, a Roman mosaic pavement, painting and photographic exhibitions. There is a tea room and picnic sites.

How to get there: the vineyard lies just to the west of Yeovil. Follow the signs off the A30 or A303 to Brympton House.

Nearby attractions: Montacute House, Yeovil.

Recommended pubs, restaurants and hotels in the area: Le Tire Bouchan restaurant (South Petherton).

Montacute House near Yeovil

CASTLE CARY VINEYARD
Mr and Mrs P.C. Woosnam Mills
Honeywick House
Hadspen
Castle Cary
Somerset BA7 7LP
☎ (0963) 50323

The vineyard (a member of the EVA, the South West Vineyards Association and Taste of Somerset) covers 5 acres and another 5 acres are to be planted. Varieties grown are Müller-Thurgau on an acre, accounting for 30 per cent of production, Seyval Blanc 0.5 acres (15 per cent), Madeleine Angevine planted in 1983 on 0.5 acres (15 per cent), Huxelrebe planted in 1984 and 1985 on 1.25 acres (35 per cent), Schönburger planted in 1986 and 1987 on 1.25 acres (5 per cent), and Regner planted in 1988 on 0.5 acres and not yet in production. There is half an acre each of Schönburger and Regner new vines, not yet in production. The vineyard is at 300ft above sea level in a fold of hills half a mile to the east of Castle Cary on a south to south-east facing slope. The soil is fine sandy loam. The vineyard is usually fairly frost free and enjoys a mild climate generally with warm rather humid south-westerly winds.

The vineyard was started in 1979 with the planting of just over half an acre of Müller-Thurgau, and a further half an acre plus was planted every year until 1988 when the present acreage was reached. Pruning starts in November soon after the harvest is over and continues until March. All the vines are trained on the Double Guyot system and are sprayed just before flowering. After the fruit has set there is a regular spraying programme against mildew and botrytis every 10 to 14 days.

The harvest usually starts in the third week of October and lasts for 3 or 4 days. The time it takes to pick is gradually increasing as new vines start to yield grapes and others mature giving bigger crops. Huxelrebe is usually the first variety to be harvested, followed by Madeleine Angevine, Müller-Thurgau, Seyval Blanc and Schönburger.

The vineyard does not have its own winery and the grapes are taken by road to Wootton Vineyard near Shepton Mallet for vinification. Castle Cary has its own fermentation tanks at Wootton.

The first vintage was in 1983 and production was about 4,500 bottles of fruity, dry white wine which was awarded the EVA Seal. In 1984, 6,500 bottles of a similar wine were produced and again it was awarded the EVA Seal. Since then harvests have been hit by bad weather although the quality of the limited quantity of wine has been high and each vintage has still been awarded the EVA Seal. Production in 1985 was 1,000 bottles which halved in 1986 and 1987. The 1987 wine currently on offer is a blend of all the varieties. It is a medium dry white, with a good fruity nose, and a fresh, very fruity taste.

Most of the wine is sold from the vineyard direct to the public, but it is sold through a number of branches of Waitrose, in local wine merchants and at the London Hilton. The vineyard is run by the owners with the help of a farm labourer. Expansion plans include converting the existing old cider house into a modern winery and doubling the vineyard acreage.

Visiting times: daylight hours from May to October to tour the vineyard, and all year round for wine sales. There is a vineyard shop which also sells cider, apple wine, home preserves and fresh vegetables in season. Organised tours for groups can be arranged.

How to get there: the vineyard lies to the east of Castle Cary which is on the A371 Wincanton to Shepton Mallet road. Approach on either the A359 or A303 and follow the signs for Castle Cary. In the village take the minor road signposted to Cole which leads you to the vineyard.

Nearby attractions: Stourhead Gardens, Longleat House, Sparkford Motor Museum, Fleet Air Arm Museum, Yeovilton.

Recommended pubs, restaurants and hotels in the area: The George (pub, Castle Cary), Holbrook House Hotel (Wincanton), Bonds Restaurant (Ansford).

COXLEY VINEYARD

Bill Austin
Coxley
Nr Wells
Somerset BA5 1RQ
☎ (0749) 73854

The vineyard covers 4 acres planted equally with Seyval Blanc, Schönburger and Reichensteiner. There have been no changes to the varieties grown in recent years and there are no new, as yet unproductive vines.

The vineyard was planted in 1981 on sandy loam on almost level ground about 40ft above sea level. All the vines are trained and pruned according to the Double Guyot system but there is a major problem with starlings. The vineyard is run by the owner with help drafted in at harvest time.

The vineyard does not have its own winery and the grapes are taken to Wraxall Vineyard for vinification under contract. The 1987 wine produced was 100 per cent Seyval Blanc medium dry, with a pale straw colour, with a huge nose, fresh and appley, with good balance and acidity and a long finish. Annual production is about 20,000 bottles.

Visiting times: any reasonable time. The wine is sold direct to the public from the vineyard by the bottle and case, and through the owner's restaurant, as well as in Peter Dominic and Bottoms Up. The wine shop sells a number of other English wines as well as a comprehensive range of European and Australian wines. The vineyard also offers accommodation in luxury en suite bedrooms, with facilities for the disabled.

How to get there: the vineyard is signposted half way between Wells and Glastonbury on the A39.

Nearby attractions: Bath, Wells, Wookey Hole, Glastonbury and Longleat House.

DUNKERY VINEYARD

Derek and Val Pritchard
Ordesa
Wootton Courtenay
Nr Minehead TA 24 8RF
☎ (064384) 505

The vineyard is the major importer and supplier of grafted vines, and also imports and supplies all types of viticultural accessories and winemaking materials and

Brympton Vineyard

Coxley Vineyard

equipment. It is a member of the EVA and South West Vineyards Association and covers an acre and there are no plans to expand at present. It comprises 2,150 vines made up of Senator, Kerner, Kernling, Riesling, Kettern-Riesling, Pinot Gris, Pinot Noir, Reichensteiner, Schönburger, Freisamer, Ehrenfelser and Madeleine Angevine. The owners do all the vineyard work and winemaking themselves and also own and work two small vineyards in the Saar Valley at Kanzemer and Wiltinger Schlossberg. The early plantings of Siegerrebe have been grubbed up because they were ripening too early and suffering from serious wasp damage. There are also experimental plantings of the red varieties Dornfelder and Dunkelfelder, and Phoenix, Orion, Silvaner, Holder, Valrebe and Abondant.

The vineyard is in the Exmoor National Park, in the lee of the Dunkery range of hills, the highest point of which is the famous Dunkery Beacon. The vineyard is on Devonian red sandstone soil, one of the great vineyard soils in Europe. It is planted on a steep sloping site, the average gradient approaching 30 per cent and due to its sheltered position, has a very special microclimate.

The Minehead weather station frequently records the highest summer temperatures in Britain. The daily maximum temperatures recorded in the vineyard are usually 11°F (6°C) above the weather station figures. Night-time temperatures are relatively cool, partly due to the south to south-east facing slope, and this combination enables the wine to have very racy acidity.

The vines are trained on either the Single or Double Guyot system with arched canes. There is a high leaf wall and the vine growth is topped using a motorised back-pack leaf cutter. Spraying is carried out using a motorised back-pack sprayer.

The harvest usually starts at the end of September or early October and continues until late November. Madeleine Angevine is the first variety to be picked. Senator and Reichensteiner are harvested in the middle of the month and Schönburger towards the end of October.

At the end of October or in early November the Kernling, Kerner, Freisamer, Pinot Noir and Pinot Gris are harvested, and the final grapes to be picked are from the Ehrenfelser and Riesling vines, usually between the middle and late November. The grapes are picked by hand and emptied into a stainless steel crusher and destalker. They are then pressed in a water powered hydropress which operates at a maximum three-bar pressure. A rubber bag exerts pressure against a stainless steel cage, and the juice is gently pressed out. The crushing and pressing is carried out very quickly after picking. Fermentation takes place in stainless steel or fibreglass tanks and all the wines are fully fermented to dryness and quickly racked off the dead yeast cells.

The winemaking is carried out with the minimum possible amount of racking, filtering and sulphuring. The relatively high acidity preserves the wine and retains its freshness for many years.

There have been only small harvests since 1986 but the superb autumn weather in 1987 enabled the late-ripening varieties to reach high natural sugar levels. However wasp and bird damage, mainly blackbirds and thrushes, decimated the crop in 1988.

Visiting times: by appointment. The vineyard has a purpose built winery, approximately 600sq ft. The wine is only sold locally to date and demand far exceeds supply. There are magnificent views of Exmoor from the vineyard and birdwatchers will enjoy seeing green woodpeckers, buzzards, long tailed tits, goldcrests and many other species around the edge of the vineyard.

How to get there: follow the A39 westwards almost to Minehead until you see Dunster Castle on the left hand side. Turn left (south) through the village of Dunster, then after about 2 miles take the turning on the right signposted to Wootton Courtenay 1.25 miles. As you approach the village, the vineyard is clearly seen ahead of you.

Nearby attractions: picturesque villages of Dunster, Selworthy, Bossington, Luccombe, many good local walks, and good riding and hunting.

Recommended pubs, restaurants and hotels in the area: The Dunkery Hotel, Wootton Courtenay.

MONK'S VINEYARD
High Compton Vines (Organic)

Mr and Mrs Raimund Herincx
Larkbarrow
East Compton
Pilton
Shepton Mallet
Somerset BA4 4NR
☎ (0749) 4462

Monk's Vineyard (a member of the EVA) covers 2.5 acres and the 2 acres for the High Compton were planted in February and April, 1989.

Monk's Vineyard was planted in 1987 with 750 vines of Müller-Thurgau, 1,200 Madeleine Angevine, 1,000 Seyval Blanc, 250 Chardonnay and 250 Pinot Blanc. An extra 250 Müller-Thurgau were planted in 1989 using 2-year-old vines so that all are now in their third year of growth.

The Müller-Thurgau are being grown conventionally and are planted 6ft apart with 6ft between the rows. All the other varieties are being trained and pruned using the Gobelet system, and are spaced 3ft apart with 6ft between rows.

High Compton Vines is an experimental vineyard and vine nursery. Altogether twenty-one varieties are being grown. The main varieties are Freisamer, Seyval Blanc and Chardonnay, each with 250 vines. The Chardonnay vines have been grown from both hard and softwood cuttings taken from Les Pucelles and Le Monrachet in Burgundy, courtesy of the owners.

Other varieties grown, in small stands of between twelve and fifty vines, are Frontignan, Bacchus, Regner, Sauvignon Blanc, Schönburger, Faber, Sylvaner, Siegerrebe, Chenin, Pinot Blanc (Weissburgunder), Reichensteiner, Scheurebe, Kanzler, Gewürztraminer, Kerner, Chasselas d'Or, Chasselas Rosé and Gold Riesling.

There have been no changes to original varieties planted in Monk's Vineyard, although the future of Müller-Thurgau is uncertain. Monk's Vineyard occupies about 3 acres, of which 2.5 acres have been planted. The vineyard lies at about 300ft above sea level on a loamy soil overlying limestone, in the last outcrop of the Mendips west of Pilton. The land lies north to south with a slightly unfavourable slope down to a stream for Monk's Vineyard, but an exceptionally favourable one for High Compton.

The vineyard has windy conditions in the winter which is often advantageous in preventing frost which affects lower placed vineyards in the valleys and dells.

Pruning is designed to develop the vines as bushes up to 3ft or so tall. The aim is to get the fruit growing nearer the ground so that it benefits from light and heat reflected from the limestone, and is protected from the wind so is not exposed to damage in the winter or spring.

Spraying takes place between June and September at approximately two-week intervals at Monk's Vineyard. Wettable sulphur is applied in August and a copper spray between September and October.

The first small harvest is expected in 1989, and for the first 2 or 3 years the winemaking will be contracted out. The vineyard is to install its own winery in renovated buildings. Extra land is available if required. The owners also have an interest in vegetable research in Bedfordshire and some vines are grown there as a back up for High Compton Vines.

The vineyard sells vines, the usual varieties as well as less known ones and expects this to be an expanding market as the interest in viniculture grows in the south-west.

Visiting times: the vineyard will be open to the public as soon as facilities and staff allow.

How to get there: the vineyard is a mile west of Pilton Manor on the A361.

Nearby attractions: Cheddar Gorge, Wookey Hole, Stourhead Gardens, Alfred's Tower, Nunney Castle, Glastonbury Tor, Wells Cathedral, Bath.

Recommended pubs, restaurants and hotels in the area: Blostin's Restaurant (Shepton Mallet), Apple Tree Pub (West Pennard).

Nunney Castle, near Frome

MOORLYNCH VINEYARD

Tom and Judith Rees
Moorlynch
Bridgwater TG7 9BU
☎ (0458) 210393

The vineyard covers about 16 acres and is planted with fourteen different varieties — twelve white wine grapes and two reds. There are no plans to extend the present acreage.

White varieties are Müller-Thurgau, Seyval Blanc, Madeleine Angevine, Würzer, Schönburger, Huxelrebe, Faber, Findling, Optima, Bacchus, Regner and Reichensteiner. The red varieties are Cabernet Sauvignon and Blauburger.

In recent years plantings of Chardonnay and Madeleine Angevine Oberlin have been removed, and plantings of Seyval Blanc, Faber, Würzer and Müller-Thurgau increased.

New plantings of as yet unproductive vines include 2.5 acres of Findling, a Müller-Thurgau clone, 2 acres of Seyval Blanc, and half an acre of Würzer.

The vineyard at Spring Farm was established in 1981 when about 8 acres were planted. The acreage has been steadily expanded and now covers about 16 acres of which half was in production in 1988. Besides the varieties for the blended wines and varietals produced on the estate, a number of experimental varieties have been introduced.

The vineyard lies on the south facing slope of the Polden Hills, overlooking the peat moors of Sedgemoor. The soil is a relatively shallow silty clay loam overlying blue lias, and this local limestone rock gives a firm character to the wines which those from more acid soils tend to lack. The vineyard receives about 27in of rainfall a year, is frost free, and exposed to westerly winds. It is generally a warm, early site. The vineyard suffers from damage by rabbits and birds.

The vines are pruned from December to April and three training systems are used — Double Guyot, Geneva Double Curtain and Open Lyre, which produces a divided canopy with spur pruning to a fruit bearing wire at about 2ft 6in off the ground. There is regular summer spraying at approximately 10- to 14- day intervals.

The harvest starts in the first fortnight of September with Madeleine Angevine, and the following varieties are then picked in order of Huxelrebe, Müller-Thurgau, Schönburger, Seyval Blanc and finally Würzer, usually in the last fortnight of October.

The Lyre trained vines ripen early, and the Lyre trained Schönburger will be picked around the same time as the Müller-Thurgau. The grapes are picked by hand and transferred to a grape trailer which mills them, and then straight to the automatic, pneumatic Willmes press. The juice is settled out before racking and fermentation in fibreglass tanks.

All the wines are cold stabilised in a refrigerated tank before sterile sheet filtration.

Any sweet reserve which needs to be added to finish the wines comes from their own grapes. It is produced from Reichensteiner grapes grown in a polytunnel. Nitrogen and carbon dioxide are used to protect the wine from oxidation during the post-fermentation handling and bottling.

Production in 1983 was 9,000 bottles which rose to 16,000 for the next three vintages. Bad summers hit the harvest in 1987 and 1988 and production fell to 11,000 and 6,000 bottles respectively.

The winemaker is Tom Rees and he is assisted in the vineyard and winery by two workers. Most of the wine is made from a blend of Madeleine Angevine, Seyval Blanc and Müller-Thurgau. The named grape of the single varietals must account for at least 85 per cent of the final wine. All seven wines produced in 1987 were awarded the EVA Seal of Quality. Wines produced are: Moorlynch Somerset, a blend of Müller-Thurgau and Seyval Blanc, medium dry, light, fruity and fresh; Moorlynch Dry, good clean fruit and attractive flowery nose. Good with food; Moorlynch Medium Dry, made from the three main blending varieties plus Huxelrebe, light, fruity and fresh; Moorlynch Medium, good fruit and balance and a clean finish; Moorlynch Schönburger, dry, aromatic with a spicy taste and melony nose; Moorlynch Würzer, crushed blackcurrant-leaf nose and delicate spicy character, from this Gewürztraminer and Müller-Thurgau cross. Moorlynch Faber, a French style wine in its depth and body, from this Pinot Blanc and Müller-Thurgau cross has an English floweriness on the nose and is aromatic. The 1988 Würzer crop was too small to justify a separate vinification.

Almost half the wine produced is sold direct from the vineyard. Until 1988 about a third of the production was marketed through Wines of England and went mainly to Waitrose, Sainsbury and Peter Dominic. Russell and McIver and Buckingham Vintners handle the London sales.

Visiting times: the shop is open all year round and the wine bar from 10.30am-6pm. The rest of the estate is open from 1 May to 30 September from 10am-6pm. There is no entry charge, and there are facilities for the disabled. The vineyards and winery buildings can be visited. There is a vineyard trail and guide, and a wine shop which also sells apple cider and apple wine (made from local apples) farm and local produce, and home made bread. Other attractions include a wine bar, which also serves coffee and light lunches. Guided tours for parties and organised tastings for up to forty can be arranged. The vineyard is part of Spring Farm which is also open to the public. It has a number of farm animals including sheep, cattle, pigs and poultry, all free ranging. Entry to the vineyard and farm is free.

How to get there: Moorlynch is 5 miles west of Glastonbury, 7 miles east of Bridgwater and 14 miles north of Taunton. It is well signposted from both the A39 and A361 roads.

MUMFORDS VINEYARD

Mr and Mrs W.A. Cox
Mumfords
Shockerwick Lane
Bannerdown
Bath BA1 7LQ
☎ (0225) 858367

The vineyard (a member of the EVA and the South West Vineyards Association) covers 4 acres and varieties planted are Madeleine Angevine, Reichensteiner, Kerner, Madeleine Sylvaner, Leon Millot and Triomphe D'Alsace. All were planted in 1986. The vineyard is on a south facing slope, about 200ft above sea level in the Avon Valley. The soil is silt over limestone brash and just alkaline. The climate is mild.

All the vines are trained using the Double Guyot system and are pruned and trained between December and March. There is a regular programme of spraying from May to September at approximately 3-week intervals. Sulphur and zinc are used to protect against fungus diseases, and there is also summer trimming and training.

The harvest usually starts in late September or early October with Madeleine Angevine and Madeleine Sylvaner, while Kerner, Leon Millot and Triomphe D'Alsace are picked in late October. The first vintage was in 1988.

The vineyard has its own small winery with modern stainless steel milling and fermentation equipment. It is designed to be operated by one person with hoists and bins to handle the harvest in batches so that quality can be controlled at all stages.

The wines produced so far are Madeleine Angevine, which is an English Loire-style wine, and Kerner, similar to a Riesling in style. The wine is sold locally at present, and the vineyard also sells apple wine. The vineyard and winery is set in the 6-acre grounds of an attractive country house close to Bath. Both are run by the owner and his wife. There are no expansion plans for the immediate future.

Visiting times: by appointment.

How to get there: take the A4 east of Bath to Batheaston. Turn into Bannerdown Road, signposted to Colerne. After about half a mile, turn right into Shockerwick Lane and the vineyard is 100yd on the right hand side.

Nearby attractions: Bath.

OATLEY VINEYARD

Iain and Jane Awty
Cannington
Bridgwater TA5 2NL
☎ (027867) 340

The vineyard (a member of the EVA and the South West Vineyards Association) covers 7 acres of which 5 acres are currently planted. The varieties are Kerner, Kernling and Madeleine Angevine. All the vines are recently planted.

The vineyard is between 105ft and 135ft above sea level, in open, rolling farmland between the Quantock Hills and the Bristol Channel. It is on a gentle south to south-east facing slope, sheltered to the north and west by woods of deciduous trees and to the south by higher ground. It is on red Quantock sandstone sandy loam and well drained in parts.

The vineyard is in the rain shadow of the Quantocks with a low annual rainfall for Somerset (between 24in and 29in), and high winter and summer temperatures — the average January temperature is 41°F (5°C), and the average July temperature is 60°F (16°C).

The vineyard was established in 1986 and there has been a planting programme of about 2 acres a year since then. The work in the vineyard is now changing from an establishing programme of spring planting, autumn and winter trellising and little spraying to a more permanent pattern of pruning from December until March, summer spraying and tucking in of shoots, weed control, October bird scaring and a

Looking towards Bridgwater from the Quantock Hills

late October to early November harvest.

All the vines are currently trained on the Bordeaux Lyre or Flat Trellis systems, with grassed alleys to minimise the use of herbicide sprays. The vineyard planted its mid-season and late varieties first and these are ready for harvest in the last week of October and first week of November respectively. The Madeleine Angevine are likely to be the first to be harvested when they become productive.

All the work in the vineyard is done by the owners, family and friends. The first 2 acres of vines were harvested in 1988 in a single day with friends helping — and a barrel of beer as bait! In future vintages, the pickers will be refreshed with the estate's own wine and the harvest is likely to last between 2 and 3 days.

The vineyard does not have its own winery and the grapes are taken by road for vinification under contract by Colin Gillespie of Wootton Vineyard. The 1988 harvest yielded only 250l of must from 2 acres of 3-year-old wines after a cold wet season. The wine at the time of writing was not ready to bottle.

Visiting times: by appointment. The vineyard is next to a country farmhouse and traditional stone and tile farmyard which will in due course be converted to a winery. Other expansion plans include increasing the vineyard acreage to 7 acres. The vineyard is part of an agricultural enterprise which also includes geese, hens, pigs, sheep and ponies.

How to get there: take the A39 from Bridgwater west through Cannington, and then after about 1.5 miles turn right at the signpost for the vineyard.

Nearby attractions: Quantock Hills, the coast and Somerset Levels.

PILTON MANOR VINEYARD

J.M. and M.A. Dowling
Pilton
Shepton Mallet
Somerset BA4 4BE
☎ (074989) 325

The vineyard (a member of the EVA, the South West Vineyards Association and Taste of Somerset) extends to 23 acres of which 8 acres are in production, and the remainder will come into production in 1991 and 1992. Varieties of vines planted including unproductive vines are: Bacchus on 1.28 acres accounting for 6.4 per cent of production, Huxelrebe 4.98 acres (25 per cent), Müller-Thurgau 4.7 acres (23.5 per cent), Reichensteiner 2.42 acres (12 per cent), Schönburger 2.37 acres (12 per cent), Seyval Blanc 4.23 acres (21 per cent), and others 0.58 acres accounting for 3 per cent of production.

Plantings of new, as yet unproductive vines are: Bacchus 1.28 acres, Huxelrebe 2.19 acres, Müller-Thurgau 1.16 acres, Reichensteiner 2.42 acres, Schönburger 0.79 acres, Seyval Blanc 1.07 acres, and others 0.5 acres.

The vineyard is planted on the site of a medieval vineyard dating from the twelfth century. The manor house, which dates back to the thirteenth century was originally the summer dwelling of the abbots of Glastonbury. Pilton Manor was the first of the modern Somerset vineyards.

The vineyard enjoys a southerly aspect on 5° to 10° slopes, at an elevation of between 125ft and 230ft above sea level. The soil is marl overlying limestone which overlies clay and blue lias. The climate is mild with flowering occurring one to two weeks earlier than in the south-east, although rainfall is slightly too high, averaging 36in annually.

The vineyard was established in 1964 and planted in 1966 and 1968. It enjoys its own sheltered microclimate which means that even in poor years — like 1988 — yields and quality are better than average.

Pruning starts in December and continues until March. New vines are planted in March and others are tied down in April. Budburst is in May and the first spraying normally takes place at the end of this month. Spraying and weed control then continue throughout the summer. Flowering takes place in July, and August is spent clipping and tucking in.

The harvest starts in early October and continues through to early November. Huxelrebe is the first variety to be picked from early to mid-October. Müller-Thurgau is picked from the middle to end of October, Seyval Blanc from the end of October to early November, with Schönburger the last variety harvested in early November. The grapes are collected by trailer and pressed immediately using Willmes and Howard presses.

The must has sulphur dioxide added and is rested for 24 hours, and the clear juice is then racked off. Sugar and acidity levels are adjusted where necessary, dry cultured yeasts are then added and fermentation starts within 24 hours. Fermentation continues for several weeks in cool conditions. The wine is then racked and filtered in November or December. It is fined and final adjustments are made for protein and acidity before bottling in March under sterile conditions.

Production over the last 5 years has been: 1984 (21,000l), a very big year and perhaps some overcropping affected quality; 1985 (5,600l), a low yield and hardly any Huxelrebe; 1986 (4,100l), another low yield because of weather, but the Seyval Blanc was of good quality; 1987 8,375l, low yield but very good quality for Huxelrebe and Müller-Thurgau. 1988 9,000l, another low yielding year, Huxelrebe yields were 1,600l an acre, and Müller-Thurgau only 560l an acre but of excellent quality.

The 1987 vintage wines were: Seyval Blanc, medium, light and fresh and very appealing, best drunk young; Huxelrebe, medium dry, good body with typical peachy flavour, and Müller-Thurgau, a medium dry with high quality, full flavoured, typical flowery nose, needs bottle age to develop and promises to be one of the best vintages. The wines are sold direct from the winery, by mail order, and exported to Holland, Germany and Italy.

The winery has been completely refurbished and expanded during 1988 and 1989 utilising the old stone built buildings. There is new bottling, sterilisation and fermentation equipment.

The owner is 'always on the look out for suitable land for planting'. Much of the original vineyard planted in the 1960s now needs to be replanned and replanted. Many of the vines first planted are now getting too old, and some of the varieties are not perhaps the most suitable and were planted too close together making them costly to manage as very little machinery can be used.

The vineyard has a long history of winemaking and there are conducted tours of the thirteenth-century wine cellars. Other attractions include tours, tastings, and a vineyard trail (opened 1989). There is a wine bar and restaurant with a patio overlooking the vineyard. Pre-booked tours for twenty to forty-five people can be arranged for summer afternoons or evenings. There is also a thirteenth-century square dovecote.

Visiting times: open 11am-5pm Wednesday to Sunday from May to September.

How to get there: the vineyard is well signposted on the west side of the village of Pilton, off the A31, between Shepton Mallet and Glastonbury.

Nearby attractions: the Somerset Vineyard Trail, Glastonbury Abbey, Wells city and cathedral, Wookey Hole, Chewton Dairy (cheesemaking) and Pilton Church.

Recommended pubs, restaurants and hotels in the area: Brottens Lodge, Oakhill (restaurant), Swan Hotel, Wells.

**STAPLEGROVE VINEYARD
& COOMBE VINEYARD**

**Mr M.M. Cursham
Staplecombe Wines
Burlands Farm
Staplegrove
Taunton TA2 6SN
☎ (0823) 451217**

Staplegrove Vineyard covers 3 acres, and Coombe Vineyard extends to an acre. Varieties planted are Madeleine Angevine 1.65 acres, Huxelrebe 0.55 acres, Reichensteiner 0.3 acres, Kerner 0.36 acres, Siegerrebe 0.29 acres, Ehrenfelser 0.14 acres and trial varieties 0.08 acres. There have been no changes to varieties planted and there are no new, as yet unproductive vines.

Staplegrove Vineyard is about 90ft above sea level, on level and south-west facing land. It is on well drained sandy clay loam on river valley alluvium. It is sheltered and warm but frosty. Coombe Vineyard is 225ft above sea level and south-west facing. It is on sandy loam on Quantock shales. It is exposed but warm and frost free. Both vineyards have above average rainfall at about 31in. They enjoy mild winters, dry springs and autumns and wet summers.

Pruning starts in mid-November and continues until mid-March. All the vines are trained on the low wire, cane replacement Double Guyot system with a leaf wall at 4ft. The rows are 6.5ft apart, and the vines 6ft to 6.5ft apart.

Spraying with fungicides takes place six to eight times from June onwards. There is no problem from powdery or downy mildew, but botrytis is difficult to control.

The harvest usually starts at the end of September with Siegerrebe being picked first, normally between 26 and 29 September. This is followed by the harvesting of the Madeleine Angevine between 1 and 8 October, and then Huxelrebe on about 15 October, Reichensteiner about 20 October, Kerner 31 October and Ehrenfelser last, about 5 November.

The grapes are transported to the winery in 22lb baskets. They are crushed and de-stemmed and sulphur is added at the rate of 40 parts per million free sulphur dioxide. The grapes are then pressed in an automatic hydraulic press with a capacity of a quarter of a ton. The juice is allowed to settle overnight, and it is then racked as it is transferred to the fermentation tanks of 600l, 800l and 2,500l capacity. The must is chaptalised, the yeast added and fermentation started.

The first racking takes place 3 weeks after the end of fermentation. There is a rough filtering in the middle of January with haze correction and acidity trim. There is sulphite stabilisation in mid-March. *Süss* reserve is added, which is made from the vineyard's own grapes, and the wine is bottled about the middle of April.

Production over the last 5 years has been: 1984 — 10.162 tons of grapes which produced 6,010l of wine, an average yield of 4,400l a hectare. The quality of the vintage was good; 1985 — 8.466 tons of grapes and 4,829l of wine, an average of 3,500l a hectare. The vintage was 'popular'; 1986 — 6.963 tons of grapes and 3,750l of wine. An average of 2,700l a hectare and an 'indifferent' vintage; 1987 — 9.539 tons of grapes, and 5,468l of wine. An average of 4000l a hectare, and an 'adequate' vintage; 1988 — 7.624 tons of grapes producing 4,712l of wine, an average of 3,300l to the hectare.

The current wines are: Staplecombe Dry 1987, a blend of Madeleine Angevine 40 per cent, Kerner 30 per cent, Reichensteiner 20 per cent, and Ehrenfelser 10 per cent. It contains 14oz per litre of residual sugar and is 10.4 per cent volume.

Staplecombe Medium 1987, a blend of Huxelrebe 60 per cent and Siegerrebe 40 per cent. It has 20oz per litre of residual sugar and is 10.9 per cent volume. Both wines have been awarded the EVA Seal of Quality.

The wine is sold direct to the public from the vineyard, in bulk to national outlets, and marketed at trade shows.

Visiting times: by appointment at any convenient time. The vineyard has a fully equipped winery capable of handling 8,600l of wine, and makes wine for other producers. The vineyard and winery is run by the owner with the aid of seasonal help.

There are no plans to extend the vineyard at present. It is part of an agricultural enterprise which also includes sheep. There are free tastings and tours will be arranged if possible.

How to get there: take the A361 Taunton to Barnstaple road, and at Staplegrove traffic lights turn right into Manor Road. Go past the church on the left and turn into Rectory Road. Follow the road for about half a mile until you come to a T-junction, turn left and the vineyard is 100yd on the left.

Nearby attractions: Quantock Hills.

Recommended pubs, restaurants and hotels in the area: Castle Hotel, Taunton.

WHATLEY VINEYARD

Michael Witt
Whatley
Frome BA11 3LA
☎ (037384) 467

The vineyard was established in 1979 and the first vines planted the following year. It is in the grounds of a large old rectory. The winery was built in 1986. There are no expansion plans although in 1989 a trial was being conducted by erecting four large polytunnels over the Schönburger. The vineyard is worked by Michael and Robin Witt, and Robin is also the winemaker. He

spent two seasons working with Colin Gillespie at Wootton.

The vineyard (a member of the EVA and the South West Vineyards Association) covers 2.42 acres of vines planted between 1980 and 1986. Varieties planted are: Seyval Blanc 0.42 acres, Madeleine Angevine 0.3 acres, Reichensteiner 0.5 acres, Schönburger 0.5 acres and Huxelrebe 0.4 acres. There have been no changes to the original varieties planted, and all the vines are now producing.

The site is flat at about 390ft above sea level, and well protected by windbreaks of

specially planted alders. The soil is a good loam overlying marl. Climatic conditions have not been favourable since 1986 because of the very wet summers. All the vines are trained on the Double Guyot system, weed control is by cultivation and hoeing and the use of herbicides is kept to an absolute minimum. Fungicide sprays are applied as and when necessary taking the weather conditions into account.

The vineyard has yet to have a 'typical' harvest because the bad weather has affected yields. The 1988 vintage should have been the first when all the vines were fruiting, but the crop was so small that all the grapes were picked together and blended. The grapes are picked by hand and taken to the winery where they are passed through a mill before being loaded into a basket press. The must is settled overnight, and then racked into stainless steel 1,000l fermentation tanks.

After fermentation the wine is racked at Christmas and then goes through a rough filtration at the end of January. Between 2 per cent and 5 per cent *süss* reserve is added, and then the wine is sterile filtered and bottled about the middle of March.

Production has steadily declined over

the last 5 years because of the weather even though more and more vines were becoming productive. In 1983 production was 5,500 bottles of Seyval Blanc, but this fell to 2,500 bottles in 1984, 1,200 in 1985 and 1986 and 900 bottles in 1987. The 1988 harvest should have been the first one to have all the varieties picked to make single varietal wines. The yields were small, and all five varieties were blended to produce 750 bottles of wine. The vineyard is only selling Seyval Blanc, and in 1987 it was made as a medium wine with a good fruity nose and well balanced.

Visiting times: 1989 — 1 April to 31 October, Tuesday to Sunday 10am-6pm. 1990 — 1 April to 31 October, Wednesday to Sunday 10am-6pm, plus bank holiday Mondays.

All the wine is sold through the farm shop and cookery school. The winery is in a converted farm building. It is small but works well. Other attractions include a walled herb garden, and the Grange Cookery School, which offers a variety of residential cookery courses using local fresh produce. There are guided tours of the vineyard, winery and herb garden with a talk on wine growing and the use of herbs, which can be followed by a tasting and meal in the seventeenth-century cellars.

How to get there: the vineyard is to the west of Frome and just south of Mells. Take the A361 Frome to Yeovil road, and the vineyard is clearly signposted just past the turn offs to Nunney. Turn right and follow the signs to the vineyard.

Nearby attractions: Longleat House, Stourhead House and Gardens, Bath, Wells, Cheddar, Sherborne and Glastonbury Tor.

Recommended pubs, restaurants and hotels in the area: Homewood Park Hotel.

WOOTTON VINEYARD

Major Colin Gillespie
North Wootton
Shepton Mallet BA4 4AG
☎ (074989) 359

The vineyard (a member of the EVA, the South West Vineyards Association, and with three other vineyards of the export company, Wines UK Ltd) covers 6 acres with a further acre still to be planted. Expansion plans include planting the additional acre and slowly replacing the existing vines as they reach 25 years of age. Varieties planted are Müller-Thurgau on 2.66 acres which accounts for 50 per cent of production, Schönburger on 2 acres (25 per cent), Seyval Blanc on an acre (25 per cent), and Auxerrois on 0.33 of an acre, accounting for 'almost nil' production.

There have been no changes to the varieties planted originally in 1971 and the additional acre will be planted with Schönburger and Seyval Blanc. The existing acreage of Müller-Thurgau will be replaced in the years ahead.

The vineyard is situated at between 70ft and 200ft above sea level on a south facing slope in the foothills of the Mendips. It is free from spring and autumn frosts and coastal fog although perhaps a bit too wet. The wind from the south-west is not excessive and there is no problem from hail.

The bulk of the vineyard is trained and pruned on Guyot trellises. There have been experiments with the Bordeaux Lyre and Geneva Double Curtain systems. Production from all systems seems to be identical over the years.

The new acre will be planted on steep slopes on the Mosel Gobelet system and will have no wires. There is a continuous programme of spraying during the growing system.

The winery at Wootton makes wine for fifteen small vineyards and can handle 75 tons of contract fruit which is vinified and sent back in their own label bottles.

The harvest of Wootton grapes has to dovetail in to the contract winemaking. Generally, the Müller-Thurgau are picked first because they are more vulnerable to botrytis. The earliest they have been picked is 4 October and the latest start is 5 November. The Seyval Blanc and Schönburger are kept on the vines because they do not rot, but there is a serious problem with birds and insects. Although there are nets for most of the vineyard, they are only used on the edges where the birds congregate.

The grapes are transported to the winery in a Chemo trailer which can take a ton of fruit. There are two German presses, a Howard 700l, and a Willmes 500l, which together can handle about 10 tons of grapes a day.

Crushing and pressing is always on the day of picking. The clear juice is racked after 12 hours, and the lees is filtered through an earth filter. After chaptalisation, fermentation is started using a German yeast. The temperature of the fermentation is between 59°F (15°C) and 68°F (20°C). The winery has forty-nine fermentation tanks.

After fermentation the wine stays on the yeast lees until December when it is racked off and filtered. The wine then goes through a series of analysis in the winery's laboratory to check alcohol, acid and sulphur dioxide, and is bottled in March. Bottling can run into several weeks, and in big years has been as late as September.

Latterly the warm winters have not provided the cold temperatures needed for tartaric acid in the wine to be deposited as crystals, and the winery has now been equipped with refrigeration to cool the tanks. The bottling machine is an eight-head model from Italy, and more than adequate for the winery's maximum capacity of 100,000 bottles a year.

Production over the last 5 years has been: 1984 — a big year with more than 30,000 bottles; 1985 — some lovely wines including the Gore Bore Trophy winner; 1986 — 12,000 bottles and a very good vintage; 1987 — 12,000 bottles, excellent vintage, two silver medal winners, and 1988 — 5,000 bottles, high sugar but low yields. The wines currently available are: Müller-Thurgau 1986, a medium wine full of flavours; Müller-Thurgau 1987, a silver medal winner, dry with a long after taste; Seyval 1987, a classy dry, bottled late so missed the wine competitions, and Schönburger 1987, a medium dry, silver medal wine, with Muscat flavours. The wine is sold direct from the winery and by many restaurants and hotels. It is exported when available through Wines UK Ltd.

The winery buildings date from the sixteenth century and combine rustic English charm with the ambience of a continental establishment. It is fully equipped with the latest equipment.

Colin Gillespie and his wife work in the vineyard and winery with two staff from the village. Up to twenty pickers are recruited for the harvest, and two or three extra hands for bottling. Expansion plans include planting the additional acre and slowly replacing the existing vines as they reach 25 years of age. The enterprise also includes 20 acres of grass which are grazed by black Welsh sheep.

Visiting times: Monday to Saturday 10am-1pm and 2-5pm. The wine shop sells wine, the vineyard's own coarse grained wine mustard, and a special Somerset punch made from apples to a 200-year-old recipe, which can be served hot or cold. It also sells vines. Visitors are welcome during opening hours to walk in the vineyard. Tours and tastings can be arranged for groups of between twenty-five and forty people. Catering can be provided.

How to get there: the vineyard lies to the south of Wells and west of Shepton Mallet between the A371 and A361. It is well signposted from the A361 and the A39.

Nearby attractions: Wells, city and cathedral, Glastonbury Abbey, Wookey Hole, Somerset Farm Museum and Cranmore Railway.

Recommended pubs, restaurants and hotels in the area: North Wootton Crossways Inn, with food and reasonable accommodation.

WRAXALL VINEYARD

A.S. and D.J. Holmes
Shepton Mallet BA4 6RQ
☎ (074986) 486

The vineyard (a member of the EVA, the South West Vineyards Association and Taste of Somerset) covers 5.75 acres. Varieties are Seyval Blanc on 2.25 acres and accounting for 45 per cent of production, Müller-Thurgau on 2.25 acres and accounting for 35 per cent of production, and Madeleine Angevine on 0.5 acres, and accounting for the remaining 20 per cent of production.

An impressive rack of Wootton Vineyard wine

Preparing the vineyard for the harvest

In recent years a number of experimental plantings—Kerner, Auxerrois, Zweigeltrebe, Wrotham Pinot, Gagarin Blue and Pinot Noir — have been grubbed out and replaced with Madeleine Angevine. There is just over 0.5 of an acre of new, as yet unproductive Madeleine Angevine vines.

The vineyard is planted on a good south facing slope at the bottom edge of the Mendips and rather exposed to winds. The soil is excellent — deep loam overlying clay. It is not a good suntrap and exposure to the southwesterly winds can sometimes be a drawback although this problem has partly been helped by tall windbreaks.

The vineyard was founded in 1973 when the family acquired the 10-acre site. Five acres of vines were planted in 1974 and trained on the high wire Geneva Double Curtain system. The vines are trained along wires 5ft high and the annual growth is allowed to hang down. The varieties planted were Müller-Thurgau and Seyval Blanc, the two most commonly grown in England at the time. In 1977 as a result of its promising performance on trial, an acre of Madeleine Angevine was planted.

The first commercial harvest was gathered in 1976 and since then the vineyard has been making good consistent wine both for itself and other local growers. Pruning starts in January and continues until March. All the vines are trained and pruned according to the Geneva Double Curtain system.

Tar oil is sprayed during the winter and there is mildew control throughout the summer using a tractor-mounted mist-blower sprayer. There are usually between five and six applications of spray during the summer. Weed control in the vine rows is done by hand using herbicide sprays.

The average harvest yields about 12,500 bottles. The Madeleine Angevine is usually the first variety to be picked and ready in late September or early October. The Müller-Thurgau is normally picked in the middle of October and the Seyval Blanc late in the month.

In a good year with decent yields the harvest takes 2 to 3 weeks. The grapes are picked with the help of friends and local pickers and milled and pressed in the purpose-built winery. The grapes are crushed through a de-stalking machine and pressed using wooden slat-sided presses. Fibreglass fermentation tanks are used. Between 6 and 8 weeks after fermentation the wine is racked to other tanks, and then coarse filtered, usually in February. It is sterile filtered before bottling, normally in April.

The 1987 is regarded as the best vintgage to date. Wines produced are: Wraxall Müller-Thurgau–Seyval, crisp, clean medium dry to dry, fragrant nose, fruity and with a crisp, clean finish. It is more like a Loire-style than German and Wraxall Madeleine Angevine, medium dry with more distinctive flavour. Separate wines are made from Müller-Thurgau and Seyval Blanc in years when there is a surplus of either variety.

Visiting times: casual visitors are welcome all year round and pre-booked groups from June to September. As much of the wine as possible is sold from the vineyard. There are a few long standing trade customers, and the wine is sold in some hotels, restaurants and at the occasional show or fair. The vineyard does not have its own shop, but wine, cider and other local wines can be purchased at any time. Rooted vines and cuttings are also sold. The wine bar is open to the public 4 days a week (Thursday to Sunday) from June to September and serves local food.

How to get there: the vineyard is signposted just off the A37, 5 miles south of Shepton Mallet.

Nearby attractions: Glastonbury Tor, East Somerset Railway at Cranmore, Fleet Air Arm Museum, Yeovilton, Montacute House, Lytes Cary Manor, Tintinhull House and Garden, Barrington Court, Hadspen House and Brympton d'Evercy.

The Fleet Air Arm Museum, Yeovilton

Avon

THORNBURY CASTLE VINEYARD

Maurice Taylor
Thornbury
Nr Bristol BS12 1HH
☎ (0454) 418511

Thornbury Castle merits a special mention in any guide on English vineyards. It is the only Tudor castle in England operated as an hotel, and it is set in its own magnificent grounds, which includes the vineyard and walled garden. Although the vineyard is not open to the public, the wines can be drunk in the sumptious hotel and restaurant.

The one-acre vineyard is planted with only Müller-Thurgau, and the vines were planted about 12 years ago. The grapes are vinified and bottled by the Three Choirs Vineyard at Newent in Gloucestershire.

The hotel, once owned by Henry VIII, has won many accolades for its luxurious accommodation and cuisine, and has been rated 'one of the 300 best hotels in the world'. The former dungeons house an exceptional cellar of fine and rare wines. Work on the castle started in 1511 for Edward Stafford, the third Duke of Buckingham, who 10 years later was executed for treason. Henry VIII and Anne Boleyn stayed here and Mary Tudor lived here for many years.

Facilities include personally guided tours of the area, ballooning from the castle, clay pigeon shooting and the restaurant. The castle has a helicopter pad but likes to be advised about landings in advance.

Visiting times: the vineyard is not open to the public, but the restaurant is open all the year for luncheon and dinner, with the exception of 10 days in January. The hotel is open thoughout the year, other than for 5 days over Christmas.

How to get there: Thornbury Castle lies on the northern edge of the small town of Thornbury, 5 miles from the Severn Bridge, and the junctions of the M4 and M5 motorways. From London leave the M5 at junction 20, from Wales leave the M4 at junction 21. From the West Country leave the M5 at junction 16, and from the Midlands at junction 14.

Nearby attractions: Slimbridge Wildfowl Trust, Berkeley and Sudeley Castle, Badminton House, Castle Combe, Lacock, Bath, Chepstow and Cheltenham — all with their racecourses — and Bristol.

WASHINGPOOL VINEYARD

C.R. and A.M. Wright
Washingpool
Severn View
Washingpool Hill
Ridgeway
Bristol BS12 2SD
☎ (0454) 617410

The vineyard (a member of the EVA and the South West Vineyards Association) covers an acre with a further 5 acres still to be planted when the owner is certain he can make a 'presentable wine'. Varieties grown are Siegerrebe 300 vines, Triomphe D'Alsace 330 vines, Leon Millot 200 vines, Madeleine Angevine 200 vines, Riesling 75 vines, Chardonnay 170 vines and Pinot Noir 75 vines. The Riesling is being grubbed out during 1989 and replaced with Huxelrebe.

The vineyard is on a south-west facing slope on sandy loam overlying sandstone, at about 525ft above sea level, overlooking the Severn estuary. The vineyard is exposed to the prevailing south-west winds, but sheltered from the north and east winds.

All the vines are trained and pruned on the Double Guyot system. Weed control is by cultivation and there is a spraying programme to combat mildew and botrytis. The first vintage was harvested in 1988 on single Guyot. The vines grow below the house and the garage is used as the winery. A 901 hydro press is used which works on three bar water pressure.

The yield from the first vintage was about 1.5 tons of grapes from six varieties, and the harvest was spread out. Fermentation took place in a variety of containers, mostly old fruit juice barrels, and the varieties were fermented separately.

At the time of writing the wine had not been bottled, but the owners intend to bottle the varieties individually to see how they develop. However, the aim eventually is to produce blended wines.

Visiting times: none at present, although seriously interested people could ask for an appointment.

How to get there: head for Bristol on the M5 and leave the motorway at junction 16 taking the A38 towards Thornbury. After about 2 miles you reach the village of Ridgeway, take the first left down Washingpool Hill, and the vineyard is on your left.

Devon

DOWN ST MARY VINEYARD

Leigh Barclay and Tony Sandbach
The Old Mill
Down St Mary EX17 6EE
☎ (03633) 300

Work on the vineyard is carried out almost entirely by the owners who live on the premises. The winemaker is Tony Sandbach. The vineyard (a member of the EVA and the South West Vineyards Association) covers 3.5 acres with a further 2 acres to be planted in 1990. The varieties planted are Huxelrebe 0.5 acres, Madeleine Angevine 0.7 acres, Reichensteiner 0.4 acres, Schönburger 0.5 acres, Siegerrebe 0.9 acres, and experimental varieties 0.3 acres.

The vineyard is 4 years old, there have been no changes to the original varieties planted, and all the vines are new and as yet unproductive. The vineyard is on a steep, south facing slope in mid-Devon about 300ft above sea level. The climate is equable and the soil is silty clay loam.

The vines are pruned in February and March and trained on the Double Guyot system. Minimal spraying is carried out using traditional sulphur and copper based fungicides to combat mildew and botrytis.

The various varieties were selected to give a staggered harvest. Madeleine Angevine and Siegerrebe will be the first varieties to be picked, and Schönburger the last.

The vineyard was planted in 1985 and only a small non-commercial harvest was gathered in 1988. The policy will be to crush and lightly press the grapes on the same day as harvesting and to cold ferment the must so as to preserve the full flavours of the grapes. The winery is under construction in an old water mill.

Visiting times: by appointment at present until sales commence in 1990. Vines and honey are already on sale from the vineyard. Beekeeping is one of the vineyard's other enterprises. There are tasting facilities and an informal picnic site and tours of the vineyard can be arranged.

How to get there: take the A377 Crediton to Barnstaple and a short way after passing through the village of Copplestone take a left turning signposted for Down St Mary. At the village green take the lane signposted for Zeal Monachorum. The Old Mill is three quarters of a mile down this road beside the river.

FOLLYMOOR VINEYARD

Mr and Mrs Cliff Leslie
Moorlake
Crediton EX17 5EL
☎ (03632) 2767

The vineyard is 6 miles out of Exeter, on a gentle south facing slope in the Yeo Valley on Devon red soil. The vineyard benefits from its location in the lee of Dartmoor. It was established in 1988 and the vines will be trained on the Double Guyot system in due course. All the vineyard work is carried out by the owner. It is part of a 4-acre site with the house and garden extending to an acre, the orchard an acre and the vineyard 2 acres. If the present planting is successful it is planned to expand the vineyard after 5 or 6 years.

The vineyard (a member of the EVA and the South West Vineyards Association) covers approximately 2 acres of recently planted vines and there are plans to

Down St Mary, the house and vineyard

increase the plot by a further acre depending on the success of the present project. Varieties planted are divided equally between Reichensteiner and Kernling. None of the vines is yet productive.

Visiting times: none at present but hopes to open to the public when the vineyard is established.

How to get there: directions from the owners.

HIGHFIELD VINEYARDS

I.M. and J.M. Fraser
Long Drag Hill
Tiverton EX16 5NF
☎ (0884) 256362

The vineyard (a member of the EVA and the South West Vineyards Association) covers 3 acres. Varieties planted are Madeleine Angevine 0.5 acres, Kernling an acre, Siegerrebe 1.5 acres plus four tunnels containing Scheurebe and Gerwürztraminer.

There have been no changes to the original varieties planted, but there is an acre each of Siegerrebe and Kernling vines which are new, and as yet unproductive.

The vineyard is situated on a south facing slope about 400ft above sea level. It is on sandy loam soil with good drainage and enjoys a humid and warm climate.

There is a tendency for generally mild damp winters with little sun and above average rainfall in the summer necessitating a spray programme every 10 days during the ripening period to combat mildew and fungal diseases.

Pruning starts in January and continues until March. The vines are trained on the Double Guyot and Pendalbogen systems of training. During this period fertiliser is applied.

In March and April weed control starts in earnest and there is general post and wire replacement. In late April and May there is budburst and the spraying programme starts. In June there is disbudding and spraying continues, and from July to October there is summer pruning and regular spraying. The vines get a winter wash during November and December. The harvest generally starts at the end of September or early in October with Siegerrebe being the first variety to be picked. It is followed by Madeleine Angevine with Kernling last. The vineyard uses a fairly ordinary grape crusher which gives the option of de-stalking. A basket type hydraulic press is used, and German plastic fermentation tanks are used.

Wines currently produced are all varietals — Siegerrebe, Madeleine Angevine and Scheurebe. In 1988 the three wines from the previous vintage all won top awards from the South West Vineyards Association's annual competition. The Siegerrebe was judged the best estate made wine of any year in the competition. The vineyard is run almost entirely by the owners except during the harvest and bottling time when extra help is recruited.

Visiting times: open all the year, Monday to Saturday 10am-6pm, closed Sunday. The wine is sold direct from the winery shop on the vineyard and through normal retail outlets. The old coach and stable block has been converted to the winery and shop. The enterprise also specialises in miniature geraniums and ivies, and manufactures specialist chutneys and mustards. There are tasting facilities and vineyard tours with catering which can be arranged in advance.

How to get there: the vineyard is well signposted and is a mile out of Tiverton on the A373 to Witheridge.

LODDISWELL VINEYARD

R.H. and B.E. Sampson
Lilwell
Loddiswell
Kingsbridge
South Devon TQ7 4EF
☎ (0548) 550221

The vineyard (a member of the EVA, the South West Vineyards Association, Devon Fare and the South and West Devon Tourist Attractions) covers 7 acres. Four acres were planted in 1977 and it was extended to its present acreage in 1986. There are no plans to expand the vineyard at present.

The original plantings were an acre each of Huxelrebe, Müller-Thurgau, Reichensteiner and a mixture of Siegerrebe, Bacchus and others. In 1986 the vineyard was expanded with the planting of 1.75 acres of Reichensteiner, a quarter of an acre each of Siegerrebe and Seyval Blanc and half an acre of assorted varieties. All the 1986 plantings are as yet unproductive.

The vineyard is situated in south Devon about 4 miles from the sea. The site is 300ft to 345ft above sea level and faces south-

south-west. The soil is medium loam overlying Devonian shale and is free draining. Average rainfall is 41in a year.

As the vineyard is situated in the heart of the South Hams it is affected by a maritime climate, giving warm winters and an early spring, rarely suffering from a frost after the second week of April. In the late seventies and early eighties the summers were good, but since 1985 the cold weather experienced in July and August has had a detrimental effect on the crop.

After experimenting with a small trial plot planted in 1972, the commercial vineyard was planted in 1977 with 6,000 vines, all on the Double Guyot system. The new vineyard is trained on the Karl Merz system. The buds burst in April and flowering starts during the first week in July and in warm weather the berries are fully set by the third week of the month. Each cane carries two or three bunches of grapes which slowly swell and mature. There is a programme of spraying during the summer to protect against a number of mildews.

The vineyard established a section of seven polytunnels in 1981, extended to ten in 1983, covering 700 vines of the three main varieties, so the harvest normally starts with the early varieties from the tunnels in September, finishing with the outdoor varieties in mid-October.

The tunnel grapes have high sugar and low acidity, and in good years about 20 per cent of this production is blended with the outdoor grapes to provide a better balance of acids and increase the overall sugar content to enhance the quality of the wine. The vines in the tunnels do not receive any irrigation, but the ground is well manured to provide nutrients and hold the moisture levels.

To protect the vines and the tunnels, natural windbreaks have been planted. These were originally willows, but have now been replaced with Italian Alder and Western red cedar where winter protection is also required.

The grapes are hand picked into flat polythene buckets, then transferred into bins and transported to the winery, where they are crushed and pressed. The juice is left to settle for 12 hours before the clean juice is pumped to the cellar for fermentation. A low temperature German style yeast is added and fermentation usually lasts for about 3 weeks. All testing and adjustment for specific gravity and acidity are done before fermentation.

The winery equipment includes a Ross crusher and de-stemmer, a Vaslin 300l rotary press and a Vaslin 1,300l automatic rotary press. There is a Mono pump, Seitz bottle sulphuriser, a Friederick filler, Cavomatic ten bottle filler, corker and capper, and a Purdy special labeller.

The winery has seventeen fibreglass tanks ranging in size from 300l to 2,500l, and with a combined capacity of 23,600l. When fermentation ceases, the wine is racked on the next two consecutive weeks and then left for about 4 weeks. It is then tested for levels of sulphur dioxide, acidity, alcohol, volatile acidity, protein and so on. Any adjustments are made at this stage. At the end of January the wines receive their first coarse filter and then a secondary filtration, before being bottled in late spring. The wine is then stored in bottle for 10 to 12 months before capping and labelling for sale.

Production in 1983 was 12,000 bottles, and this rose to 19,000 in the bumper year of 1984. Since then production has been hit by bad summers, 1985 — 7,000 bottles, and in 1986 and 1987 8,000 bottles each. Production in 1988 was 9,200 bottles. All the wines submitted since 1983 have received the EVA Seal of Quality and many have won prestigious awards.

Wines currently produced are: Loddiswell Huxelrebe 1985, commended by the South West Vineyards Association in 1986, and Loddiswell Medium Sweet, 1986 gold medal, and also commended by the South West Vineyards Association, 1987.

All wines prior to 1986 have been sold. There are a few remaining stocks of 1986 and half the 1987 vintage has already been sold. About three-quarters of the wine produced is sold through the vineyard shop, about 15 per cent is sold to hotels and pubs, and the remaining 10 per cent is sold to the distributive trade.

Visiting times: Easter to end of October 1-6pm Monday to Thursday, and Sundays in

July and August together with bank holiday weekends. The vineyard is run with the help of one full-time worker, and a part-time student helper during the summer. The owners conduct tours of the vineyard and the winery. There is a shop and tea room. The vineyard shop also sells apple wine and vines. There are guided tours, tastings, a video of the vineyard year, children's play area, tea room, picnic area and ample car parking. Groups (minimum twenty) are welcome if arranged in advance.

How to get there: the vineyard is situated 2 miles north of Loddiswell and 2 miles south of California Cross, off the former B3196. From Exeter take the A38 to Plymouth. After South Brent take the Wrangton Cross turn-off and follow the signs to Loddiswell. The vineyard is well signposted.

Nearby attractions: Dartington Cider Press Centre, Bowden House, Kingsbridge and its miniature railway, Cookworthy Museum of rural life, National Shire Horse Centre, Yealmpton, Kitley Caves, Saltram House, Dartmoor and the Dartmoor Wild Life Park and Falconry Centre.

MANSTREE VINEYARD

Mr and Mrs G. Symons
Shillingford St George
Exeter EX2 9QR
☎ (0392) 832218

The vineyard (a member of the EVA and South West Vineyards Association) covers 3.3 acres with a further 17 acres under consideration. Varieties planted and in production are Müller-Thurgau 0.54 acres, which will eventually account for 15 per cent, Madeleine Angevine 0.15 acres (7 per cent), Seyval Blanc 0.15 acres (7 per cent), and Chardonnay 0.45 acres (14 per cent). Varieties of new, as yet unproductive vines are Bacchus 0.94 acres (25 per cent), Seyval Blanc 0.74 acres (20 per cent), and Schönburger 0.4 acres (10 per cent).

The vineyard is in the lee of Dartmoor and Haldon Hill on the west side of the Exe estuary. The area has one of the driest summer climates in the UK. The vineyard is situated on old red sandstone on a steep southern slope between 150ft and 200ft above sea level.

The average rainfall is about 31in a year, with proportionately higher precipitation in winter than average. The high ground to the west gives a break in the cloud cover leading to above average sunshine levels for the area. The proximity to the estuary reduces the severity of frosts even though the vineyard is in a valley, and the site has very good air drainage.

The vineyard gets its name from the road that passes it and from a nearby field, indicating it was once the site of a gallows for the execution of sheep stealers and other felons. The owner of the vineyard is a descendant of the poet A.E. Houseman.

All the vines are trained and pruned according to the Double Guyot system. The rows are 10ft apart and the vines spaced 4ft apart in the rows. They are treated with a tar oil wash prior to winter pruning. There is routine fungicide spraying from budburst onwards to protect against powdery and downy mildew and botrytis. Action has to be taken to control wasps but so far birds have not proved a problem.

The vineyard uses pre-emergent herbicides and keeps the soil bare during the growing season using spot treatment when necessary. The gravelly nature of the bare soil gives good heat reflection and with the very open drainage there is little problem from erosion.

The harvest usually starts in the middle of October with Madeleine Angevine and Müller-Thurgau being harvested. The Seyval Blanc is normally picked in late

Exeter Cathedral

October, and the Chardonnay in early November. The other varieties when in production should fit into this pattern. The current harvest, depending on volume, is gathered within 2 days.

The vineyard does not have its own winery and the grapes are taken by road to Wootton where Major Gillespie makes the wine under contract, carrying out the pressing, vinification and bottling.

The first harvest was in 1984 when 1,200 bottles of medium dry Seyval Blanc were produced. This rose to 2,500 bottles in 1985. A medium dry blended wine was produced together with a medium blend to which *süss* reserve was added. In 1986 1,500 bottles of medium blended wine was produced, again with the addition of *süss* reserve and in 1987, 700 bottles of a blended medium dry which was awarded the EVA Seal of Quality. The 1988 harvest yielded about 1,300 bottles, but at the time of writing had not been returned from the maker. The 1986 was not a vintage year, but the wine has continued to develop in the bottle and created a very appealing fruity bouquet. The 1987 produced the vineyard's best wine to date, with good body and fruit, and very smooth. Most of the wine is sold locally from the vineyard, or through wholesalers to inns and hotels.

The vineyard is part of an agricultural enterprise which also includes a large pick-your-own fruit farm, with fifteen different soft fruits grown on 12 acres, and a seventy-head intensive bull beef unit. More than thirty types of dried flower material are also grown on the farm, and sold in bunches or arrangements. They are available from the farm shop between June and October, and from the farmhouse by appointment during the rest of the year.

The vineyard is run by the owner with the help of a full-time student. Temporary and casual staff taken on to help with the 'pick-your-own' and dried flower business also help out with summer pruning.

About half the vine stock is planted on its own roots, the rest on grafted German rootstock. The vineyard is part of a 17-acre sloping site running down the valley and all suitable for planting. A feasibility study is currently underway to assess the economics of expansion. One avenue being explored is that production from an expanded acreage could be sold under contract to other vineyards who are actively seeking grapes to meet their demand for English wine.

Visiting times: the vineyard and 'pick-your-own' is open to visitors free of charge 9am-6pm 7 days a week from the middle of June to the end of July, and from 9am-5pm Monday to Friday in August and September, 9am-1pm, Saturdays and closed on Sundays. At other times by appointment. The vineyard offers tastings and there is a children's farm trail. There is a picnic site with panoramic views, ample car parking, toilets and play area. There are also the 'pick-your-own' and dried flower enterprises.

How to get there: the vineyard lies south of Exeter, less than a mile and a half from the city boundary at Alphington. Follow the road through Alphington to Shillingford St George, and the vineyard is well signposted.

Nearby attractions: Devon and Exeter racecourse, Powderham Castle, Exeter Cathedral and Exeter Maritime Museum.

Recommended pubs, restaurants and hotels in the area: The Huntsman (Ide), The Nobody Inn (Doddiscombeleigh), The Devon Motel (Matford, Exeter).

SAUL'S VINEYARD

Dr Nigel Kemp
Saul's Farm
Wembworthy
Nr Chulmleigh EX18 17RW
☎ (0769) 80750

The vineyard (a member of the EVA and the South West Vineyards Association) covers 3.27 acres and a further 2 acres are planned, one each of Seyval Blanc and Madeleine Angevine. All the vines are trained on the Guyot system and varieties planted are: Pinot Blanc, 1,000 vines planted in 1986 on 0.96 acres which will account for 30 per cent of production, Schönburger, 1,000 vines planted in 1986 on 0.8 acres (25 per cent), Huxelrebe, 1,000 vines planted in 1987 on 0.85 acres (25 per cent), and Bacchus, 700 vines planted in 1987 on 0.66 acres which will account for 20 per cent of production. The first vintage is expected in 1989 with Pinot Blanc being harvested.

The vineyard is in mid-Devon, half way between Exmoor and Dartmoor in the Taw valley. It is on a sunny, south to south-east facing slope between 200ft and 300ft above sea level. It is well protected from the prevailing westerly winds and rain, as well as from the north on mid-Devon loam overlying sandstone.

Weed control is by the use of plastic mulch in the rows of vines, with grass grown in the lanes. The application of herbicide and pesticide sprays is kept to the absolute minimum.

Visiting times: by appointment only from 1990. The vineyard, which surrounds a thatched farmhouse, is worked by the owner and his wife. There is also a cider orchard, woodlands, wetlands, stream and forest, all of which attract a great deal of wildlife.

How to get there: turn off the Exeter to Barnstaple road at Eggesford Station (19 miles from Exeter). Cross the railway crossing and continue towards Wembworthy. At the top of the hill, turn right and continue through the forest and after about half a mile the vineyard and thatched farmhouse will be seen on a facing slope.

Nearby attractions: the Taw river, Forestry Commission forest at Eggesford.

The Guildhall, Totnes

SHARPHAM VINEYARD
Mr M.A. Ash, Miss C.F. Ash and Mr M. Sharman
Sharpham House
Ashprington
Totnes TQ9 7UT
☎ (080423) 203

The vineyard (a member of the EVA and the South West Vineyards Association) covers 4.75 acres, 0.5 acres planted in 1989, and a further 3.25 acres to be planted in 1990 to bring the total area under vines to 8 acres. The first vines were planted in 1981 with further plantings in 1984, 1987 and 1989.

The varieties planted are Reichensteiner 2 acres, Huxelrebe 1.25 acres, Madeleine Angevine 0.8 acres (0.5 acres planted in 1989), Pinot Noir 0.33 acres, and others 0.33 acres. A further 3 acres of Madeleine Angevine are planned for 1990.

In the last few years Seibel and Gewürztraminer have been grubbed out as well as some inferior Madeleine Angevine. All were replaced by better strains of Madeleine Angevine. The acreage of new, as yet unproductive vines is Reichensteiner 1.5 acres, and Huxelrebe an acre.

The vineyard is set in typical picturesque rolling Devon countryside, dominated by the river Dart which flows right past the bottom of the vineyards. The vineyard is on the side of an east-west valley that runs down to the river Dart. The slope is quite steep and curves round at each end to form a huge amphitheatre.

Sharpham House with its imposing Georgian façade, is set on a rise and is often mistaken for a Calendar house. The area was once volcanic and an old volcano can still be seen on the farm. The soil is red Devon loam.

The vineyard has a unique microclimate because of its sheltered location on a south facing slope protected from the prevailing south-west winds by the surrounding hills. Rainfall is below average for the area and the proximity of the river means there is little risk from frosts.

From January to March the vines are pruned and trained using either the Double Guyot system or Double Pendelbogen method. In April and May there is vigorous growth and the major task is controlling weeds. A minimum spray programme is used, however, and it is based on sulphur, zinc and copper, always with an eye on the weather to ensure the timing is right. Flowering and trimming of the vine tops takes place in late June or July.

At present the wine is made elsewhere but a purpose built winery is under construction and should be completed in 1990. The harvest at the moment is geared to picking the grapes as fast as possible and transferring them by road to the winery also as quickly as possible.

It is the Madeleine Angevine that can sometimes ripen as early as September, and it is followed by the Reichensteiner and Huxelrebe through October and the Pinot Noir last in November if the weather holds. The harvest has been as early as September but usually takes place in October. The vineyard has a full time manager and employs casual staff occasionally when necessary. Harvesting involves about twenty pickers for just a day.

The area is fortunate in that the weather often stays fine, well into November, and the pickers have the pleasure of picking the ripe red grapes in the November sun with the leaves of the vine turning glorious shades of red and yellow.

The first small harvest was gathered in 1986 when 365 bottles were made. In 1987, 520 bottles of wine were made and the 1988 vintage is expected to yield 1,200 bottles from a good crop despite the poor summer. The crop yielded the equivalent of 3 tons an acre. The 1986 produced a blend of Madeleine Angevine and Huxelrebe which has now developed into a delicate medium dry wine. The 1987 wine was the same blend, and produced a lively medium dry wine with a powerful bouquet. The 1988 blend has Reichensteiner added for the first time, but at the time of writing had not been bottled.

Visiting times: visiting times for 1990 have yet to be finalised so by appointment until then. The wines are sold in local pubs and village shops. Because of the limited supply to date no effort has been made to extend sales outside the locality. The winery, tasting area and wine shop are due for completion in 1990. Other facilities will include vineyard trail, picnic area, farm and riverside walks. The vineyard sells locally produced organic cider and red wine vinegar. The winery farm shop will sell other products from the estate, including cow, goat and sheep cheeses, fruit, vegetables and eggs.

How to get there: take the A381 Dartmouth and Kingsbridge road south from Totnes. After about 2.5 miles take the road signposted to Ashprington. The vineyard is part of the Sharpham estate and is on the banks of the river Dart.

Nearby attractions: Totnes, Berry Pomeroy Castle, Compton Castle, Dartmouth, Torquay and Kingsbridge, many beaches, Buckfast Abbey, Dart Valley steam railway, Devon Shire Horse, Dartmoor.

Recommended pubs, hotels and restaurants in the area: the vineyard can recommend many excellent local pubs and accommodation to suit all tastes and pockets.

WHITSTONE VINEYARDS

George and Laura Barclay
Bovey Tracey
Devon TQ13 9NA
☎ (0626) 832280

The vineyard (a member of the EVA, the South West Vineyards Association and Devon Fair) covers 1.5 acres and no futher expansion is planned. Varieties are an acre of 700 Müller-Thurgau vines and half an acre of 300 Madeleine Angevine vines. Each variety accounts for 50 per cent of production. There have been no changes to the varieties planted, and there are no new, as yet unproductive vines.

The vineyard is on a south-west slope over the Bovey Valley looking towards Dartmoor at a height of between 250ft and 350ft above sea level. The soil is acid and rocky but drains well. The vineyard gets quite a lot of rain and sea mists being on the seaward side of Dartmoor.

In the last 10 years there has also been a change in the prevailing winds which have gradually swung round from south-westerly to north-westerly bringing colder air in during the growing season.

The vineyard was started in November 1974 by the Barclays, an American couple who have lived in England for about 20 years. The first harvest was gathered in 1978 when twenty-four bottles were produced. In 1981, with almost all the vines productive, 650 bottles were produced and the first commercial sales were made. By 1984 the vintage was yielding 12 tons of grapes.

All the vines are trained and pruned on the Geneva Double Curtain system. Winter pruning starts in December and takes until March, all the work being carried out by the owners. The vineyard does not usually require fertiliser dressing but is treated with lime because of the acidity of the soil. There is a regular spraying programme at approximately 2 week intervals, which starts in June and continues until September to protect against various types of mildews. Weedkiller sprays are used as required using a back-pack sprayer. The entire vineyard is netted about mid-September until picking to protect the grapes from bird attack.

Müller-Thurgau is the first variety to be picked, usually in the first or second week of October. It is followed by Madeleine Angevine about a week later. The volunteer pickers are all friends and neighbours, so the grapes are always harvested at weekends. A picking team of about fifty can pick each variety in about 3 hours at the rate of about a ton an hour. The vineyard does not have its own winery and the grapes are taken by road immediately to Wootton Vineyard in Somerset for vinification and bottling.

Whitstone, like a number of other vineyards which contract their winemaking to Colin Gillespie, has its own fermentation and storage tanks at Wootton, so that its must and wine can be kept separate from that of other producers.

The wine is tasted in January and a final decision on how to finish it off is made by Whitstone. It is then bottled in March or April and moved back to Whitstone Vineyards.

In 1984 production was 12,000 bottles,

Sharpham Vineyard

Compton Castle, a place of interest near Sharpham Vineyard

9,000 Müller-Thurgau and 3,000 Madeleine Angevine. In 1985, after a bad summer, production was 2,000 bottles, 1,000 each of Müller-Thurgau and Madeleine Angevine. In 1986 only 1,000 bottles were produced and a blend of the two varieties was made because of such poor yields. The 1987 production was 2,000 bottles, 800 of Müller-Thurgau and 1,200 of Madeleine Angevine, and the 1988 production is about 1,200 bottles although the mix was not known at the time of writing.

Due to bad weather the levels in recent years has fallen and the 1988 vintage was particularly disappointing, especially after the tremendous potential shown earlier on in the year.

Wines produced include: 1986 Madeleine Angevine–Müller-Thurgau blend, bone dry, crisp and fruity (each bottle was numbered because of its rarity), 1987 Müller-Thurgau dry, fruity with a smokey aftertaste, an excellent aperitif and 1987 Madeleine Angevine , dry and fruity and good with food. The 1988 is not available yet but will probably be a blend. All of the wines since 1981 have won the EVA Seal of Quality. Most of the wine is sold from the farm gate but there are regular sales to local restaurants and hotels, and some sales in London and Scotland.

Visiting times: by appointment any time. From 1 June to 1 September, Monday to Friday before noon for buying wine. August open days are every Tuesday and the bank holiday from 10am-5pm. Closed Sundays. The vineyard does not have its own winery but there is a small tasting room and shop overlooking the vineyard, which also sells vines, vegetables, herbs and items promoting the vineyard. Special group tours lasting about an hour can be arranged for any time of the year but summer evenings are best. Groups are limited to thirty people.

How to get there: the vineyard is on the edge of the village of Bovey Tracey. Take the A38 Exeter to Plymouth road and follow the signs to Bovey Tracey. The vineyard is on the right off the A382 road to Moreton Hampstead just after leaving the village.

Nearby attractions: Dartmoor, Devon Guild of Craftsmen Centre and Museum in Bovey Tracey, Drogo Castle and Compton Castle, Saltram.

Recommended pubs, restaurants and hotels in the area: The Nobody Inn, Doddiscombeleigh.

YEARLSTONE VINEYARD
Gillian Pearkes
Bickleigh
Nr Tiverton
☎ (03635) 302

The vineyard is a member of the EVA, the South West Vineyards Association, Devon Fare and Devon Harvest, both marketing organisations to produce food and drink from the county. It covers 2 acres with plans to expand it up to 5 acres by 1990. Varieties planted are Madeleine Angevine on 0.5 acres which accounts for 35 per cent of production, Siegerrebe on 0.5 acres (35 per cent), Chardonnay and Pinot Noir on 0.33 acres (15 per cent), and other red varieties on 0.33 acres accounting for the remaining 15 per cent. There is also a 0.33-acre plot devoted to trial and research work. In 1983 and 1984 the Siegerrebe, Chardonnay and red wine areas were all increased.

The vineyard is situated in the valley of the river Exe on a hot, quite steep sided valley with an alluvial plain of water meadows at river level. At Bickleigh the river Exe is joined by its tributary the Little Dart which creates the dramatic due south facing amphitheatre-like site on which the vineyard is situated.

The famous Devon red soil, a silty clay loam, covers the fragmented Devonian sandstone and mudstone to a depth of between 9in and a foot.

Although it is a fertile but very hungry soil the owner can exercise total control over the vigour and nourishment of the vines. A vine kept on poorer soil and on the hungry side of well fed will produce grapes and ripen them well, whereas a richer soil produces masses of cane and leaf, and due to the massive growth at the hottest time of the year which usually coincides with flowering, is unable to cope with setting and

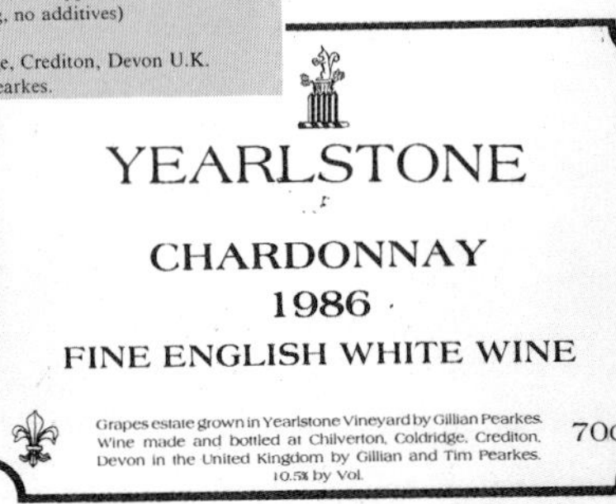

yearlstone
FINE ENGLISH TABLE WINE
from
devon
MADELEINE ANGEVINE
Estate Grown and bottled in the Exe Valley by Gillian Pearkes.
Chilton, Bickleigh, Tiverton, Devon, United Kingdom.
70cl
minimum contents

Various products from the Yearlstone Vineyard, Devon

yields are hit.

The vineyard has a remarkably favourable microclimate and enjoys an early spring and a long, late warm autumn. Being situated in the giant amphitheatre rising from river level to 500ft above sea level, the site is very open and dry and sunny. The vineyard often enjoys sunshine when it is raining just to the north or south and gets an average 28in to 30in of rainfall a year.

The vineyard was planted in 1976 by Gillian Pearkes, and is laid out on traditional French and German lines, vines spaced 4ft apart in both directions, a system which is highly labour intensive in that most of the work is necessarily done by hand. The high density of vines per acre means each vine bears a relatively moderate crop of grapes, but on an acreage bases the overall crop is high as is the quality and ripeness of the grapes.

It is run by Gillian with the help of one full-time worker. The aim has always been to have the highest possible input of technical viticulture, to keep ahead of trouble wherever possible, and to use as many aids as possible to achieve a good flowering and set however awkward the weather conditions. The winemaker is brother Tim, who also produces the apple wine and cyders, and looks after visitors.

The vineyard is visited by many viticulturalists and winemakers from all parts of the world, and Gillian travels abroad extensively researching and lecturing. In 1984 she was a guest speaker at the first Cold Climate Viticultural Conference in Oregon.

Winter pruning starts in January and continues into February. All the vines are trained and pruned according to the Double Guyot system. During March and April the vineyard is manured, trellises are repaired and the programme of weed control starts.

The first spray application takes place in April or May, and disbudding takes place to reduce the number of buds between twelve and fourteen on each vine. There is a second spraying in June or July, the vines are topped and flowering takes place. In mid-July there is a third spray and topping continues, and in August the final spray is applied.

The harvest usually starts between 15 and 21 September with Siegerrebe being the first variety to be picked. Madeleine Angevine is usually picked around the 28 September and the red varieties and Chardonnay is harvested from 21 October.

With the exception of the section devoted to Chardonnay, with some Pinot Noir and Pinot Gris, three early ripening varieties were deliberately planted which can be harvested fully ripe in good years and nearly ripe in the off years. These varieties give wines with good extract, natural sugar, balance and body. The Siegerrebe ripen every year to 80 Oechsle by the 15 to 21 September.

The staggered harvest begins with the 0.33 acres of Siegerrebe, a Madeleine Angevine cross with Gewürztraminer, which ripens to the most glorious old gold dull red colour with the most exotic spicy aroma. Yield ranges from 0.5 tons to 2 tons an acre, and hopefully will rise to 3 tons as the new area starts to bear fully in 1989 and 1990. The yield depends on the weather during flowering as Siegerrebe is a very temperamental variety and requires hot, dry bouyant conditions at this time. Between 10 per cent and 15 per cent of noble rot is welcomed as this increases the complexity of the wine.

By 25 to 28 September picking of the Madeleine Angevine has started. Being a very thin skinned variety the grapes become more vulnerable to wind and rain and subsequent botrytis damage as they ripen. They are checked daily and at the first sign of botrytis the decision is taken to start picking.

As the vineyard aims to make a French rather than a German style wine, it tries to avoid the Germanic noble rot flavour, preferring instead, an Alsatian clean, dry, natural style.

It usually takes 5 days to harvest the Madeleine Angevine and an Oechsle level of between 65° and 75° is reached according to the year from a yield of between 1.5 tons and 2 tons.

From 14 to 21 October, and sometimes as late as 24 October, the Triomphe D'Alsace and Leon Millot grapes are picked for the red wine. The Leon Millot are totally disease free and require no spraying, but the Triomphe D'Alsace can attract odium as they ripen and this is combatted by a sulphur spray in early September.

The Leon Millot are always a few days behind the Triomphe D'Alsace from budburst to veraison, but seems to catch up by the harvest. The aim is to harvest all the red wine grapes in one day. The Oechsle rating ranges from 65° to 75° in average years and up to 97° in hot years like 1983 and 1984. The yield is from half a ton to one ton, but this will increase as the new area comes into full Double Guyot production by 1989. The Chardonnay, Pinot Noir and Pinot Gris are the last grapes to be picked, normally on or about 24 October. The Chardonnay has tough dark, glossy leaves and fairly thick skinned grapes which helps it restrict fungal attack and it is usually harvested clean. In hot summers, the Chardonnay is usually vinified alone, but in lesser years the Pinot Noir gives backbone and longevity, and the Pinot Gris imparts complexity. In cooler summers the Chardonnay delivers about 60° Oechsle, and 70° Oechsle in fine, hot summers.

The winery has an electric mill and a large centre screw hydraulic basket press. On arrival at the winery, the white grapes are gently milled just to break the skins. The second batch is milled immediately the first batch is put into the press so that from batch two on, they enjoy half an hour to three quarters of an hour skin contact to increase flavour.

The grapes are pressed gently and slowly, the press is then emptied and the second batch is pressed. The pulp from both pressings is then broken up and pressed out a second time, again gently to ensure that none of the harsher acids and tannins are extracted which can taint a delicate wine. The must is vatted, tested for sugar and acidity and sulphured.

The red wine grapes are gently milled, and then transferred to vats. Once the first load has been tipped in, the yeast is added so that is placed near the base of the pulp which encourages an earlier and more thorough start to the fermentation.

The pulp is pushed down two or three times a day, and on the eighth day the free run juice is removed. The pulp is gently pressed out once more and the extraction added to the free run juice. Experience has shown that the maximum colour and flavour has been extracted by the eighth day, and if left longer the alcohol starts to reduce the colour.

For white wines, a long, slow cold fermentation is encouraged using cold fermentation yeasts. Having studied at the Stats Domain at Schloss Böckelheim, Nederhausen on the Nahe, Gillian is convinced that a long slow fermentation over many weeks is needed to produce the full flavours and delicacy of English wines. The yeasts used can function happily at between 41°F (5°C) and 45.5°F (7.5°C). She believes hot fast fermentations taking 5 to 6 days boil away the finer flavours and more delicate bouquets which are so important in English wines.

Once fermentation ceases, the wines are racked and the vats topped up. The winery then waits for a very cold frosty spell in January to cold stabilise the wines during which the tartrates drop out naturally. The wines, once stabilised, are coarse filtered and re-vatted to await bottling in April.

Prior to bottling, the wine is passed through a non-asbestos sheet filter, and if *süss* reserve is being added to the Siegerrebe at 2.5 per cent, this wine is then run through a membrane filter in line between the sheet filter and the bottling head.

The red wine has a spell of maturation in new French Tronçais oak *barriques* for 4 to 6 months according to the vintage. This converts the wine from a bright purple colour and a raw, earthy fiery taste to a smooth, mellow, complex harmonious and garnet coloured wine, with a lovely smokey back flavour.

The red wines are fined with the whites of four eggs for each 225l *barrique* in the January of the second year when the wine is 15 months old. The wine is racked off after 45 days, then bottled in May or June. The egg white fining renders the wine clear and supple, and the winery tries not to have to filter it before bottling. The wine is then laid down in bottles until the following December at the earliest, and for a year if possible.

Wines produced are: Madeleine Angevine, a clear natural delicate wine, with a spring flower bouquet, and big fresh grapey flavour with great length on the palate. It is very elegant; Siegerrebe, a medium dry wine with fresh peaches bouquet, a rich spicey, honeyed muscat flavour, and smooth gentle finish; Chardonnay — Special Private Reserve — the wine is fermented and matured in lightly toasted new French Limousin oak casks, and late bottled when ready after a mellowing malolactic fermentation in June. It has a big, flowery, buttery Chardonnay nose, considerable depth, backbone and elegance with a lovely smokey back flavour which comes from its contact with the oak; Riesling, a fresh lemony bouquet, elegant, racy acidity, fine soft honeyed finish and good length and red wine, a lovely deep garnet colour, smooth rich mellow flavour, and elegant smokey back flavour from its maturation in wood. It is a complex and well balanced wine that will continue to improve over several years.

The winery also sells cooking wine, made from young vines not rated highly enough to be released as a single varietal wine, apple juice and vintage and non-vintage cyders, made from undiluted pure apple juice. The spelling distinguishes it from cider, which is made by covering the apple pulp from the first pressing with water, and then pressing out the diluted juice.

Up to 4,545l of cyder are made each year using fruit from their own traditional cyder apple orchards, or from fruit bought in from neighbouring orchards in the Exe valley.

Visiting times: winery and shop are open daily 10am-5pm, vineyard visits and winery tours and tastings by appointment. The winery shop sells wine by the bottle and case, apple juice and cyders. The wines are sold from the vineyard and to many hotels, restaurants, wine merchants, wine shops and tourist centres and are regularly used at county and local council banquets and at tourism events.

The vineyard has a large airy winery, with adjoining laboratory and administration area. It is large enough to cope with the one or two larger harvests of each decade, but does not make wine for other growers. The vineyard is part of a small agricultural enterprise which also includes a small flock of Suffolk sheep and 3 acres of cyder apple orchards.

How to get there: from Exeter take the A377 through Crediton and Copplestone. Opposite the Lion Garage at Morchard Road turn left on to the B3200. After about 3 miles turn left on to the road signposted for Chilverton. After half a mile turn left and Chilverton is the first house on the left.

Nearby attractions: Bickleigh Castle, Tiverton Castle, Bickleigh Craft and Farm Centre, Killerton House and Gardens (NT), and Knightshayes House and Gardens (NT), and Tiverton, with its award winning small town museum and church.

Cornwall

MOUNTS BAY VINEYARD
Peter Rogers
Tolver Water
Long Rock
Penzance TR20 8YG
☎ (0736) 60774

The vineyard covers 6 acres of which 4 acres are planted. Varieties include Madeleine Angevine, Huxelrebe, Siegerrebe, Leon Millot and Triomphe D'Alsace. There have been no changes to the varieties planted in recent years, but there are 2 acres of new, as yet unproductive Weisser Burgunder vines.

The vineyard is on a south facing slope looking out over the bay and is on granite and clay. The climate is mild and moist. The vineyard was established by the present owner in 1984 with an initial planting of 4,000 vines. The land was originally a small holding. A further 2,000 vines have since been added making a total of 6 acres in all. The vineyard and winery is worked by the owner with the help of one full-time worker.

The first harvest was picked in 1986 and yields so far have been poor because of the bad weather. All the varieties are picked around the middle of September by hand and the winery uses an electrical crusher and a hand press.

Wines produced are: Madeleine Angevine, a superior white wine with a fine Muscat nose; Huxelrebe produced from grapes which usually have high sugar and acid readings; Siegerrebe with full bouquet and spicy flavour; Leon Millot, an experimental red and Triomphe D'Alsace, a full bodied wine which needs to be aged for at least 2 years before bottling.

Mounts Bay Vineyard

Expansion plans include a garden centre and extending the restaurant. The vineyard is part of an agricultural enterprise which also involves soft fruit, including strawberries, raspberries, gooseberries, blackberries and loganberries.

Visiting times: from Easter to November 10am-5pm. The wines are sold from the vineyard through its restaurant and shop which also sells country wines, mustards, pickles, chutneys, jams, honey, local sweets, home-made ice cream and so on. There are tasting facilities, restaurant, vineyard trail, picnic sites and parking. Tours of the vineyard and winery can be arranged. There is also a garden shop selling young vines, herbs, perennials and shrubs, wooden tubs, terracotta containers and hanging baskets. The main building which houses the tea room, licensed restaurant and shop was built in 1984. A conservatory overlooking the main planting area, and another where visitors use barbecue facilities, has since been added. A path leads from the main building to the vineyard bottling plant, a former stable block, where all the equipment necessary for processing the grapes is housed.

How to get there: the vineyard is to the north-east of Penzance, just to the south of the B3311 Gulval to Ludgvan road. It is clearly signposted.

Nearby attractions: St Michael's Mount, beaches, Penzance and Newlyn.

PENBERTH VALLEY VINEYARD

D.R. Bryant
St Buryan
Penzance
No telephone

The vineyard (a member of the EVA and the South West Vineyards Association) covers 1.6 acres and a further 0.5 acres is being considered. More than half the production comes from Triomphe D'Alsace with the remainder coming from Siegerrebe, Madeleine Angevine, Leon Millot, Pinot Noir and Chardonnay. There have been no changes to the varieties planted, and all the vines are productive.

The vineyard is 2 miles from Lands End, located in the Penberth Valley. It enjoys a maritime climate and is planted on light, loamy soil which is slightly acidic. It is on a south facing slope. The vineyard enjoys warm springs and summers not as hot as those further inland because of the moderating influence of the sea. Winters are mild but gales can be a problem.

The vines are trained using the spur, cordon cane and head cane pruning methods. Botrytis damage can be severe and there is a regular spraying programme to protect against this and other diseases.

The harvest starts towards the end of October and occasionally into early November with the white grape varieties, followed by the red grape varieties. The winery is located in an old Cornish stone barn with traditional slate roof. The red wine grapes are fermented in wooden casks after crushing and later stored in casks. The white varieties are fermented in glass jars and stored for a short period in casks before being transferred again to glass jars. Because of the wine making methods used, the winery is more labour intensive than many others. The wines produced are sold locally through wine merchants. The vineyard and winery is worked by the owner with the help of a casual hand and is sited in a very picturesque valley now under National Trust supervision, half a mile from the sea.

Visiting times: none at present but the vineyard can be seen from public footpaths and there is access to the cove at the foot of the valley.

How to get there: the valley runs down to the sea 2 miles east of Lands End and is only accessible by footpath.

POLMASSICK VINEYARD

G and B Musgrave
Polmassick
St Ewe
St Austell PL26 6HA
☎ (0726) 842239

The vineyard was established in 1978 and was the first commercial vineyard in Cornwall. It was sold as a productive vineyard to the present owner in 1986. It is a member of the EVA and the South West Vineyards Association and covers 1.5 acres. Varieties planted are Müller-Thurgau on 0.81 acres and Seyve Villard on 0.27 acres which each account for 50 per cent of production at present. There is also 0.4 acres of Kernling not yet in production. Some Müller-Thurgau has already been grubbed out and replaced with Kernling, and further replacements of Müller-Thurgau are planned in 1989.

The vineyard is in south mid-Cornwall, at an average height of 150ft above sea level. It is on a very steep, south facing slope but sheltered, and on coarse, stony ground of sandy clay loam. It experiences damp and windy conditions, but the location is well sheltered and much of the production is in polytunnels.

Most of the vines are trained and pruned on the Double Guyot system but there is some Single Guyot. Pruning takes place in January and February, and tying and cutting starts towards the end of February. The spraying programme starts after budburst, usually in late April. There is summer pruning, and the harvest starts normally in early to mid-October. The vines get a winter wash between December and January.

When the harvest starts about a ton of grapes is picked a day, starting with the Müller-Thurgau. The harvest normally lasts about 4 days. The grapes are crushed as they come into the winery using a hand-operated crusher. They are then transferred to the vertical wooden-slatted press. The must is pumped direct from the press-receiving vat into carbon dioxide filled storage vessels where sulphur is added.

After being left to settle for 2 days, the must is racked and acidity, sugar and sulphur dioxide levels are checked and adjusted. The starter yeast is added and fermentation begins. The must usually has an Oechsle level of between 62° and 72° naturally, and this is adjusted to 82°.

The wine is racked late to encourage malolactic fermentation. The winery uses a two stage coarse and sterile filtering machine before the wine is bottled. All the wines are bottled dry.

Although the quality of the vintages has been consistent over the last few years, the quantity of the harvest has varied enormously because of the bad weather.

All the wine has been sold from the farm gate for the last 2 years because of the low production, but there are sales through a local brewery in good years when volume production is greater. The vineyard has a potential acreage of 7 acres and a number of varieties were planted on an experimental basis in the spring of 1989 to determine which will be used for the new commercial plantings. It is part of an agricultural enterprise which also includes sheep and cattle.

Visiting times: 23 May to the last Sunday in September, Tuesday to Sunday 11am-5pm. Open bank holiday Mondays. The vineyard has its own winery shop which sells wines and local cider. Other sales include vines, Polmassick glasses and decanter corks, and sheep skins. Refreshments are available. There is also an interesting collection of animals and birds, including Soay sheep, Dexter cattle and Falabella horses, the smallest horse breed in the world. There is a covered tasting area and picnic site, and a self-conducted farm trail.

How to get there: the vineyard is signposted to the south of the B3287 which runs from Tregony to join the A390 Truro to St Austell road. It is about 3 miles north-east of Tregony and about 5 miles south-west of Truro.

Nearby attractions: Mevagissey, Roseland Peninsula, beaches.

Recommended pubs, restaurants and hotels in the area: The Crown (St Ewe), Barley Sheaf (Gorran Churchtown) and Kilbol House Hotel (Polmassick).

Chapter 8
East Anglian Vineyards

Essex

BRIGHTLINGSEA VINEYARDS
M.J. Murphy
68 Red Barn Road
Brightlingsea CO7 0SL
☎ (020630) 2026

The vineyard has been arranged so that it can be worked 'as a one man band'. It is set on the edge of a small holiday town and has been, and will remain, a slowly developing attraction. A 10-year plan began in 1985 to bring the vineyard and smallholding to 'acceptable levels of production and satisfaction.'

The vineyard (a member of the EVA and East Anglian Wine Growers Association) covers 4 acres of new, as yet unproductive vines. Varieties planted are Müller-Thurgau, Bacchus, Senator, Pinot Noir and Gewürztraminer. The vineyard is 45ft above sea level at the river mouth and planted on sandy loam. It has a dry cool climate.

All the vines are trained on the Guyot system and pruning starts each year in January together with tying down. There is a programme of spraying and de-foliation from May to September and the grapes are ready for harvesting at the end of October. The first full harvest will be gathered in 1989. The vineyard plans initially to sell the main crop to other winemakers and to process the grapes from the smaller yielding varieties itself. Each year it will gradually increase its self-production capacity.

Visiting times: by appointment. Vines are sold and tasting facilities, picnic sites and other facilities will be developed from 1990.

How to get there: from Colchester take the B1027 to Thorrington, then the B1029 to Brightlingsea. Red Barn Road is on the northern edge of the town.

Nearby attractions: Brightlingsea, sailing and regattas.

Recommended pubs, restaurants and hotels in the area: Brightlingsea Hall, The Swan Hotel, and Jacobes Hall.

Norfolk

LEXHAM HALL VINEYARD
W.R.B. Foster and Partners
Lexham Hall
Nr Litcham
King's Lynn PE32 2QJ
☎ (0328) 701288

The vineyard (a member of the EVA and East Anglian Wine Growers Association) covers 8 acres. Varieties in production are Müller-Thurgau on 4.08 acres and accounting for 13.6 per cent of production, Reichensteiner 0.84 (27.8 per cent of production), Scheurebe 2.24 acres (28.5 per cent), and Madeleine Angevine 0.84 acres and 30.1 per cent of production.

In recent years there has been a reduction in the acreage of Müller-Thurgau and further plantings of Madeleine Angevine and Seyval Blanc. There is a further acre of

— *Location of the Vineyards in East Anglia* —

Essex
1 Brightlingsea

Norfolk
2 Lexham Hall

Cambridgeshire
7 Chilford Hundred

Suffolk
3 Bruisyard
4 Giffords
5 Helions
6 Shawsgate

Seyval Blanc not yet in production.

The vineyard is on a south facing site on the northern slopes of the Nar Valley, approximately half a mile downstream from the village of East Lexham, notable for its Saxon round towered church. The vineyard is on sandy loam and receives an annual average rainfall of 23in. The vineyard is on the North Norfolk coast which exercises some influence on the weather, but it also has its own microclimate due to the south facing amphitheatre-like situation. It was mostly planted between 1975 and 1977. The vines are trained on the High Culture system and are supported by a 6ft trellis with 4ft between the vines and 8ft between the rows.

Pruning takes place between January and March. The vineyard is dressed with fertiliser in March and a spraying programme starts at the end of May and continues until October to protect against mildews and botrytis. The harvest spans mid- to late October to mid-November, and the winter is spent repairing the trellises.

The average harvest starts around 15

October and continues until 10 November. Madeleine Angevine is the first variety to be picked, followed by Reichensteiner, Müller-Thurgau with Scheurebe last. About a dozen pickers collect the grapes using secateurs to cut the bunches which fall into buckets. The buckets are then empted into a 700l grape transporter.

It takes approximately 2lb of ripe, juicy grapes to make a single bottle of wine and an average crop yields sufficient for 2,000 bottles an acre.

The grapes are transported to the winery and then pumped into a 700l Vaslin horizontal press. After pressing they are pumped into settling tanks and left to settle out for 4 or 5 days. The juice is then racked into clean tanks and the yeast starter injected into the must to start fermentation following chaptalisation.

The tanks are cooled to keep the maximum temperature below 59°F (15°C) during fermentation. The fermentation usually lasts about ten days and the wine is then allowed to settle out. It is then filtered into clean tanks, tested for acidity and sugar levels and treated as necessary. It is then filtered again and left to rest until the end of March, or beginning of April when it is bottled. A twelve-head bottling machine is used, capable of handling 5,000 bottles a day.

Production in the bumper year of 1984 was 9,846l. This fell to 2,522l in 1985 and 2,750l the following year. In 1987 the vineyard was hit by terrible weather and production fell to just 400l, but the 1988 harvest saw a major improvement with production topping 7,300l. The wine is ready for drinking in the July following the harvest.

The white wines, which have received the EVA Seal of Quality, are dry, fragrant and fruity, reminiscent of the Upper Moselle and Alsace.

The vineyard is worked by the owner with the aid of one full-time worker and casual staff brought in as required, mostly during the harvest. The vineyard is part of an agricultural enterprise which also includes arable, forestry and pigs. The wine is sold from a small winery shop and the estate office at Lexham Hall, through off-licences, wine merchants, hotels and restaurants.

Visiting times: by appointment. Vineyard and winery visits can be arranged for parties of ten to fifty people. There are tastings in the winery and catering can be arranged.

How to get there: the vineyard is signposted 2 miles to the west of Litcham off the B1145 Norwich to King's Lynn road.

Nearby attractions: Castleacre Castle and Priory and East Lexham Church.

Recommended pubs, restaurants and hotels in the area: Bull Inn (Litcham), George and Dragon (Newton), Ostrich (Castleacre), Grady's and George Hotel (Swaffham).

Suffolk

BRUISYARD VINEYARD

Ian and Eleanor Berwick
Church Road
Bruisyard
Saxmundham
Suffolk IP17 2EF
☎ (072875) 281

The vineyard (a member of the EVA, East Anglian Winegrowers Association, British Herb Trade Association and British Herb Society) covers 10 acres of Müller-Thurgau. There have been no changes in the plantings in recent years and all the vines are productive. There are no plans to expand the vineyard which is also part of an agricultural enterprise which includes a herb garden. It was planted between 1974 and 1975 — 5 acres in each year. The vines are spaced 4ft apart in rows 8ft apart, and there are 13,000 vines in all. They are grafted on to American phylloxera-resistant rootstocks imported from Switzerland. The vineyard has 2,500 posts and 54 miles of wire and is 100ft above sea level, on a slight south facing slope, so that there is some elevation to the sun. The soil is a sandy clay loam.

The vineyard nestles in the Alde Valley so is protected from the worst of the weather. There are trees planted round the perimeter so the wind is prevented from blowing the warmth out of the vineyard.

All the vines are trained and pruned according to the cane replacement, or Double Guyot system. Weed free ground conditions are maintained to ensure that all available warmth is reflected from the earth back up to the vines. Pruning starts in late December or January and it takes until the end of April to prune and tie down all the vines.

During the winter a granular fertiliser is applied in the vineyard to replace lost nutrients. It is high in phosphate and potash, and low in nitrogen because the aim is not to encourage too much leaf growth. Farmyard manure is not used because it gets washed into the ground and is taken up by the vines and can be tasted in the grapes. Contact herbicides are used in March to burn off any green weeds that are growing, as well as pre-emergent herbicides.

The vine growth starts about 3ft above the growth to protect young shoots from frosts in the spring. The rows of vines are planted running north to south, so that one side of the vine gets the morning sun, and the other side gets the sun in the afternoon. The vine needs an average temperature of 50°F (10°C) for about ten consecutive days for the buds to burst and the shoots to start growing. This usually occurs in late April or early May and the young shoots are very susceptible to late spring frosts.

The vines are sprayed every 10 days with wettable sulphur after budburst to protect against mildew, and the vineyard is sprayed four times a year as a protection against botrytis. The last spray is applied about 6 weeks before the harvest, so that if the weather conditions are suitable, about 10 per cent of the crop is infected with the noble rot, botrytis.

Flowering takes place about mid-July when the vines should have reached the top of the trellises. If it rains during flowering, the pollen sticks to the stamens and the berries do not set which means a low yield. The pollen is air borne so needs warm, dry weather plus a light breeze for a good set.

In 1981 it rained on 10 of the 14 days of the flowering period and the eventual harvest yielded 8,000 bottles of wine. In 1983 there was no rain at all over the flowering period and 49,000 bottles of wine were subsequently produced.

In August the vines have usually grown 2ft to 3ft above the top of the trellis, and the tops are cut off, level with the top of the trellis. This stops the vine growing and all its energy goes into the ripening of the grapes.

Ian Berwick is the winemaker and he is assisted by five permanent staff, and plenty of casual local labour brought in at harvest time which starts in late October. The vineyard is netted in the final weeks before picking to protect the grapes from the birds. It takes about 2 weeks to net the whole 10 acres.

The grapes are picked when they reach a minimum specific gravity of 1,060°. The vineyard looks for quality and expects to harvest between 2 tons and 3 tons of grapes an acre, compared with a continental yield of 6 tons and more. If the weather looks like remaining fine, the grapes are left on the vines to increase their sugar content even more.

The entire crop is gathered in 10 days using a small army of pickers. The bunches are cut off the vines using secateurs and put into buckets which, when full, are emptied into the grape trailer moving up and down the rows. The 2-ton trailer, when full, takes the grapes straight to the press room for splitting and pressing.

A large screw auger runs along the bottom of the trailer and is driven by a shaft from the tractor. This moves the grapes to the back of the trailer into the berry mill, splitting the grapes which are then pumped along a pipe into the press. The mill has to split the skin of every grape but must not damage the stalks or pips because too much tannin will be released into the wine, making it harsh and bitter. It takes about 4 minutes to split and offload the 2-ton trailer loads of grapes.

The press is a unit with the trailer, capable of holding 2 tons of grapes, and fully automatic. The programme is selected according to the ripeness of the grapes. Ripe grapes release their juice more readily than unripe grapes so require less pressing. When the press is started the drum full of split grapes slowly rotates in an anti-clockwise direction, and the two large discs at either end slowly start to move towards each other pressing the juice out of the grapes. The juice escapes through holes in the side of the drum, and is collected in the juice tray underneath the press before being pumped into vats in the winery.

When the discs are about 18in apart in the centre of the drum they stop automatically and start to move backwards. This leaves a cake in the middle of the press which is broken up and then pressed again to extract more juice. Each press load has a lot of gentle pressings. An average load will have about twenty-five pressings and will take about 2 hours. The bone-dry pulp, or pomace, is then spread back on the vineyard as a mulch.

Before the vats are filled with grape juice they are pre-filled with carbon dioxide gas to prevent the liquid coming into contact with air risking oxidisation. When the vats have been filled, the juice is then left for 24 hours to settle and to allow the pips and bits of skin etc to fall to the bottom. After this period, the clear juice is then drawn off into clean vats, again pre-filled with carbon dioxide. The juice is corrected by adding sugar and adjusting the acidity, a cultured yeast is injected and fermentation started.

About a week before the main harvest, a small quantity of grapes are picked and pressed by hand. The juice is heat sterilised and put in a small vat together with the wine yeast which starts to multiply rapidly. This is then used as the starter wine for the main fermentation. A few litres of this starter wine is added to the juice in the big vats, and the yeast is so active that it swamps any wild yeasts that may still be present in the wine juice.

The temperature of the fermentation is controlled so that it is not too fast. This is done by cooling down the tanks by running cold water over them. If the weather is very cold, heaters are brought into the winery to

Bruisyard Vineyard

keep the temperature up. The fermentation normally takes about three weeks. After fermentation, the wine is allowed to settle so that dead yeast cells fall to the bottom of the tank and the clear wine can be drawn off into clean vats, this time pre-filled with nitrogen to prevent any air entering.

The wine is filtered three times before bottling. The first is a coarse filtration to remove any yeast cells that have not settled out naturally. The wine then undergoes a sterile filtration before being returned to the vats to mature for up to 6 months, and it gets a second sterile filtration to polish it and make it crystal clear immediately before bottling in April or May. It is bottled on a semi-automatic line which can handle 800 bottles an hour, corked, capsuled and labelled. It is then packed in boxes and stored upside down for at least a month before being offered for sale.

Average production is about 2,000 cases a year. Wines produced are a medium dry fruity wine with a little sparkle, as well as a dry and medium wine made from grapes bought in from other English vineyards. The wine is sold from the winery shop, occasionally to British Embassies, and to a wide range of wine merchants all round the country, including Grants of St James's.

Visiting times: Easter to the end of November daily 10.30am-5pm. The vineyard and winery are open to the public as well as the herb and water gardens. There are tasting facilities, a picnic area, children's play area, shop selling English wines, local crafts, gifts and souvenirs, a tea room and ample car parking. Conducted tours for parties of twenty or more, which last about an hour and a half, are by appointment only.

How to get there: the vineyard lies to the north of the B1119 Saxmundham to Framlingham road, and south of the A1120. If travelling north on the A12 Saxmundham, turn left on to the B1119 and then follow the signposts for Bruisyard. The vineyard is well signposted on all the approach roads.

Nearby attractions: Framlingham Castle, Easton Farm Park, Helmingham Hall,

Saxtead Windmill, Glemham Hall, Snape Maltings and Woodbridge Tide Mill.

Recommended pubs, restaurants and hotels in the area: Crown Inn (Westleton), Marlborough Hotel (Ipswich), White Horse Inn (Easton) and Seckford Hall Hotel (Woodbridge).

GIFFORDS VINEYARD

John and Carol Kemp
Gifford's Hall
Hartest
Bury St Edmunds IP29 4EX
☎ (0284) 830464

The vineyard is part of a small agricultural enterprise which also includes cut flowers, bees, free range chickens and a flock of Hebridean sheep, a rare breed.

The vineyard (a member of the EVA and East Anglian Wine Growers Association) covers just 2 acres at present which is likely to be doubled in size in 1990. There is an acre of Madeleine Angevine which accounts for about 40 per cent of production, and an acre of Bacchus (40 per cent) and 300 vines each of Reichensteiner and Pinot Noir which make up the remaining 20 per cent of production. All the vines were planted over 1986 and 1987 and are not yet productive. The first real crop is expected in 1989.

The vineyard is flat but in rolling countryside, in one of the highest parts of the county, about 300ft above sea level and very exposed. 'We are waiting to prove we can grow vines before expanding further.'

The vineyard is exposed to a lot of wind but is relatively frost free. A great deal has been spent on firm trellising and stainless steel wire, and all the vines will eventually be trained on the Double Guyot system — most are on the single Guyot at present. Spray is applied as necessary and there is not a regular spraying programme.

About 1cwt of grapes — Madeleine Angevine and Reichensteiner — were picked last year in mid-October. A nice floral bouquet is apparent.

Visiting times: by appointment from 1990.

How to get there: directions from owners.

Giffords Vineyard

HELIONS VINEYARD

Jasper Grinling
The Old Vicarage
Helions Bumpstead
Nr Haverhill
Suffolk CB9 7AS
☎ (044084) 316

The vineyard (a member of the EVA) has one full-time worker and gardener and covers an acre split equally between Müller-Thurgau and Reichensteiner. There have been no changes to the varieties planted in recent years and there are no new, as yet unproductive vines. The vineyard is low lying close to the Suffolk and Cambridgeshire borders. It is on loam overlying clay, very well drained and has an open aspect receiving east, south and west sun, and protected from the north by hedges.

The vines are planted in rows running north to south. The vines are planted 4ft 6in apart, in alleys 5ft apart and there are 11,000 vines to the acre. Pruning takes place in January and February, and there is a preventative spray programme against diseases which starts in the spring and continues through the summer. There is also summer pruning. The vines are all trained on the Double Guyot system. The grapes are picked in late October and the Reichensteiner is harvested first as it ripens earlier, about a week before the Müller-Thurgau.

The vineyard does not have its own winery and the grapes are sent for vinification at High Weald Winery run by Christopher Lindlar. Production in 1984 was 5,000 bottles, 3,000 in 1985 and 2,000 in 1986. There was no production in 1987 because heavy rains in July destroyed the flowering. Production in 1988 was about 500 bottles. A single blended wine is produced using equal proportions of the two varieties. It is sold through local shops, pubs and restaurants and to private customers.

Visiting times: by appointment.

How to get there: the vineyard is in the centre of the village of Helions Bumpstead, opposite the village green.

Recommended pubs, restaurants and hotels in the area: The Eight Bells (pub, Saffron Walden).

Wine from Helions Vineyard

SHAWSGATE VINEYARD

Ian S. Hutcheson
Shawsgate
Badingham Road
Framlingham IP13 9HZ
☎ (0728) 724060

The vineyard was established in 1973 on 13 acres and was bought by Ian Hutcheson in

Shawsgate Vineyard shop

1985 since when it has undergone major restoration. It covers 21 acres of which 18 acres are planted with five distinct vineyards each surrounded by either natural or artificial windbreaks. The vineyard is a member of the EVA and East Anglian Winegrowers Association, and hopes to expand its tourist facilities as quickly as possible.

There are 11 acres of Müller-Thurgau which accounts for all the production at the moment. New, as yet unproductive varieties planted over the last 3 years are Seyval Blanc 5 acres, Reichensteiner an acre, and half an acre each of Bacchus and Chardonnay. A sixth variety, Triomphe Spéciale was planted on half an acre in spring 1989. The rows of vines are planted north to south.

The vineyard is 15 miles north-east of Ipswich, and a mile north of the small market town of Framlingham. The geography of the area is of gentle undulating countryside with old woodland areas, much damaged in the hurricane of October 1987. The climate is generally good with about

Framlingham Castle, a place of interest near Shawsgate Vineyard

21in of rainfall annually and good sunshine hours. The soil is medium to heavy loam. In recent years there has been a large amount of rain during July, the most important month because of flowering, and this has led to a very large reduction in yield. The winters are usually cold but dry, and there is a great deal of wind which tends to reduce the microclimate within the vineyard.

Pruning begins in January and usually takes about three and a half months using a staff of three. All the existing vines are trained and pruned on the Double Guyot system but the new vines on the recently planted acreage will be trained using the Geneva Double Curtain method. Spraying takes place at approximately ten-day intervals during the growing season to prevent mildew and botrytis. It is occasionally necessary to spray for caspid early on in the season. This is a small bug that attacks the leaves rendering them useless for photosynthesis. A winter wash can also be applied to combat dead arm disease. The vineyard adopts the policy that spraying prevention is far better than cure as far as vines are concerned.

The harvest usually starts around the third week of October. Only Müller-Thurgau is being picked at present and the order of picking from the various vineyards is dependent on ripeness. The first vintage of Seyval Blanc is likely to be picked in 1989 although it is expected to be small. It will be picked after the Müller-Thurgau. This will fit in the with the vineyard's current operation. A small quantity of Seyval Blanc is purchased from a neighbour and this is processed soon after Shawsgate has finished its own harvest of Müller-Thurgau.

Before the vineyard built its own winery, it picked under contract and had to harvest a large quantity each day so employed between twenty and thirty pickers. Now that it processes its own grapes the number of pickers has been reduced to fifteen, and picking is related to the winery's daily needs.

The grapes are picked into a ton fibreglass grape trailer which also has a berry mill through which the grapes, stalks and all pass. The berry mill breaks the skin of the grapes before pressing. The trailer load is discharged directly into the press in about three minutes enabling it to return to the vineyard quickly. The press holds 1.2 tons and is fully automatic. It takes between 2 and 3 hours to press a batch of grapes, but the timing is very dependent on quality. From the press the must is pumped into stainless steel tanks where it is allowed to settle for 2 days, after which time fermentation is started. A few weeks after fermentation has ceased the wine is racked. It is left on the lees for some time, but is racked off before bad flavours start to be taken up. The wine is usually racked a number of times before bottling which usually takes place in May.

The wines are filtered using a plate and sheet filter. Just before bottling, the pressure in the tank is increased slightly so that the wine does not have to be pumped out. Because of the pressure it naturally passes through the filter into the vacuum filter.

The bottles are assembled next to an automatic bottle steriliser from where they are placed on to the filter, filled and corked. The corking machine has a carbon dioxide attachment which creates a vacuum within the bottle to ensure better keeping quality. The bottles are then stacked into a bin. Each bin holds 700 bottles and these are held in the adjacent refrigerated storage area.

Production in each of the last 5 years has been hit by bad weather. Many of the vines planted by the original owner are having to be retrained from new canes brought up from the original graft, so the yield potential of many of the original vines has been lost. The vineyard has averaged about a quarter of a ton an acre over the last 5 years, but the few new vines that are coming into production look promising. As the new canes from the old vines are brought up, the improvement in health of the vine and its yield potential can be seen.

In 1984 and 1985 the harvest of Müller-Thurgau was sold under contract. In 1986 a medium dry Müller-Thurgau was made in the new winery. The entire crop was lost in 1987 because of the hurricane, and the 1988 harvest of Müller-Thurgau and the bought in Seyval Blanc was still in tanks at the time of writing.

The 1986 was described in the 1988 International Wine and Spirit competition as having 'a big, powerful nose with fruit behind it. Immature, needs keeping, a serious wine, crisp and stylish.' The winery also produces an apple dessert wine.

All the wine produced is sold through the vineyard shop as production is still limited. The first wines are expected to be sold to the trade in the summer of 1989. The winery was purpose built in 1987 and consists of the winemaking area, where all the processing takes place, a refrigerated bottle storage area, and a laboratory and office. The shop is attached to the main building. The capacity of the winery is about 100,000l indoors with a further 50,000l immediately adjacent outdoors. The vineyard is managed by Robert Hemphill who is also the winemaker, aided by an experienced German winemaker who acts as consultant.

Visiting times: April to October, daily 10am-5pm and by appointment after that time. Coaches and parties of twenty or more by appointment. The shop is fairly small and is to be extended in the near future. It sells wine and apple wine and cider, vines, dried flowers and vine garlands, jams, wine related products, wine books and literature, T-shirts, sweatshirts and aprons and pottery with grape motifs. A children's play area is beside the winery, and attractive gardens and a vine nursery are nearby. There is a walk around most of the property accessible to visitors. Tastings can take place in the shop or at tables outside. Other light refreshments are available and there is also a picnic site. Guided tours are available on the hour which includes a tasting and walk round the vineyard.

How to get there: the vineyard is signposted a mile north of Framlingham.

Nearby attractions: Framlingham Castle, a mile away, Minsmere bird reserve, Easton Farm Park, Saxstead Mill.

Recommended pubs, restaurants and hotels in the area: Victoria Pub (Earl Soham) and Railway Bar and Crown Hotel (Framlingham).

Cambridgeshire

CHILFORD HUNDRED VINEYARD
S. Alper
Chilford Hundred
Chilford Hall
Linton CB1 6LE
☎ (0223) 892641

The vineyard (a member of the EVA and East Anglian Winegrowers Association) covers 20 acres. There are no plans to expand the vineyard. Varieties planted are Müller-Thurgau, which accounts for 50 per cent of production, Huxelrebe (20 per cent), Ortega (20 per cent), Schönburger (7 per cent) and Siegerrebe (3 per cent).

There have been no changes to the varieties planted in recent years, and there are no new, as yet unproductive vines, but there is a small experimental area devoted to new clones developed for their suitability for the English climate.

The vineyard is on a south-west facing slope in rolling countryside in south Cambridge close to the Essex border. It is about 270ft above sea level, below the crest of a hill which deflects the cold north and easterly winds and ensures the vines enjoy maximum benefit from summer sunshine. It is on soils of flinty loam over chalk, and flinty gravel over sand. Both soils are ideal for vines and typical of the soils found in many parts of Bordeaux. The climate is marginal. It suffers the general East Anglian problem of east winds in winter and south-westerly winds in the summer. It enjoys a generally reasonable September and October.

When the vineyard was established and the first vines planted in 1973 it was decided to train them on the Lenz-Moser system of wide spacing between the rows. This assists growth, giving more soil per vine and affording them more light. The vines are now pruned between January and March according to the Double Guyot system.

The vines are hand hoed to keep down weeds thus avoiding the need to use herbicides and insecticides. There is a programme of organic spraying, however, which starts after budburst and is repeated at about 14-day intervals after flowering. A natural copper sulphate mixture is used to protect against fungal diseases.

The harvest usually starts in the third week of October and lasts between 2 and 3 weeks depending on the weather and the size of the crop. The picking order is normally Siegerrebe, Ortega, Huxelrebe, Müller-Thurgau and finally Schönburger.

The grapes are hand picked and transferred to the vineyard's winery in converted old farm buildings. The grapes are unloaded into the crusher and partially de-stemmed and then pumped into a ton Vaslin Veritas ten-rotary press. The pressing of each full load takes about 2 hours. Each ton of grapes produces about half a ton of juice which falls into a tray and is pumped to settling tanks where it rests for 24 hours to let the solids drop to the bottom of the vats. The clear juice is then pumped to fresh tanks where the starter yeast culture is added. If there is not enough sugar in the grapes to produce the correct level of alcohol, the juice is chaptalised.

Fermentation is carried out in fibreglass tanks and lasts between 2 and 3 weeks. The must is bentonited prior to fermentation. After fermentation the wine is coarse filtered, and fined if necessary. It is fine filtered at the end of January after which blending of the five varieties takes place to produce the vineyard's two commercial wines. No more than three varieties are used for either blend, one dry and the other medium dry using *süss* reserve. It is then left to settle for a further 3 months and bottled in April using a vacuum filter. As bottling affects the wine, it is left to settle again for up to 6 months before being offered for sale.

Production has varied enormously over the last few years because of the weather. The characteristic of the Chilford Hundred is a good clear colour, fragrant nose, fruity body with good acidity. In 1984 17 tons of grapes were harvested and all went into the production of a medium dry wine, soft and easily approachable. In 1985 the harvest yielded 12 tons, all of which was used to make a dry wine. It had lots of flavour and developed quite slowly. It is improving in bottle and does not like to be served too cold. The 1986 vintage was 9 tons of good quality grapes. The wines produced were clean, fresh and quite soft. In 1987 a single ton of grapes was picked after storm damage. The 1988 harvest yielded 7 tons of first class grapes, however, and should produce fine wines. About 70 per cent of the wine is sold from the vineyard, shop or the catering outlet. The vineyard has a modern press house and winery, and the cellar is a partially buried building, built in 1974 using reclaimed materials.

Visiting times: 1 May to 1 October 10.30am-5.30pm daily, 2 October to 30 April 9am-5.30pm Monday to Friday (call at office) and Saturday and Sunday 2-4.30pm in December only. There is a shop which sells wine, vines and vinegar and wine accessories and home-made and local produce such as jams, biscuits, honey, mustards, chutneys and hampers. There is ample parking and catering. There are a number of barns, some of which have been converted for conferences, exhibitions and functions. There is also a collection of old agricultural implements and a silk screen printing press which specialises in fine art work but visiting is by appointment only.

How to get there: the vineyard is well signposted to the north of Linton off the B1052 which runs between Saffron Walden and Newmarket. It is 10 miles from Cambridge.

Nearby attractions: Imperial War Museum (Duxford), Wimpole Hall (NT), Anglesey Abbey (NT, Cambridge), Saffron Walden, Newmarket.

Recommended pubs, restaurants and hotels in the area: Pear Tree (Hildersham), The Crown (Little Walden), and Three Hills (Bartlow).

— Additional East Anglian Vineyards Open to the Public —

Boyton Vineyard
Hill Farm, Boyton End, Stoke-by-Clare, Suffolk CO9 4AN
☎ (0440) 61893
Open: May to October 10am-4pm for sale of wine. Other times by appointment.

Cavendish Manor Vineyard
Nether Hall, Cavendish, Sudbury, Suffolk CO10 8BX
☎ (0787) 280221
Open: daily 11am-4pm for visits and wine sales. Guided tours and tastings by appointment.

Elmham Park Vineyard
Elmham House, North Elmham, Norfolk NR20 5JY
☎ (036281) 571
Open: for wine sales, visits, guided tours and tastings by appointment only.

Felsted Vineyard
Cricks Green, Felsted, Great Dunmow, Essex
☎ (0245) 361504
Open: for wine sales and visits by appointment only.

Harling Vineyard
Eastfield House, East Harling, Norwich, Norfolk NR16 2NA
☎ (0953) 717341
Open: for wine sales and visits by appointment only. Wine festival held in September.

Highwaymans Vineyard
Risby, Bury St Edmunds, Suffolk IP28 6QP
☎ (0248) 810969
Open: for wine sales and tasting by appointment, guided tours available.

Mersea Island Vineyard
Rewsalls Lane, East Mersea, Colchester, Essex CO5 8SX
☎ (0206) 384560
Open: for wine sales 9.30am-1.30pm daily except Thursdays. Vineyard open: beginning May to end September except Thursdays. Guided tours available.

New Hall Vineyard
Chelmsford Road, Purleigh, Maldon, Essex CM3 6PN
☎ (0621) 828343
Open: for vineyard visits and wine sales Monday to Friday 10.30am-6pm, Saturday and Sunday 10.30am-1.30pm. Guided tours available.

Priory Vineyards
Priory Place, Little Dunmow, Essex CH6 3HY
☎ (0371) 820577
Open: for wine sales, vineyard visits and guided tours, by appointment only.

Pulham Vineyard
Mill Lane, Pulham Market, Diss, Norfolk IP21 4XL
☎ (0379) 76672
Open: for shop and vineyard May to September 9am-7pm, October to April 10am-3pm. Guided tours available.

Staverton Vineyard
The Rookery, Eyke, Woodbridge, Suffolk IP12 2RR
☎ (0394) 460271
Open: for wine sales, weekdays 9am-5pm. Vineyard visits by appointment.

Willow Grange Vineyard
Street Farm, Stone Street, Crowfield, Ipswich, Suffolk IP6 9SY
☎ (044979) 234
Open: for wine sales and vineyard visits, Friday to Sunday. Other times by appointment. Guided tours available.

Chapter 9
Vineyards of Central England

Northamptonshire

BRAUNSTON VINEYARD
Colin and Penny Duns
Checkley Close
69 High Street
Braunston NN11 7HS
☎ (0788) 890278

The vineyard is near to the site of a Roman vineyard and grapes were produced in the area until the Middle Ages. Braunston Vineyard was established in 1979. Expansion plans include increasing the vineyard to a maximum 1.5 acres with wines made from the existing vineyard and the new 8-acre vineyard established at Staverton about 4 miles away. The vineyard (a member of the EVA) covers 2 acres of which half an acre is planted. Varieties are Madeleine Angevine which will account for 85 per cent of production and Seyval Blanc, the remaining 15 per cent. The Madeleine Angevine should be in production in 1989 and the Seyval Blanc in 1991. The vineyard was planted with Müller-Thurgau as well, but these vines were grubbed out and replaced with the Seyval Blanc. The vineyard is at a height of 360ft above sea level on a slope facing south towards the banks of the Grand Union Canal. The soil is well drained loam on a strata of sand and clay sub-soil. Braunston has the distinction of being situated further inland than anywhere else in the UK, and because of this has low rainfall and beneficial microclimate.

All the vines are trained on the Double Guyot system. Pruning takes place each year between January and March, and pruning continues throughout this period unless there are hard frosts. In March the vineyard is ploughed and rotavated. The weeds between the rows are sprayed with herbicide in April and budbust can occur at the end of the month or early in May. Between May and September there is a regular programme of foliar spraying with an atomiser spray against mildew using wettable sulphur, Zineb and Foliar Feed. In September the vineyard is netted and fenced against badgers, and the harvest takes place from September into October.

The harvest normally takes place during late September in a good year but can be delayed until the first week in October in bad years. Early varieties picked in order in previous years were Madeleine Angevine, Seyval Blanc and Müller-Thurgau.

The harvest is completed in as short a period as possible, usually within a week if labour is available. The grapes are picked by hand and taken immediately to the winery and pressed as soon as possible — always within 4 hours of picking. All grapes are passed through a powered mill with automatic de-stemmer and pressing is then carried out using a hydraulic central screw and traditional basket press.

The must is sulphured and allowed to settle for 24 hours and then racked for fermentation into stainless steel vats. Acidity levels are adjusted with Acidex as required and the must chaptalised to the correct must weight before fermentation which takes place in a traditional stone barn with constant temperature, and is usually completed within 7 to 10 days. The wines are racked twice before filtration,

Braunston Vineyard

about 3 weeks after fermentation and then again after 4 weeks. The final filtration takes place using an Elva 8in plate filter immediately before bottling on a line capable of handling 500 bottles an hour.

Production has varied enormously in the last few years and after a crop equivalent to 750l an acre in 1984, which doubled to 1,500l in 1985, there was no crop at all in either 1986 or 1987. In 1988 the Madeleine Angevine was harvested for the first time and yielded about 400l an acre.

The wines currently produced are a dry white table wine, and a medium dry. Apart from degrees of dryness they are reminiscent of muscat in style, although with a traditionally English bouquet, and reminiscent of English summer gardens. They are both full, fruity wines with strong finish and are all sold locally.

The vineyard has a traditional Northamptonshire stone winery situated in the grounds of a listed Jacobean house. Colin Duns, the owner, is also the winemaker and John Fretter is the vineyard manager.

Visiting times: the vineyard can be visited by appointment, May to October, 10am-12noon and 3-6pm. Wines are available for tasting and purchase. The vineyard also sells vines.

How to get there: follow the A45 from Daventry signposted to Coventry. Turn right 4 miles from Daventry after crossing the Grand Union Canal and follow the signs for Braunston. The vineyard and winery are situated behind the first stone house on the right after the church.

Nearby attractions: Oxford, walks along Grand Union Canal and Braunston — Canal Centre, local crafts and boat trips.

Recommended pubs, restaurants and hotels in the area: Plough Inn (Braunston), Admiral Nelson and The Boatman (both canalside pubs in Braunston).

STAVERTON VINEYARD
Colin and Penny Duns
Napton Road
Staverton NN11 7HS
☎ (0788) 890278

The vineyard (a member of the EVA) has recently been planted by the owners of Braunston in the neighbouring village. The two vineyards will be operated as separate entities, although the Staverton wine may be produced at Braunston in the short term. Staverton is expected to produce its first small harvest in 1990 and a winery is expected to be operational by 1992 when the vineyard reaches full production. It covers 2.5 acres with a further 6 acres planned. It is planted with 2 acres of Madeleine Angevine and half an acre of Seyval Blanc. The first plantings took place in 1988 and the expansion is expected to take place in 1990.

The vineyard is at an average 360ft above sea level, on a south facing slope running down to a brook. The soil is well drained loam on a strata of sand and clay sub-soil. The vineyard is situated at maximum distance from the sea with favourable micro-climate and low rainfall.

All the vines are trained and pruned according to the Double Guyot system. Pruning takes place between January and March except during periods of frost. In March the vineyard is ploughed and rotavated. Weed control starts in April with a herbicide application between rows. There is a regular spraying programme between May and September against fungal diseases, and in September the whole vineyard is netted and fenced against badgers. Initially the wines will be made by Colin Duns at Braunston with John Fretter managing the vineyard.

Visiting times: not applicable at present, but will be open to the public once the vineyard is productive.

How to get there: directions from the owners when applicable.

Nearby attractions: many country walks and a golf club in the village.

Recommended pubs, restaurants and hotels in the area: Staverton Park Country Club and The Countryman, Napton Road, Staverton.

Buckinghamshire

HALE VALLEY VINEYARD
Antony and Carol Chapman
Hale Lane
Wendover HP22 6NQ
☎ (0296) 623730

The vineyard (a member of the EVA and the Thames and Chilterns Vineyards Association) covers 2 acres planted in April 1988. There are 400 vines each of Bacchus, Kernling and Findling, none of which are yet productive. The vineyard is on a south facing slope on chalky soil. It is run by the owners who plan initially to have the grapes vinified under contract. There are no plans to expand.

Visiting times: none at present but those seriously interested in viniculture might ring for an appointment.

How to get there: directions from owners.

Worcestershire

ASTLEY VINEYARDS
Michael and Betty Bache
The Crundels
Astley
Nr Stourport-on-Severn DY13 0RU
☎ (02993) 2907

The vineyard (a member of the EVA and the South West Vineyards Association) covers 5 acres. Varieties planted are Müller-Thurgau on an acre which accounts for 20 per cent of production, Huxelrebe on 1.25 acres (25 per cent), Kerner on 1.5 acres (30 per cent) and Madeleine Angevine on 1.25 acres and accounting for 25 per cent of production. There have been no changes to the original varieties planted and there are no new, as yet unproductive vines.

The vineyard is in the Severn Valley between 150ft and 190ft above sea level. It is on sandy loam, well sheltered from the prevailing winds and planted in three blocks, on a site almost certainly used for vine growing until the Middle Ages. The steep south facing slope beside the Norman church is still known as the Vineyard. The owner's named their home, Crundels, after a local word which denotes a southward-facing sandstone bank. It was on this feature that they first established their vineyard in 1971.

The first experimental years clearly established that the distinctive sandy loam of this part of the Severn Valley, combined with the favourable microclimate, produced high-quality wines with individual character.

The main 4-acre vineyard was planted in 1979 and 1980 and the wines produced were Huxelvaner, Astley's own name for a blend of the vigorous Huxelrebe and the Müller-Thurgau, as well as Madeleine Angevine, Kerner and a blend of all four.

Almost all the vines are trained on a modified Double Guyot system on high trellises. There is also some experimentation with the Single Guyot and Silvoz methods. Weeds are controlled by a combination of mechanical and chemical means, using a cultivator and flail mower and applications of herbicides. There is a regular spraying programme to protect against fungal attack and botrytis throughout the year.

The harvest starts between 5 October and 20 October with Huxelrebe and Madeleine Angevine being picked first. The Müller-Thurgau is usually harvested about 2 weeks later, and the Kerner can be anything between 2 and 4 weeks after the first picking. The grapes are taken in bushel boxes for crushing, pressing and vinification in Astley's own fermentation tanks at the Three Choirs Vineyard at Newent in Gloucestershire.

Production in the bumper year of 1984 was 23,500 bottles which fell to about 8,000 in 1985 and about 5,000 in 1986 because of bad weather, and down to about 2,900 in 1987 after the very wet summer. The 1988 vintage is expected to yield about 5,800 bottles. The award winning Kerner 1986 is now sold out but the 1987 is a fresh dry wine with an attractive hint of citrus flavours and a subtle Kerner nose.

Other wines produced include Astley Severn Vale, a medium blend of the vineyard's four varieties. It has a flowery nose and good fruit on the palate with enough body to accompany both meat and fish dishes. There is also a medium Huxelvaner, a blend with fine bouquet and flinty palate, and Madeleine Angevine, a dry wine with powerful nose and distinctive character, reminiscent of a fine Gewürztraminer.

The vineyard has a fine tradition of award winning wines, has won many gold medals and been awarded the prestigious President's Trophy of the EVA on three occasions. Every wine produced since 1983 has won at least one award. About 70 per cent of the wine is sold through the vineyard's own licensed shop. The rest is sold to a number of local restaurants and wine merchants. For 3 years wine has been exported to Germany and the vineyard has supplied British Embassies in Tokyo, Ankara, and The Hague. There has also been some export to the USA.

The vineyard is worked by the owner with the help of some regular part-time staff and casual labour brought in to assist with the pruning and picking. There are no plans to expand the acreage at present, although there will be a small increase in the experimental area on a steep south facing slope.

Visiting times: organised parties (minimum twenty) are welcome during the summer for talks, tastings and tours. Customers are free to walk round the vineyard and the vineyard shop is open throughout the year. There are no catering facilities but there are picnic areas.

How to get there: the vineyard is in Astley which is south of Stourport-on-Severn and north of Worcester and lies between the B4196 and the river Severn. If entering the village from the south on the B4196, the vineyard is signposted as a turning off to the right.

Nearby attractions: Worcester city and Cathedral, Great Witley, Stourport-on-Severn, Bewdley, Severn Valley steam railway, Wye Forest, Hartlebury Castle and Worcester County Folk Museum.

Recommended pubs, restaurants and hotels in the area: The Elms (Abberley), The Manor Arms (Abberley) and The Hundred House (Great Witley).

TILTRIDGE VINEYARD
Mr and Mrs P. Barker
Upper Hook Road
Upton-on-Severn WR8 0SA
☎ (06846) 2906

The vineyard (a member of the EVA) covers about 2.15 acres. The first plantings took place in 1988 when a quarter of an acre each of Huxelrebe and Seyval Blanc were planted. In 1989 a further acre is due to be planted, divided between Huxelrebe and Schönburger, and a further 0.66 of an acre is to be planted in 1990 but a decision on varieties is still to be made.

The vineyard is in the Severn Valley and enjoys a mild air flow from the Bristol Channel. It is 125ft above sea level on a south-east facing slope. The soil is clay silt with poor natural drainage which has been improved by installing land drains. The vines are all trained and pruned according to the Double Guyot system.

The vineyard does not have its own winery at present and when the vines are in production the grapes will be vinified under contract for the foreseeable future. The vineyard plans to sell as much wine as possible from the premises.

Visiting times: the vineyard is not yet open to the public but visitors seriously interested in viticulture could ring for an appointment.

How to get there: directions from owners.

Nearby attractions: Upton-upon-Severn, Malvern and Ledbury.

West Midlands

HALFPENNY GREEN VINEYARD
Martin Vickers
Upper Whittimere Farm
Halfpenny Green
Bobbington
Stourbridge DY7 5EP
☎ (038488) 387

The vineyard (a member of the EVA and the South West Vineyards Association) covers 3 acres of which half an acre is currently in production. These productive vines are divided equally between Seyval Blanc, Reichensteiner and Huxelrebe which each account for a third of production. There are also a number of varieties planted which are not yet in production. These are Huxelrebe 1.4 acres, Reichensteiner 0.6 acres, Seyval Blanc 0.5 acres and Madeleine Angevine 0.1 acres, as well as small quantities of Pinot Noir, Bacchus, Regner, Faber and some experimental varieties. There are plans to expand the vineyard with a further 2 acres of vines in 1990.

The vineyard is on south-east and south-west facing slopes in a large basin of fertile agricultural land between the Severn Valley at Bridgnorth and Wolverhampton. It is on the borders of Staffordshire and Shropshire, on light sandy loam over sandstone. It is free draining and at an altitude of about 315ft above sea level. The vineyard is in an area which enjoys early springs with soil temperatures and rainfall above average.

All the vines are trained and pruned using the Double Guyot method which has been modified slightly so that the system is very low because the site is rather exposed. There is a programme of spraying throughout the growing season to combat fungal diseases.

As only half an acre is in production, the

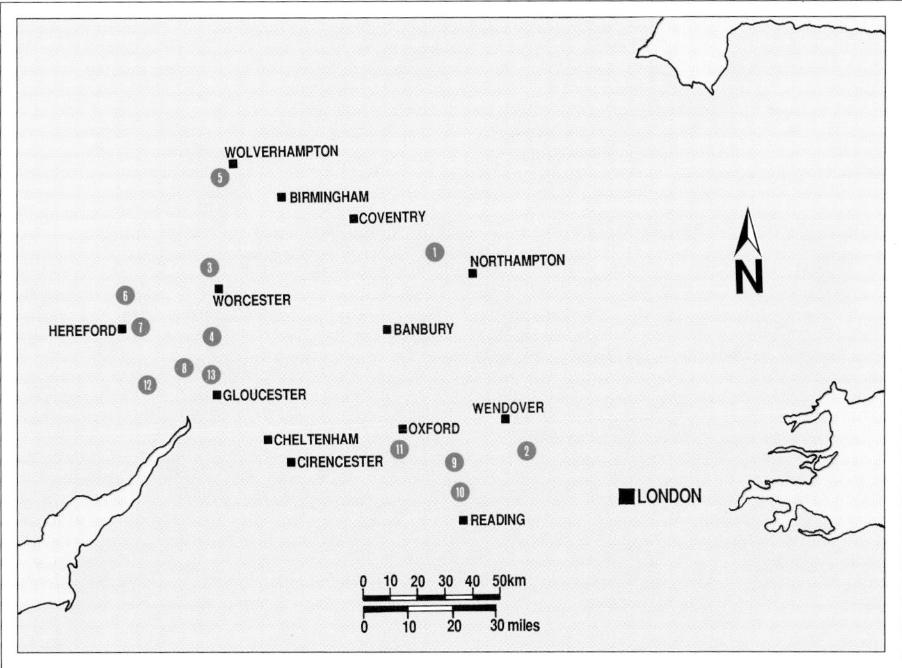

— *Location of the Vineyards in Central England* —

Northampton
1 Braunston
1 Staverton

Buckinghamshire
2 Hale Valley

Worcestershire
3 Astley
4 Tiltridge

West Midlands
5 Halfpenny Green

Herefordshire
6 Broadfield
7 Hagley
8 Halfpenny

Oxfordshire
9 Old Luxters
10 Clapcot
11 Bothy

Gloucestershire
12 St Anne's
13 Three Choirs

harvest usually takes only a few hours to gather. Picking normally takes place in the last week of October. The vineyard does not have its own winery, and the grapes are taken by road for vinification under contract at the Three Choirs Vineyard at Newent in Gloucestershire. The first harvest was in 1985 when 120 bottles were produced blending all three varieties, and that policy is still practised. Production in 1986 was 260 bottles, none in 1987 and about 100 in 1988. No wine has been sold commercially to date.

When the vineyard is mature it will be an extremely attractive site commanding stunning views across open countryside. More than 350 trees have been planted around the site both as windbreaks and to enhance the landscape. Expansion plans include the increased acreage, the building of a winery and opening to the public. The vineyard is part of an agricultural enterprise which also includes a 750-acre arable farm.

Visiting times: not open to the public yet, but those seriously interested in viticulture may ring for an appointment.

How to get there: the vineyard is just outside the village of Halfpenny Green on the Wolverhampton road.

Nearby attractions: Weston Park, Black Country Museum, West Midlands Safari Park and Ironbridge Gorge.

Herefordshire

BROADFIELD VINEYARD

Keith James
Broadfield Court Estate
Bodenham
☎ (056884) 483 (estate office)

The vineyard (a member of the EVA) covers 12 acres, with a further 3 acres due to be planted in 1989 and a further 5 acres in 1990. Varieties planted are Reichensteiner which accounts for about 60 per cent of production, Müller-Thurgau 20 per cent and the remaining production comes from Huxelrebe and Madeleine Angevine with a very small amount of Seyve Villard. In recent years the acreage of Huxelrebe has been increased and the Müller-Thurgau has been introduced. There are new plantings of Madeleine Angevine which are as yet unproductive.

The vineyard is on a south-south-west facing slope with the Calderwell brook running at the bottom. The escarpment is between 210ft and 240ft above sea level. The site is well sheltered and has its own excellent microclimate retaining the warmth once it has built up. It is on red clay loam. The average annual rainfall is about 27in, the weather is normally mild but there can be exceptionally cold winters — in January 1982 a temperature of -17°F (-27°C) was recorded. The climate is ideal for ripening grapes even in the worst English summers.

Broadfield was mentioned in the *Domesday Book* of 1085 as part of the Todeni estates. By the end of the fourteenth century, however, the land had passed into the hands of the Dinmore preceptory of the Knights Hospitallers of the Order of St John of Jerusalem.

The first vines were planted at Broadfield in 1971 — Müller-Thurgau and Seyve Villard — and the first vintage produced in 1975. A further 500 Reichensteiner vines were planted in a sloping field facing south-west immediately next to the gardens.

Reichensteiner was planted because of its ability to ripen consistently even in the poorest summer with high sugar readings. The alcohol content of the Reichensteiner 1985 for instance, was 11.3 per cent. The Huxelrebe vines crop heavily but were badly hit by the exceptionally cold winter of 1982 when the variety was nearly destroyed, for this reason further plantings are being restricted. Both the Müller-Thurgau and Seyve Villard stood up well to the cold weather.

All the vines are trained on the Double Guyot system and there are 1,000 vines to the acre. Pruning takes place in February and March. The harvest usually starts around 20 October and picking lasts between one and two weeks depending on conditions and the size of the crop. The vineyard does not yet have its own winery although one is to be installed when the vineyard's production reaches 25,000 bottles. The grapes are currently sent by road for vinification under contract at Pilton Manor or Three Choirs.

Reichensteiner and Huxelrebe grapes are taken to Pilton Manor in Somerset in late October from which dry wines are produced. The Müller-Thurgau and Reichensteiner for blending, together with the Seyve Villard are taken to Three Choirs in Gloucestershire from which medium and sweet wines are produced. The juice is siphoned off the presses into Broadfield vats where it is fermented and bottled in the following March.

Production has varied enormously over the years from 9,000 bottles in 1983, to 28,000 in the bumper 1984 and it has tailed off each vintage since because of the bad weather. In 1985 production was 9,000 bottles, 1986 6,000, 1987 5,000 and 1988 about 3,000. The quality of the wine has been very consistent and well received. Yields have been low in recent years but sugar content has been high and so providing the right material for producing quality wines.

Wines produced are Reichensteiner and Huxelrebe which are generally dry and similar to a Loire in style. The Seyve Villard and a blended Reichenster and Müller-Thurgau which is medium dry are also manufactured. The wines are of distinctive flavour and bouquet, and mature well in the bottle. After a few months they settle down and develop over a number of years. Vintages of the early eighties are still drinking well. Most of the wine is sold direct from the vineyard to restaurants and hotels, although it is stocked by fine wine merchants.

The vineyard is part of a 1,000-acre estate with ample room for expansion on sloping hillsides between 300ft and 400ft above sea level. Other activities include 350 cows milked at two dairy farms, and a similar number of followers being reared. About 80 per cent of the cattle feed is grown on the estate. There are 350 acres of cereals about a third of which goes for seed. There is also about 150 acres of woodland and this is being developed.

Visiting times: May to September 11.30am-3pm daily except Sunday. Parties by arrangement, minimum twenty people. There is a shop selling wines and vines, light refreshments are available and there is ample parking and picnic facilities. The vineyard is beside 4 acres of traditional English gardens which can also be visited. A farm trail is planned.

How to get there: the vineyard is 2 miles west of the A49 Hereford to Leominster road. From Hereford take the A49 for about 8 miles and then turn right on to the A417. Follow this road for about 2 miles, and then turn left opposite the Jet Garage. The vineyard is signposted about a mile down the road. If travelling from the south on the A49, the A417 turning is on the left about 4 miles out of Leominster.

Recommended pubs, hotels and restaurants in the area: The Green Dragon (hotel and restaurant, Hereford), and Talbot Hotel (Leominster).

HAGLEY VINEYARD

John Dorrell
Hagley Court East
Bartestree HR1 4BX
☎ (0432) 850284

The vineyard (a member of the EVA) covers 9.25 acres and is owned by a farmer who has retired after a lifetime in large scale agricultural and horticultural production. Varieties planted include Madeleine Angevine on 4 acres which accounts for 40 per cent of production, Seyval Blanc on 2 acres (20 per cent), Huxelrebe on 1.5 acres (15 per cent) and Reichensteiner on one acre (10 per cent). The rest of the acreage is planted with Müller-Thurgau, Kerner and Freisamer which make up the remaining production. The main plantings took place in 1985 and 1986 with a smaller acreage added in 1987. The first crop is expected in 1989.

The vineyard is 4 miles east of Hereford at an altitude of between 270ft and 300ft above sea level. It is on a south facing slope and rather exposed to westerly winds. The soil is a gravel cap at the top end merging with old red sandstone loam. The site is in the rain shadow of the Black Mountains which accounts for the low annual rainfall of about 24in but the vines receive high levels of light. It is in a well known fruit growing area. All the vines are trained and pruned on the Open Lyre system. The rows are 9ft apart and the vines are spaced at 4ft 6in intervals.

Under this system the vine is trained so that it resembles an inverted umbrella and there is a gap of at least 30in at the top of open 'Y' which allows maximum penetration of light and sunshine. There is some summer pruning and the growing tips of the vines are trimmed mechanically.

There is a regular spraying programme during the growing season at approximately 14-day intervals. Downy mildew poses a problem every year but is contained. There is little experience of harvesting yet but the Madeleine Angeveine is expected to be the first variety to ripen and the Kerner last.

Visiting times: not open to the public, although people interested could ring to ask for an appointment.

How to get there: directions from owners.

HALFPENNY VINEYARD
Giles Cross
Halfpenny House
Common Hill
Fownhope HR1 4QA
☎ (0432) 77348

The vineyard (a member of the EVA) covers 0.6 acres divided equally between Bacchus and Seyval Blanc. The first plantings took place in May 1987. It is at an altitude of 120ft above sea level on a south facing slope with good protection. The soil is clay with a reasonable loam overlay, but with a high ph because it is situated on a limestone ridge. The weather in the vineyard seems to be affected by a 'window' in the lee of the Welsh hills — the Black Mountains and Brecon Beacons.

Since planting, the vines were pruned in January 1988 and trellis training started for a modified Geneva Double Curtain system. A regular programme of spraying against disease and weeds is undertaken through the growing season.

The vineyard hopes to gather its first harvest in 1990. It does not have its own winery and the grapes will be vinified under contract elsewhere.

Visiting times: not open to the public although people interested could ring to ask for an appointment.

How to get there: take the B4224 from Newent (Gloc) to Fownhope and turn right at the church into the very narrow lane. The vineyard is half a mile down the lane on the left.

Nearby attractions: The Wye Valley Walk from Hay to Chepstow, Symonds Yat.

Recommended pubs, restaurants and hotels in the area: Green Man (Fownhope), and Green Dragon (hotel and restaurant, Hereford).

Oxfordshire

BOTHY VINEYARD
Roger and Dorothea Fisher
Bothy Cottage
Frilford Heath
Abingdon OX13 6QW
☎ (0491) 681484

The vineyard is run by the owner, a professional civil engineer, and his wife, an entomologist. Casual labour is brought in as required. The vineyard is a member of the EVA and was the founding vineyard in the Thames and Chilterns Vineyards Association. It covers 3 acres and is to be extended by a further 2 acres. Varieties grown are Huxelrebe, Perle, Ortega and Optima. There have been no changes to the varieties planted since the vineyard was established in 1978-9 and there are no new, as yet, unproductive vines.

The vineyard is south of Boars Hill, to the west of Abingdon, on land sloping gently to the south. There are distant views across the river Ock to the Berkshire Downs in the Vale of the White Horse. The vineyard has an annual rainfall of about 24in with little variation throughout the year. The climate is generally warm with low humidity but occasional severe frosts in the spring.

The soil is very well drained deep sand with occasional bands of cemented concretions. The loamy top soil (full of moles) form part of the Frilford Series, only found locally.

Vine growing at Abingdon is not new and the abbey maintained a vineyard during the Middle Ages, as well as extensive farms in the parishes of Marcham, where Bothy Vineyard has been established.

The site was specially chosen for its suitability for growing vines, especially deep rooting and early flowering varieties, giving moderate yields but excellent balance of acidity and extract. Pruning starts straight after Christmas and continues until Easter. The vines are trained on both the single and double Guyot method, although experiments are being carried out on a new adaptation of the Guyot system.

The vines are spaced at 4ft 3in intervals, in rows 7ft 3in apart. The rows are divided into five blocks with two wide and two narrow paths. Green pruning takes place between July and September. Prunings are composted and winter prunings are burnt. Topping of vines is done once or twice at 5ft 9in and some de-leafing is done. Spraying by tractor takes place at approximately fourteen-day intervals, although the first spray may be by hand. Weed control is by paraquat only which is non-persistant, and by cultivating.

The harvest generally starts around the middle of October and continues until early November. The order of picking depends on the ripeness of the varieties. Picking usually takes place at the weekends with the help of friends. They are unpaid but are entertained to lunch and harvest supper. Picking is into buckets in the rows, which are emptied into crates holding about 180lb at the end of each row. The crates are then transported to the winery in a trailer pulled by a two-wheel tractor. On reception at the winery the crates are weighed and emptied into the crusher and de-stemmer, which is a hand operated model converted to electric motor drive.

The crushed grapes are taken to the press using 22.5l buckets. An elevator will be installed in due course. The varieties are weighed and crushed separately, but may be mixed subsequently for fermentation. Blending of fermented wines is not practised. If necessary, the crushed and settled juice may be de-acidified before fermentation, which is preferred to post-fermentation de-acidification.

Addition of sugar for chaptalisation, and the de-acidification are carried out in a purpose made mixing tank to the owner's design. Fermentation is carried out in 810l stainless steel tanks, with the wines being racked off into larger tanks when appropriate.

Malolactic fermentation may be induced after the main fermentation. The wines are fermented out fully and *süss* reserve used to increase the residual sugar content if a non-dry wine is required.

A highly successful sweet wine has been made by stopping fermentation. A mono pump is used in preference to centrifugal machines and gas pressure is used when possible. Minimal filtering is used after fermentation. A sterile filter is used and after stabilisation, into the bottling machine which is a four-head vacuum filling type. The bottles are stood upright for 24 hours before binning to prevent weeping through the corks. Bottle corks are given a sterile spray after corking.

The first vintage was gathered in 1982 but was very low because of severe frosts. In 1983 6,000 bottles were produced and quality was excellent, although there were some losses due to rot. A similar production was achieved in 1984, and again quality was excellent, and there was some noble rot on some varieties.

In 1985 there was only a moderate harvest and it would have been disastrous had it not been for a good autumn. About 2,000 bottles were produced, and this figure was repeated in 1986. The 1987 harvest was described as appalling with only 700 bottles produced, because of sparse flowering followed by awful weather, and in 1988 the vintage yielded 900 bottles after a good flowering was ruined by a wet July and generally cold summer.

The wines produced are: Ortega and Optima, a dry wine, very well balanced with good extract and complex flavours. It has an interesting fruity nose and is designed to accompany food and the Huxelrebe and Perle a medium dry blend, fresh and tangy with a hint of sweetness on the finish, but definitely more on the dry side than the medium. It has a flowery nose which matches the lighter style.

The present winery is in an old stone bothy, which at one time was part of the adjacent Oakley Park estate. The wide grassy paths between the vines make pleasant walking and there is an abundance of wildlife which is encouraged. A new winery is to be built shortly, and the remaining 5 acres planted.

Visiting times: any time when open, normally at weekends and some days during the week. A telephone call in advance is advised. Sales of the wine by the bottle or case are from the wine shop. The winery can be visited on request. Free tastings are usually available. Arrangements can be made for groups wishing to visit. Other products sold include asparagus, red, white and black currants, autumn raspberries and some fresh vegetables when in season.

How to get there: the vineyard is on an unnumbered road a mile north of Marcham village, 2 miles west of Abingdon.

Nearby attractions: the vineyard is in a conservation area and close to a nature reserve. Oxford and Abingdon are tourist centres, and the famous White Horse Hill is not far away.

Recommended pubs, hotels and restaurants in the area: Dog House Hotel (next door).

OLD LUXTERS VINEYARD

Chiltern Valley Wines
David and Fiona Ealand
Hambleden
Henley-on-Thames RG9 6JW
☎ (049163) 330

The vineyard (a member of the EVA) covers 3 acres planted with Madeleine Angevine, Bacchus and Reichensteiner. In the last 5 years the owners have also been engaged in establishing seventeen other vineyards in the area, most of which grow for the Old Luxters winery. This extra vineyard acreage now covers about 100 acres and at a production rate of about 5 tons an acre, should be yielding about 500,000 bottles of wine by the mid-1990s. The owners are the winemakers aided by a full-time manager and part-time help from members of the family. They plan to continue to expand the vineyard acreage, and are considering producing cider.

The vineyard is in the Chiltern Hills overlooking the Hambledon Valley, near Henley-on-Thames. The site enjoys a good temperate climate and has a chalky soil with flints (ideal for heat retention and drainage). The vineyard has revised a 2,000-year-old tradition because the Romans grew vines there. All the vines are trained and pruned on the Geneva Double Curtain system.

Harvesting is by hand and there is never a shortage of volunteers — possibly because of their traditional celebration lunch as soon as the harvest is gathered. All three varieties are picked in a single morning. Natural sugar levels are monitored daily so that the grapes are harvested at their optimum. They are crushed then pressed immediately but the fermentation is kept cool and slow — between 50°F (10°C) and 53°F (12°C) — to preserve fruitiness and flavour.

The grapes are crushed on the way to the purpose built winery and then transferred to a Willmes press. All the tanks are stainless steel and a visiting wine professor from Davis University, California, described the winery as 'one of the most impeccable I have seen in Europe'.

The sharp January frosts are used to naturally settle, clarify and stabilise the wine so that in the absence of frosts over a mild winter some tartrate crystals might form in the bottle. These are completely harmless. The wines are matured in the bottle in a temperature-controlled store and are ready for drinking in the summer following the harvest.

The winery's secret is in minimal interference by man, oxygen or infection. Enormous attention to detail is exercised particularly in maintaining sterile conditions. The aim is to use the latest technology to prevent spoilage, but 'not to seek to change, improve or otherwise interfere with the natural wine making process'.

Annual production is about 70,000 to 80,000 bottles a year and is increasing. The wine is sold direct from the winery and through a number of local outlets, and exported to New Zealand, the USA, Japan, and throughout Europe.

Four varieties of Chiltern Valley white wine are produced; dry, reserve (also dry), medium dry, and a special *cuvée*, with an extra touch of sweetness. They are blended from Madeleine Angevine, Bacchus, Reichensteiner, Müller-Thurgau and Seyval Blanc.

The winery has developed an international reputation and has won gold medals and top awards both in the UK and overseas. Against a total of 1,100 wines from thirty countries, their Old Luxters Reserve won the silver medal in a blind tasting at the 1987 International Wine and Spirit

Competition, and the trophy for the best English wine, for the second year running. The 1986 award was only 12 months after their first commercial harvest. In 1988 they won both the trophy and gold medal for the best English wine. The vineyard is in an area of outstanding natural beauty, and the winery is in buildings of historic interest.

Visiting times: by arrangement.

How to get there: take the Hambleden road off the A4155, about 5 miles from Henley-on-Thames heading towards Marlow.

Nearby attractions: Henley-on-Thames, Marlow, Oxford, and Hambleden.

CLAPCOT VINEYARD
Denys Randolph
The Cottages
Rush Court
Wallingford OX10 8LJ
☎ (0491) 34802

The vineyard covers 10 acres with a further 3 acres due to be planted in 1989. Planting started in 1987 with Bacchus 1.5 acres, and an acre each of Huxelrebe and Reichensteiner. The second plantings took place in March 1988 and consisted of a further 3 acres of Bacchus, 2 acres of Dornfelder, an acre of Madeleine Angevine and half an acre of Dunkfelder. The vineyard was pasture land until 1986 and was grazed regularly. It is on a level site, rather open to the prevailing south-westerly winds so windbreaks have been planted. The soil is a mixture of clay, chalk and sandy loam.

All the vines are trained on the Geneva Double Curtain system. In all cases, the first year growth was pruned back to the second or third buds. The 1987 vines are now all firmly established with one leg on the trellis. There is a regular spraying programme to protect against disease during the growing season. The vineyard will not take any crop from 1989 and expect to gather their first harvest in 1990.

Visiting times: not open to the public although people interested could ring to ask for an appointment.

How to get there: directions from owners.

Gloucestershire

ST ANNE'S VINEYARD
Brian and Annie Edwards
Wain House
Oxenhall
Nr Newent
☎ (098982) 313

The vineyard covers 2 acres planted mainly with Madeleine Angevine, Seyval Blanc, Triomphe D'Alsace and Müller-Thurgau. There are many other varieties being grown but only in very small quantities. There are no plans for expansion. There have been no changes to varieties planted in recent years and there are no new, as yet unproductive vines.

The vineyard is in a fairly sheltered position on well drained clay with no frost pocket, in a very rural location. The soil has a ph of 6.5. It usually enjoys a fairly mild climate with no extremes. The vineyard was planted by the present owners in 1979 and came into commercial production in 1984. More than 100 varieties are grown, most of them on an experimental basis.

Pruning takes place from January to April and all the vines are trained on the Double Guyot system. Sprays are used only when necessary to combat fungal diseases, such as mildew and weeds.

The grapes are harvested in October before too much autumn dampness has set in, and before the wasps become too much of a pest. The Madeleine Angevine is harvested first and the ripeness of the other varieties varies according to the weather. The later varieties are often picked into November.

The grapes go through an electric crusher and de-stalker, and are then pressed in a traditional basket press, before being fermented in 157l barrels.

The wine is racked as necessary, filtered and bottled using a syphon bottler. This can

Chiltern Valley Wines, Old Luxters Vineyard, Oxfordshire

cope with about 1,000 bottles a day if necessary, and is operated by a single person.

Annual production is variable according to the weather conditions, but the aver-

age over the last 5 years has been about 4,000 bottles plus.

Wines produced are Madeleine Angevine and Müller-Thurgau, both medium dry, a dry Seyval Blanc, a dry red Triomphe D'Alsace, and a medium dry rosé and blended white. All the wines are sold from the vineyard. The vineyard and winery are worked by the owners with the help of casuals brought in for the harvest. The winery is traditional using low cost machinery and operating on a small scale.

Visiting times: weekends and bank holidays 10am-7pm, Tuesday to Friday all year, 2-7pm. The public are welcome to visit the vineyard and winery free of charge, and there are short guided tours if time permits. The wine shop offers free tastings, and sells the above wines as well as vines and a range of fruit wines, including strawberry, red and white currant, Worcesterberry and

rhubarb made from local fruit at the winery. There is also a range of home made marmalades, jams and chutneys.

How to get there: from Newent, take either the B4215 north to Dymock and turn off left and follow the signs for Oxenhall, or take the B4221 through Woodyard and follow the Oxenhall signs. From Woodyard the vineyard is 1.7 miles along Horsefair Lane. The turning for St Anne's is opposite Oxenhall Church, and the vineyard is on the right a short way after a narrow bridge.

Nearby attractions: Newent Victorian Museum, and Falconry Centre.

THREE CHOIRS VINEYARD
Tom Day
Rhyle House
Welsh House Lane
Newent GL18 1LR
☎ (053185) 223 or 555

The vineyard covers 22 acres in full production, with a further 3 acres coming into production in 1989. It is planned to expand the acreage under vines with Huxelrebe, Schönburger and Seyval Blanc. The vineyard, a member of the EVA, South West Vinegrowers Association, and South West Wine and Spirit Association, is part of an agricultural enterprise which also includes 42 acres of apple orchards. Varieties planted are: Huxelrebe 1.5 acres, Reichensteiner 5.2 acres, Müller-Thurgau 7 acres, Seyval Blanc 4.4 acres, Schönburger 1.1 acres, Pinot Noir 0.66 acres, as well as some small plantings of Triomphe D'Alsace, Bacchus, Ortega and Riesling.

There have been no changes to the varieties planted in recent years but there has been a steady programme of plantings with 3 acres coming into production in 1989 and a further 6 acres the year after. This last planting includes an additional acre of Pinot Noir as well as Triomphe D'Alsace, Schönburger, Seyval Blanc and Huxelrebe.

The vineyard is on south facing slopes, on free draining red sandstone. Average rainfall is 29in a year and the vineyard is in a sheltered location, and benefits from being in the rain shadow of the Forest of Dean. The vineyard gets its name because it is close to the mid-way point between Gloucester, Hereford and Worcester in one of whose cathedrals the famous Three Choirs Festival is celebrated each year. It was planted in 1973 and the first vintage was in 1975. Early success has resulted in rapid expansion, from an experimental half an acre to 18 acres with a potential output of more than 100,000 bottles, making it one of the six largest vineyards in Britain.

It was originally planted with Müller-Thurgau and Reichensteiner and more than a dozen vines have been experimented with, including the Austrian red variety Zweigeltrebe. The vines are trained using a variety of systems—Single Curtain, Geneva Double Curtain and Double Guyot.

The vintage usually starts around the 20 October and lasts for about a month. Ortega, Siegerrebe and Huxelrebe are the first varieties to be picked, and Pinot Noir and Riesling last. In recent years there has been a rush to pick the grapes before botrytis damages the crop. In previous years a system of measuring sugars and acidities prior to harvest was adopted so that a graph could be plotted to get the optimum picking date.

The grapes are picked by hand and loaded on to Chemo grape trailers which take them to the winery. A Willmes 1,200 press is used together with an old style Willmes internal bladder press.

The winery uses both stainless steel and fibreglass tanks. Cold stores are available for either keeping the fermentation warm or for checking or stopping fermentation, as well as for bitartrate deposition.

A special neutral yeast is used to help develop the natural flavour characteristics of each variety. The fermentation is controlled so that it is slow and cool to retain freshness of flavour and fragrance. It can take between a month and six weeks.

When fermentation is complete, the clear wine is racked and stored until ready for bottling. Just before bottling it is filtered to remove any remaining solids. It is bottled cold in March to retain small amounts of carbon dioxide, to give it the slight *pétillant* for which Three Choirs is noted. All the varieties are vinified separately and the most promising varietals bottled. The remainder of the wines are separated into a medium dry and medium wine by blending according to taste. Filtering is by sheet filtration. The sweet (*süss*) reserve is made

in the winery and blended according to taste. The wines tend to be light, clean and dry in style with subtlety of delicacy and flavour.

Production over the last 5 years has been variable, often hit by the bad weather and wet summers. The cold and wet summer of 1985 could have been disastrous, but the harvest was saved by a dry September and October. The quality of the wine produced was excellent. In 1986 the quantity was down because of the weather, although the quality was superb, achieved mainly by

Three Choirs
11% Vol.
WHITE ENGLISH TABLE WINE 70cl.

the amount of sunshine in September and October after a very wet, cold summer. The vineyard was not badly affected by the storms that hit other southern vineyards during the 1987 harvest and wine was produced, although because of the poor summer the acid levels are high. In 1988 the flowering which takes place in early June was hampered by rain, and led to a bad fruit set and low yields. Quality is good, however, because a period of sunshine in late September put sugar levels up to help compensate for the high acidity levels. The vineyard expects to produce high quality wines from the 1988 harvest.

Wines produced are: Three Choirs Medium 1985 which won the vineyard title of Winemakers of the Year in 1987, and the EVA Gold Seal of Quality. It is made from the more aromatic grapes, has a full and fruity palate with good balance between sweetness and acidity. The finish has length and because of the fruity acidity it is clean and fresh; Three Choirs Medium Dry 1986, another EVA Gold Seal of Quality wine, it

Fine ENGLISH Wine
10.5% Vol. 70cl.
THREE CHOIRS
Winemasters Selection
WHITE ENGLISH TABLE WINE
Produced at Three Choirs Vineyards Limited Newent, Gloucestershire. U.K.

has excellent fruity balance, full fruit and is just off dry. Mostly a blend of Müller-Thurgau and Reichensteiner with a hint of spiciness from some of the more aromatic varieties; Three Choirs Seyval Reichensteiner 1985, EVA Gold Seal of Quality and gold medal winner. It was made after the hot summer of 1984 and has a crisp, gooseberry aroma with honeyed flavours on the palate, and a long, crisp finish. More French in style than German; Winemasters Selection Dry 1984, has a delicate flowery nose, crisp

palate and a touch of spring flowers, producing a fresh finish and Winemasters Selection Medium 1984, a powerful, but mellow rich blend of fruity aromas on the nose, lush ripe melons on the palate, and crisp finish.

Limited supplies of single varietal wines were produced in 1988, including Pinot Noir Rosé 1987 (74 cases), and Schönburger 1987 (94 cases). There will be some Pinot Noir Rosé 1988 but it will again be in short supply. The vineyard also produces a number of different types of traditional perry and cider, elderflower cordial and apple juices.

The vineyard sells wine directly to the public and to both the on and off trade, including wholesalers, independent merchants, restaurants and hotels and national wine merchants including Victoria Wine, Thresher and Peter Dominic.

The vineyard also specialises in 'own label' wines for a number of companies including Ferranti, Pilkington and Manchester United Football Club. The wine is not exported but it has been shown in Japan, Germany and France.

Visiting times: summer weekdays 9am-5pm, 10am-5pm weekends. Winter 9am-5pm weekdays only, not open at weekends until Easter and closed 24 December until mid-January.

The wine shop adjoins the winery and is open to the public for tastings and sales of wines, perry, cider, local cheese and other local food and beverage. Vines are also for sale. Individuals are welcome and there is a free map of the walk around the vineyard. A nature trail is being developed below the spectacular terraced vineyard. There is a tasting room and a picnic area overlooking a terraced vineyard. Groups, between twenty and fifty-five, receive a talk on the history of English wine and vine growing in the vineyard, followed by a tasting and slide show, tour of the winery, and lunch or supper if requested. Group visits must be arranged in advance.

How to get there: from Newent take the B4215 signposted to Dymock and Leominster. After about 2 miles turn right into Welsh House Lane which is signposted, and drive for about a mile until you see the vineyard on the right hand side of the road.

Nearby attractions: Falconry Centre (Newent), Shambles of Newent (Victorian Museum), and Butterfly Centre.

Recommended pubs, restaurants and hotels in the area: Corse Laun hotel and restaurant (Tirley) and Butchers Arms (Woolhope).

Chapter 10
Other Vineyards

Wales

The history of Welsh wine can be traced back to the twelfth century but probably pre-dates this by several hundred years or more. International wine writer and Welshman Andrew Jones, who has kindly made available his detailed research, credits the first written record of vines being planted in Wales to Geraldis Cambrensis, the twelfth-century cleric and writer.

Describing his first home at Manorbier Castle in Dyfed, he wrote 'Under its walls beside a fishpond, a beautiful garden, enclosed on one side by a vineyard and on the other by a wood'.

The next evidence of a Welsh vineyard comes in the fourteenth century. It was at Sycarth, the home of the Welsh leader Owain Glyndwr, and was described as having 'every support to hospitality, a park, warren and a pigeon house, a mill, orchard and a vineyard.'

The Dissolution of the Monasteries and the availability of cheap wine from the continent led to the decline of winemaking throughout Britain, and there was not a real revival until the middle of the 1870s.

In 1875 John Patrick Crichton Stuart, the then Marquess of Bute, was aged 26 and extraordinarily wealthy, a landowner on a massive scale with huge estates in Scotland and South Wales. A few years earlier while travelling through Europe, he was struck by the beauty of a particular *château* surrounded by vineyards and decided to copy this on one of his estates. Work had already started on rebuilding a small ruined thirteenth-century castle at Tongwynlais, about 5 miles north of Cardiff. It was to be rebuilt as a hunting lodge and it was surrounded by slopes ideal for vines.

In 1875 he sent his head gardener Andrew Pettigrew to the castle to locate the best sites for the vineyards. Two different parcels of land were chosen, a total of 3 acres, and they were planted with Gamay Noir and Mille Blanche. The Mille Blanche were not successful and were grubbed up and the whole area was planted with the Gamay. The castle was made of rough faced red stone, and known locally as Castell Coch, the Red Castle. A new age of winemaking was about to dawn, red wine produced from grapes grown in Wales at the Red Castle. *Punch* magazine wrote unkindly that if ever wine was made it would take four men to drink it — the victim, two to hold him down and one to pour it down his throat.

The vineyards prospered and others were planted. Five acres were planted near the coast at Swanbridge, and another small one at St Quentins, near Cowbridge, but this was too exposed to the wind and failed. The first wines produced at Cardiff Castle, however, were white and labelled Coteaux Champenois, or still Champagne.

The Castle Coch Vineyard was on a gentle south facing slope protected from the north by dense woodland. The soil was a light fibrous loam about 2ft deep overlying broken limestone rock. The vines were planted 3ft apart in rows 3ft apart. The first wine sold to the public was offered in 1881. In 1887 the harvest yielded 3,600 bottles and in 1893 a record 12,000 bottles were produced. By 1905 the vineyard had grown to 63,000 vines, and the wines were being marketed by London wine merchants Hatch Mansfield — from 48s a dozen for the 1885 to 36s a dozen for the 1892. The 1893 fetched 60s a dozen, compared with famous Burgundies from Pommard selling for 42s and Chambertin 66s.

The vineyards lasted until 1920 although production ceased during the war. The Castell Coch site is now part of the castle grounds, and the Swanbridge vineyard is a small orchard.

Welsh vineyards started to appear again in the mid-1960s. Vineyards were planted at Lamphey in Dyfed, and Trimsarn, near Llanelli, but both were to fail. Today there are half a dozen or more vineyards, battling against the odds and the weather, to produce Welsh wine. Thankfully, they seem to be winning.

GLYNDWR VINEYARD

Richard and Robbie Norris
Folly Farm
Llanblethian
Cowbridge
South Glamorgan
☎ (04463) 4564

The vineyard (a member of the EVA) covers 3 acres with a further acre to be planted in 1989-90, probably with Seyval Blanc or Triomphe D'Alsace. Varieties planted are in groups of Triomphe D'Alsace with Leon Millot, Seyval Blanc, and Reichensteiner with Madeleine Angevine, each accounting for a third of total production. There has been a switch in recent years away from Madeleine Angevine to Seyval Blanc. There are no new, as yet unproductive vines.

The vineyard is set in the unspoilt Vale of Glamorgan, amid rolling hills and valleys, with a small wood to the west. It is on loamy clay overlying limestone, on a gradually sloping south-south-east site. It enjoys a very mild maritime climate being only 4 miles from the sea. It also enjoys the highest mean temperatures in the country outside the south-west tip of England, and is windy which prevents botrytis setting in. Summers are quite fair compared with the rest of Wales, and there are very few severe winters.

The vineyard was planted in 1983 and all the vines are trained on the Double Guyot system 4ft apart in rows 6ft apart. There is a regular fortnightly spraying programme using zinc and sulphur, interspersed with pre- and post-flowering Bordeaux mixture and so on. The harvest usually begins between 14 and 22 October and normally takes 2 days to gather. The Madeleine Angevine is the first variety to be picked, followed by Reichensteiner, Triomphe D'Alsace, Leon Millot and finally Seyval Blanc.

The vineyard does not have its own winery and the grapes are sent by road for vinfication at Three Choirs Vineyard by Dr Kit Morris. Production in 1986 was 400 bottles, which rose to 600 in 1987 and 1,000 in 1988. The vineyard is very pleased with the quality of all the vintages to date, despite the limited production.

A rosé is currently produced which has tremendous bouquet and great character. It is light, refreshing and fruity. They hope to produce their first white wine from the 1989 vintage. The wine is sold locally to restaurants, hotels, off-licences and shops.

Visiting times: by appointment only.

How to get there: the vineyard is south of Cowbridge in the village of Llanblethian. Take the B4270 out of Cowbridge and turn left past the castle remains on the outskirts of the village. The vineyard is on the right just beyond the pub.

Nearby attractions: coastal walks, bathing, very wild area with ruined castles and small villages to explore. No major tourist attractions.

Recommended pubs, restaurants and hotels in the area: Mulligans Rest, near Cowbridge, Bea Hotel (Cowbridge), and Cross Inn (Llanblethian).

HOUSE OF CELYN VINEYARD

Alan Hann
Llwyn Celyn
Caerleon
Newport
Gwent NP6 1LS ☎ (063349) 600

The vineyard (a member of the EVA) covers 1.5 acres and varieties are Triomphe D'Alsace 950 vines, Leon Millot 140 vines, Pinot Noir 380 vines, Dornfelder 1,230 vines, Chardonnay 230 vines, and Auxerrois 330 vines.

The vineyard has planted mostly red wine varieties — only 15 per cent are for white wines — and so has been able to squeeze more than 3,000 vines into the 1.5-acre site on a 4ft square basis. All the vines are now in their third year and all are trained on the Double Guyot system. The first harvest is expected in 1990.

The vineyard is south-south-east facing, and the vines are planted in rows running north to south at an altitude of about 250ft above sea level. The slope is 1:8 on sandy clay loam with good drainage with considerable rock about 18in below the surface. This rock sub-strata has forced the vines to grow vigorously and they have come on surprisingly quickly.

The vineyard is about 10 miles up the Usk valley on nicely sloping hills. It enjoys a quite distinct microclimate giving mild conditions and better than average sunshine hours. This part of south-east Wales is one of the first regions to reach the 200 cumulative hours point in the UK.

Pruning starts each January and continues throughout February, while summer pruning takes place in July and September. There is a regular spraying programme at 3-week intervals from March to September, although it is suspended during flower set time. There are no plans at present to expand the vineyard but Alan Hann is considering establishing his own winery.

Visiting times: not yet decided at time of writing.

How to get there: from the M4 take exit 25 to Caerleon. Follow the one way system past the village green on the left and straight over the mini roundabout and head towards Usk and Llangybi. After 3 miles take a left hand turn opposite a bus stop. After about 300yd turn right up the driveway marked LLwyn Celyn.

Nearby attractions: Roman garrison at Caerleon, Usk Castle, river Usk and Cardiff Castle.

Recommended pubs, restaurants and hotels in the area: White Hart (Llangybi), Cwrt Bleddyn Hotel (Llangybi), and Alfonso's Restaurant (Usk).

LLANERCH VINEYARD (Cariad Wines)

Peter and Diana Andrews
Hensol
Nr Pontyclun
South Glamorgan CF7 8JU
☎ (0443) 225877

The vineyard (a member of the EVA, the South West Vineyards Association and Taste of Wales) covers 6 acres, 4 of which are planted with 2 acres due to be planted in 1989. An acre each of Bacchus and Reichensteiner was planted in 1987, and an acre each of Huxelrebe and Kernling in 1986. The 1989 plantings will be Seyval Blanc, Triomphe D'Alsace and Leon Millot to be trained on a modified Geneva Double Curtain system. The first harvest is expected to come from the Huxelrebe and Kernling in 1989. The vineyard is on a south facing slope overlooking the Ely valley in the Vale of Glamorgan. The soil is sandy loam. It enjoys mild, humid summers and mild, humid winters.

The Bacchus and Reichensteiner are on a modified Geneva Double Curtain system with the vines planted 5ft apart in rows 11ft apart, and the wire 5ft above the ground. The Huxelrebe and Kernling are trained on the Lyre system, with the vines 4ft apart in rows 9ft apart. The wire is about 27in above the ground. A winery is being built this year in a converted cowshed. It will make the vineyard the only one in Wales making its own wine.

Visiting times: the vineyard hopes to open to the public in 1991. It plans to sell other Welsh wines, cheeses and other local produce, and possibly trout from their own lake. When open there will be tours, gift shop, picnic area, as well as woodland and lakeside walks.

How to get there: Follow the signs from junction 34 on the M4 for a mile.

Nearby attractions: Cardiff.

MONNOW VALLEY VINEYARD
M.J.M. Clarke and R. Wilson
Osbaston House
Monmouth
Gwent NP4 5BB
☎ (0600) 3596 or 6209

The vineyard (a member of the EVA) covers an acre with a further 3 acres to be planted. Varieties planted are Seyval Blanc, Madeleine Angevine, Müller-Thurgau and Ortega. There are about 1,500 vines. The Ortega is to be replaced, while the Seyval Blanc and Madeleine Angevine will be increased in the new plantings. There will be about an acre each of these two varieties and the third will be planted with Huxelrebe. The vineyard is on a south-west facing slope above the river Monnow, 2 miles north of Monmouth, on light to medium loam.

Given a reasonable spell in late June to mid-July, over the crucial flowering period, the climate is satisfactory in an average year. Pruning can be spread from early January until March although the aim is to do it as quickly as possible. It is the largest single task. The spraying programme 'which is absolutely the heart of the job and the secret of success', runs throughout the growing season from May until the end of October or early November depending on the weather.

The vineyard was planted in 1978 and 1979 using a low Double Guyot system but has now been converted to a higher system. This has been reasonably successful but requires a lot of summer pruning. They are now converting to the Geneva Double Curtain system in the existing vineyard which will take 2 or 3 years. The new vineyard will be trained from the start on the Geneva Double Curtain system.

The harvest usually starts between 5 and 10 October because Ortega and Madeleine Angevine are both early varieties. The grapes are normally picked in a day. The two later varieties, Seyval Blanc and Müller-Thurgau are harvested between 20 and 25 October, again a day is sufficient except in the bumper years. The vineyard does not have its own winery and the grapes are taken by road to the Three Choirs Vineyard at Newent and vinified under contract. The first harvest in 1983 yielded 2,750 bottles. Production rose to 7,250 bottles in the bumper year of 1984, but fell to 1,000 bottles in 1985. It was 2,250 in 1986, and has been 1,000 bottles in each of the last 2 years. Usually a wine is made by blending together all the varieties. The wine is mostly sold locally to hotels and restaurants in Cardiff, south-east and west Wales. The bottles are labelled Gwin o Gymru — Wine of Wales.

Visiting times: by appointment.

How to get there: take the Skenfrith road north from Monmouth for about 2 miles to Monnow Hill House and the vineyard.

Nearby attractions: Wye Valley and Black Mountains.

Recommended pubs, restaurants and hotels in the area: The King's Head Hotel (Monmouth), and A Taste of Wales (Cardiff).

Yorkshire

LEVENTHORPE VINEYARD
George and Janet Bowden
Bullerthorpe Lane
Woodlesford
Leeds LS8 1NF
correspondence to:
25 Thorn Lane
Leeds LS8 1NF
☎ (0532) 667892

The vineyard covers 5 acres and has the distinction of being the most northerly vineyard in this guide. It is the only vineyard in this part of the world so far, although both the Cistercians and the Knights Templar grew vines successfully on the valley sides in the district.

Varieties planted are Madeleine Angevine on 3 acres, Seyval Blanc an acre, and Madeleine Sylvaner and Triomphe D'Al-

sace making up the remaining half an acre. There is also an experimental area carrying out trials on Ortega, Siegerrebe, Leon Millot, Joffre and Gagarin. There have been no changes to the varieties planted in recent years and there are no new, as yet unproductive vines.

The vineyard is situated on well drained sandy loam overlying carboniferous sandstone at an elevation of 75ft to 100ft above sea level. It slopes to the south on the sides of the Aire Valley looking at the river.

It is in a rainshadow caused by the Pennines which also protects the vineyard from strong westerly winds. There is a good local microclimate. The river and parallel canal nearby, with other large bodies of water, afford good frost protection at critical times of the year. The climate in this part of Yorkshire is much drier and milder than many people realise.

Pruning starts in January and continues until March. The vineyard is also dressed with fertiliser during this period. Budburst takes place towards the end of April or early May, and flowering at the end of June or into July. The harvest takes place from early October into November. From April to September there is a regular preventative spraying programme at approximately 14-day intervals.

The vineyard is split into two. Three acres are trained on the Double Guyot system with rows of white varieties 6ft apart and vines spaced at 4ft intervals. This allows a planting of 1,400 vines to the acre. The red varieties are in rows 6ft apart and the vines 6ft apart. This allows a planting density of 1,200 vines to the acre. The remaining 2 acres are planted only with Madeleine Angevine on the high Lenz-Moser system with 12ft between rows and vines planted at 4ft intervals. This allows a density of 700 vines to the acre. All the vines are planted north to south on the slopes.

The normal harvest starts in early October with Madeleine Silvaner the first variety to be picked, followed by Madeleine Angevine in the middle of the month, and Seyval Blanc and Triomphe D'Alsace at the end of October or early November. The weight of the harvest varies from a ton an acre in a poor year to more than 5 tons in a good one. The vineyard was planted in 1985 and when the vines are mature, they are expected to yield an average of about 3 tons an acre.

The vineyard does not have its own winery yet and the grapes are sold to another vineyard. It hopes to start its own winemaking in 1991. Sample wines produced so far have been: Madeleine Silvaner light dry wine with a delicate flowery lemon nose; Madeleine Angevine full flavoured, grapey dry wine with a delicate muscat nose; Seyval Blanc full flavoured dry wine with a sharp clean finish and a hint of Bramley apples on the nose and Triomphe D'Alsace deep red wine with light tannic fruity flavour, strongly hinting of berries on the nose. Each white wine has its own unique fine flavour which varies with the vintage. The reds are reminiscent of a Gamay.

Visiting times: weekends by appointment until the vineyard is fully running.

How to get there: take the A642 from the eastward bound M62. Follow the signs to Garforth through Woodlesford and over the river Aire bridge, then take the first left up Bullerthorpe Lane. The vineyard is 300yd up on the left.

Nearby attractions: Temple Newsam House, a Tudor house and ancestral home of the Darnley family, standing in 900 acres of gardens designed by Capability Brown, with farm and recognised rare breeds centre. The vineyard is on the edge of the estate. Lotherton Hall and bird gardens, Leeds (art gallery, museums) Kirkstall Abbey and Abbey House Museum and Roundhay Park.

Recommended pubs, restaurants and hotels in the area: Chequers (Ledsham) Russell's Restaurant (Selby Road, Leeds 15) and Hilton National Motel (Garforth, Nr Leeds).

LA MARE VINEYARDS
Mr and Mrs Robert Blayney
St Mary, Jersey
☎ (0534) 81178

The vineyard (a member of the EVA) covers 5 acres and does not have any expansion plans at present, mostly because of the difficulty in acquiring land. Varieties planted are Reichensteiner 2 acres, Huxelrebe an acre, Seyval Blanc 1.5 acres, Scheurebe half an acre, and an experimental half an acre of Ammensis, a hybrid from Geisenheim. Half an acre of the Seyval and the Ammensis vines are not yet productive. There have been no changes to the varieties planted. The vineyard is to the north of the island in the parish of St Mary and set round a fine eighteenth-century granite farm house. The land is flat, well drained and the soil is sandy loam.

The climate is warm and windy. The vineyard is mostly free of frosts at budburst and artificial windbreaks have been erected to protect against the wind. The climate seems to suit the varieties planted but an early onset of winter can cause difficulties in the ripening Scheurebe. Some of the vineyards are netted to keep out rabbits which can be a problem. Roses are planted among the vines for practical as well as aesthetic reasons. Roses suffer from the same mildews as vines but are affected earlier so provide a useful early warning system.

The vineyard was the first on Jersey in recent times and was established in 1972, the first vines being planted 2 years later. It was fitting as the family have been involved in the wine trade for 150 years.

The vines are trained on either the Double Guyot or Geneva Double Curtain systems. There is little evidence to date that one method is better than the other. There is a spraying programme throughout the summer using a mist blower and a minimal use of insecticides. There has been a great deal of experimentation with weed control and a number of methods have been tried.

The harvest usually starts within the first 10 days of October but is delayed if the weather is suitable. Like most northerly vineyards, they are forced to begin the harvest if the weather is unfavourable and likely to damage the fruit quality, rather than because the grapes are getting too ripe. Sugar levels are, however, usually very satisfactory.

The Huxelrebe is often the first to ripen and as the Seyval lasts well in all weathers — it is picked after the Reichensteiner. The Scheurebe is picked last, often 2 or 3 weeks after the other grapes have been gathered.

The vineyard has a modern purpose-built winery. The grapes are de-stalked and pressed and the must is cool fermented and the wine then stored in either stainless steel or fibreglass tanks. The wine is fined and filtered as little as possible, the aim being not to race the wine into the bottle too soon. It is usually bottled in the spring after the vintage.

Production has varied enormously in the last few vintages. The 1982-5 vintages were good with yields providing about 1,000 cases a year. The 1986 harvest was seriously hit because of bad weather at flowering, and the October hurricane in 1987 hit Jersey very badly and a big proportion of the crop was lost. The 1988 crop was back to the 1,000 case average.

The wines produced are: Clos de la Mare, made from Reichensteiner and Huxelrebe, this is a well flavoured wine with depth and the potential for good maturity and Seyval, a soft, elegant, refreshing varietal with attractive length, ideal with local seafood.

In excellent years, a special reserve is produced which is a lovely big wine with a depth of flavour due largely to the well ripened Huxelrebe. The wine is sold mostly on Jersey, and figures heavily in tourist and civic functions. It was served at luncheon to toast the Queen when she visited the island during her Jubilee celebrations.

Visiting times: May to October 10am-5.30pm. The vineyard is rapidly becoming one of the major tourist attractions on the island and has a number of facilities for visitors. The property is very attractive, and has at its centre an historic farmstead set in lovely grounds. There is a wine shop as well as a buttery, a vineyard trail, adventure playground and picnic areas. There are facilities for disabled.

Apart from wines, the shop also sells home-made preserves, mustards, jellies, butter and Christmas specialities. Tastings and light food are available. Out of season, the vineyard caters for tasting groups and specialist occasions. The enterprise also has its own cider orchard and makes cider and apple wine using both its own fruit and apples bought in from a neighbouring parish.

How to get there: the vineyard is well signposted, and is on the C103 north of St Mary.

Nearby attractions: parish church, Devils Hole, Butterfly Farm, Carnation Nursery and cliff path walks.

LES PERQUAGES VINEYARDS
Les Perquages Vineyards Ltd
Mont Remon, St Peter
Jersey

☎ day (0534 83416), evenings (0534) 791 63

The vineyard (a member of the EVA) covers 4 acres of which 2 acres have been planted. The aim is eventually to expand the vineyard to 8 acres. The first variety to be planted was Regner when half an acre was established. In the spring of 1989 an acre of Seyval Blanc and half an acre of Chardonnay was added.

The vineyard is in the centre of the island, planted on south and west facing valley sides enjoying a temperate maritime climate. The site is well drained on acid loam.

The vines are all trained on the Double Guyot system and pruning takes place between November and March. There is a regular spraying programme throughout the growing season. The harvest starts in late October or early November, and usually lasts for a couple of days. Regner is picked first and will be followed by Seyval Blanc and then Chardonnay.

The grapes are crushed and de-stalked using a Zambelli crusher, and then passed straight to a Howard rotapress, unless skin contact is appropriate. The must is then pumped into settling tanks, either stainless steel or glass reinforced plastic.

When the juice has cleared it is pumped into another tank and innoculated with yeast. Cool fermentation is maintained between 50°F (10°C) and 59°F (15°C). After fermentation, the wine is clarified, blended and finally bottled. The main consideration after fermentation is to prevent oxidation, and it is therefore handled as little as possible with inert gas used to protect the wine.

Production over the last few years has varied enormously from nil in 1984 and 1986, to 30 bottles in 1987 and 300 bottles in 1985 and 1988. The wine is made by Steve Duquemin, who is also managing director of the vineyard company. The wine produced is a dry white, highly aromatic, light, refreshing and fruity with a hint of grapefruit and all the wine is currently sold from the cellar door.

Visiting times: from April 1990 it will be open daily from 9.30am. The vineyard has a small winery and all the equipment is on display. It is in a beautifully scenic setting, and the property also includes woodland, willow beds and bee hives. There are cellar tastings, picnic areas and a vineyard trail.

How to get there: follow the signs for the Fantastic Tropical Gardens, and the vineyard entrance is almost opposite the gardens.

Nearby attractions: tropical gardens, strawberry farm, German underground hospital, motor museum and carnation nurseries.

— Index —

— Places of Interest near the Vineyards —

Also from MPC......

- Detailing over 3,500 vineyards open to the public
- Covers all the wine-producing areas
- Lists over 700 recommended local hotels and restaurants
- Highlights local cuisine
- Explores the history and culture of each region
- Describes the wines and tells you how to buy and ship them home

ISBN 0 86190 162 2 (paperback) £7.95